Studies in Economic Theory

Founded by: **Charalambos D. Aliprantis**

Series Editors

Nicholas C. Yannelis
University of Illinois
Department of Economics
Champaign, IL 61820
USA

Timothy J. Kehoe
University of Minnesota and Federal Reserve Bank
of Minneapolis,
USA

Bernard Cornet
Paris School of Economics
Université Paris 1 and University of Kansas

For further volumes:
http://www.springer.com/series/2584

Titles in the Series

M. A. Khan and N. C. Yannelis (Eds.)
Equilibrium Theory in Infinite
Dimensional Spaces

C. D. Aliprantis, K. C. Border
and W. A. J. Luxemburg (Eds.)
Positive Operators, Riesz Spaces,
and Economics

D. G. Saari
Geometry of Voting

C. D. Aliprantis and K. C. Border
Infinite Dimensional Analysis

J.-P. Aubin
Dynamic Economic Theory

M. Kurz (Ed.)
Endogenous Economic Fluctuations

J.-F. Laslier
Tournament Solutions and Majority
Voting

A. Alkan, C. D. Aliprantis
and N. C. Yannelis (Eds.)
Theory and Applications

J. C. Moore
Mathematical Methods
for Economic Theory 1

J. C. Moore
Mathematical Methods
for Economic Theory 2

M. Majumdar, T. Mitra and K. Nishimura
Optimization and Chaos

K. K. Sieberg
Criminal Dilemmas

M. Florenzano and C. Le Van
Finite Dimensional Convexity
and Optimization

K. Vind
Independence, Additivity, Uncertainty

T. Cason and C. Noussair (Eds.)
Advances in Experimental Markets

N. Schofield
MathematicalMethods in Economics and
Social Choice

C. D. Aliprantis, K. J. Arrow, P.Hammond
F. Kubler, H.-M. Wu and N. C. Yannelis
(Eds.)
Assets, Beliefs, and Equilibria in
Economic Dynamics

D. Glycopantis and N. C. Yannelis (Eds.)
Differential Information Economies

A. Citanna, J. Donaldson,
H. M. Polemarchakis, P. Siconolfi
and S. E. Spear (Eds.)
Essays in Dynamic General Equilibrium
Theory

M. Kaneko
Game Theory and Mutual
Misunderstanding

S. Basov
Multidimensional Screening

V. Pasetta
Modeling Foundations of Economic Property
Right Theory

G. Camera (Ed.)
Recent Developments on Money
and Finance

C. Schultz and K. Vind (Eds.)
Institutions, Equilibria and Efficiency

C. D. Aliprantis, R. L. Matzkin,
D. L. McFadden, J. C. Moore
and N. C. Yannelis (Eds.)
Rationality and Equilibrium

Guo Ying Luo

Evolutionary Foundations of Equilibria in Irrational Markets

Springer

Guo Ying Luo
DeGroote School of Business
McMaster University
Hamilton Ontario
Canada
luogy@mcmaster.ca

ISSN 1431-8849
ISBN 978-1-4614-0711-9   e-ISBN 978-1-4614-0712-6
DOI 10.1007/978-1-4614-0712-6
Springer New York Dordrecht Heidelberg London

Library of Congress Control Number: 2011942480

© Springer Science+Business Media, LLC 2012
All rights reserved. This work may not be translated or copied in whole or in part without the written permission of the publisher (Springer Science+Business Media, LLC, 233 Spring Street, New York, NY 10013, USA), except for brief excerpts in connection with reviews or scholarly analysis. Use in connection with any form of information storage and retrieval, electronic adaptation, computer software, or by similar or dissimilar methodology now known or hereafter developed is forbidden.
The use in this publication of trade names, trademarks, service marks, and similar terms, even if they are not identified as such, is not to be taken as an expression of opinion as to whether or not they are subject to proprietary rights.

Printed on acid-free paper

Springer is part of Springer Science+Business Media (www.springer.com)

To my daughters

Acknowledgements

The book owes its origin to my thesis and I gratefully acknowledge the inputs from my thesis advisor, Arthur Robson, and committee members Phil Reny, Peter Howitt, and Motty Perry. I have also benefitted a great deal from numerous individuals acknowledged in the respective published papers and seminar participants from numerous universities and conferences. Constant support from Dean Mountain is gratefully acknowledged. In addition, I would like to thank the Social Sciences and Humanities Research Council of Canada (SSHRC) for financial support. In compiling this book, I have received many helpful suggestions and comments from the editor, Brian Foster of Springer Science + Business Media. Also valuable suggestions from Nicholas Yannelis, the editor for Studies in Economic Theory has greatly improved this book.

Contents

1 **Introduction** 1
 References 4

2 **Evolution, Irrationality, and Perfectly Competitive Equilibrium** 5
 2.1 Introduction 5
 2.2 The Model 8
 2.3 The Results 12
 2.4 Numerical Illustration 24
 2.5 Conclusions 27
 Appendix 28
 References 30

3 **Evolution, Irrationality, and Monopolistically Competitive Equilibrium** 33
 3.1 Introduction 33
 3.2 The Model 37
   3.2.1 The Demand and Average Cost Functions 37
   3.2.2 The Dynamic Process of Monopolistic Competition 41
 3.3 The Results 42
 3.4 Numerical Illustration 44
 3.5 Conclusions 47
 Appendix A 48
 Appendix B 57
 References 58

4 **Evolution and Informationally Efficient Equilibrium in a Commodity Futures Market** 61
 4.1 Introduction 61
 4.2 The Model 64
   4.2.1 Speculators' Types 65
   4.2.2 Speculators in the Market Selection Process 68
   4.2.3 The Futures Market Equilibrium 70

	4.3 Convergence of Futures Market to Efficiency	71
	4.4 Conclusions	75
	Appendix A	76
	Appendix B	82
	Appendix C	84
	Appendix D	84
	References	87

5 **Natural Selection, Random Shocks, and Market Efficiency in a Futures Market** 89
   5.1 Introduction 89
   5.2 Commodity Futures Market 93
   5.3 Traders' Predetermined Behavior Rules 96
   5.4 Numerical Examples and Results 98
   5.5 Conclusions 102
   Appendix A 103
   Appendix B 103
   References 111

6 **Evolution, Noise Traders, and Market Efficiency in a One-Sided Auction Market** 113
   6.1 Introduction 113
   6.2 The Model 117
       6.2.1 Traders' Prediction Errors 117
       6.2.2 Traders' Wealth Dynamics in the Market Process 119
       6.2.3 The Asset Market Equilibrium 121
   6.3 Convergence of the Asset Price to the Fundamental Value 122
   6.4 Conclusions 126
   Appendix A 127
   Appendix B 141
   Appendix C 150
       C.1 Failure of Convergence with Too Noisy Traders 151
       C.2 Convergence when the Probability of Predicting the Fundamental Value is Allowed to be Arbitrarily Close to 1 151
       C.3 Convergence when the Probability of Predicting the Fundamental Value is Constrained to be Less than a Number Below 1 153
   References 154

7 **The Evolution of Money as a Medium of Exchange in a Primitive Economy** 157
   7.1 Introduction 157
   7.2 Framework 160
       7.2.1 Physical Environment 160
       7.2.2 The Trading Sessions 161

	7.3	Evolution of Strategies...	164
		7.3.1	Example 1: Random Sampling Among the Same Population	165
		7.3.2	The General Class of Dynamics	166
		7.3.3	Equilibria Selection.............................	169
	7.4	Mutation	175
		7.4.1	The General Class of Dynamics	177
		7.4.2	Equilibria Selection with Mutation	178
	7.5	Conclusions	180
	Appendix A	182
	Appendix B	187
	Appendix C	192
	Appendix D	193
	References	194
8	**Conclusions**	197
	Reference	198

Chapter 1
Introduction

One of the core building blocks in traditional economic theory is the equilibrium concept (e.g., perfectly competitive equilibrium, monopolistically competitive equilibrium, and informationally efficient equilibrium). Many of the classic equilibrium concepts are derived or established on the basis of the rationality of the individual participants in the sense that they are capable of maximizing their utility, or their profits or forming rational expectation in such a way that a particular equilibrium can be achieved at an aggregate level. For example, the perfectly competitive equilibrium is described to be a market equilibrium outcome in an industry with free entry and exit and completely mobile resources provided that all firms are profit maximizers. Similarly, although Chamberlin and Robinson arrive at monopolistically competitive equilibrium with different techniques, both of their original arguments for deriving this equilibrium rely heavily on rationality and purposive profit maximization. The notion of firms maximizing profits within a monopolistic context has remained in modern analyses of monopolistic competition (e.g., Spence (1976) and Hart 1985a,1985b). Also, an informationally efficient equilibrium can be achieved in the Bayesian Rational Expectation Equilibrium framework if traders are rational, in the sense that they maximize expected utility and form rational expectations. This is shown by Grossman (1976, 1978), Radner (1979), Hellwig (1980), Allen (1981), and Bray (1981). A new alternative approach to the Bayesian Rational Expectation Equilibrium framework is Maximin Rational Expectation Equilibrium (MREE), see Castro et al. (2011). This approach can be used to examine market efficiency if market individual participants are rational and able to solve the complex problem set up by MREE framework.

However, the individual's rationality has been questioned from many angles. For example, an individual participant may not be interested in pursuing maximization of its profit. Even if it is, the individual may not be able to do so due to the complex market environment, unknown information, and its computational capability constraints. If we accept the view that the individual participants cannot be rational, then, do we have to abandon all these equilibrium concepts? Is there any way we could justify the existence of all these equilibria.

The Darwinian's evolutionary idea of natural selection has been used in the early literature (e.g., Alchian (1950), Enke (1951), Friedman (1953)) to validate the profit maximization hypothesis or to justify the disappearance of noise traders (or the dominance of informed traders). For example, as Penrose (1952, 11, pp. 812) points out, "no matter what man's motives are, the outcome is determined not by the individual participants but by an environment beyond their control. Natural selection is substituted for purposive profit-maximizing behavior just as in biology natural selection replaced the concept of special creation of species". Alchian (1950) writes, "realized positive profits, not maximum profits, are the mark of success and viability. It does not matter through what process of reasoning or motivation such success was achieved. The fact of its accomplishment is sufficient. This is the criterion by which the economic system selects survivors: those who realize positive profits are the survivors; those who suffer losses disappear". Enke (1951) presents more details on how the market selection works. Enke (1951) says that "in the long run, however, if firms are in active competition with one another rather than constituting a number of isolated monopolies, natural selection will tend to permit the survival of only those firms that either through good luck or great skill have managed, almost or completely, to optimize their position and earn the normal profits necessary for survival. In these instances the economist can make aggregate predictions as if each and every firm knew how to secure maximum long-run profits". In the financial market, Friedman (1953) conjectured that noise traders gradually lose their wealth to the informed traders through natural selection, the informed traders will come to dominate the markets and drive the market to an informationally efficient outcome.

All these discussions by the early economists are descriptive in nature, Recently, there are a large number of models built in the literature to further examine these thoughts in a variety of contexts. Furthermore, in the literature using the natural selection in the markets, few models focus on addressing the eventual occurrence of the equilibrium at an aggregate level even though the individual participants are total irrational.

This book gathers some of my own work in this area and intends to address at an aggregate level the eventual occurrence of some of equilibrium outcomes through economic natural selection in a totally irrational world.

There are eight chapters in the book. Chapter 2 examines whether the concept of the perfectly competitive equilibrium would be valid if the firms are total irrational in the industry in the sense that they cannot maximize or simply are not interested in maximizing their profits. It is commonly known in any standard textbook that profit maximization is the usual prerequisite for achievement of a perfectly competitive equilibrium. This chapter presents an evolutionary model of an industry to show analytically that with the market selection criterion of making nonnegative wealth and with firms behaving totally irrationally, the industry evolves and converges in probability to a perfectly competitive equilibrium. This is accomplished by following the evolution of an industry through an infinite time horizon model where firms' outputs are chosen randomly by nature, entry occurs with no motivation and exit occurs when a firm's wealth becomes negative.

Chapter 3 examines whether the monopolistically competitive equilibrium would occur if the individual firms are not profit maximizers. In a product differentiated industry, this chapter formulates an evolutionary dynamic model where there is continuous entry of firms that randomly select their output levels on entry and fix their output levels thereafter. Firms exit the industry if they fail to pass the survival test of making nonnegative profits. Through the evolutionary process of natural selection in the market, firms that make positive profits, survive; otherwise, they disappear. This model proves that the industry converges in probability to the monopolistically competitive equilibrium as the size of each firm becomes infinitesimally small relative to the market, as the entry cost becomes sufficiently small, and as time gets sufficiently large. Consequently, in the limit, the only surviving firms are those producing at the tangency of the demand curve to the average cost curve and no potential entrant can make a positive profit by entry.

Chapter 4 presents an evolutionary model of a futures market to justify the eventual occurrence of an informationally efficient equilibrium. In this dynamic futures market, where the market participants know very little about their environment, the market, itself, by serving as a selection process of information, promotes an efficient aggregate outcome. Specifically, traders are assumed to merely act upon their predetermined trading types (buyer or seller), their predetermined fractions of wealth allocated for speculation and their inherent abilities to predict the spot price, reflected in their distributions of prediction errors with respect to the spot price. This model proves that the proportion of time that the futures price equals the spot price converges to one with probability one.

Chapter 5 follows up by adding a random shock to the futures market to see if the market is still informationally efficient. In this evolutionary model of a commodity futures market, there is a continual inflow of unsophisticated traders with predetermined distributions of prediction errors with respect to the fundamental value of the spot price. The market acts as a selection process by constantly shifting wealth from traders with less accurate information to those with more accurate information. Consequently, with probability one, if the volatility of the underlying spot market is sufficiently small, then the proportion of time, that the futures price is sufficiently close to the fundamental value, converges to one. Furthermore, the width of the interval containing the fundamental value, where the futures price eventually lies, increases as the volatility of the underlying spot market increases.

Chapter 6 uses natural selection to examine the occurrence of informational efficiency in a one-sided buyer auction market. Through the natural selection or market selection in the market, this model reaches the similar conclusion to the above. Specifically, each trader's behavior is preprogrammed with its own inherent and fixed probabilities of over-predicting, predicting correctly, and under-predicting the fundamental value of the asset. If each buyer's initial wealth is sufficiently small relative to the market supply and if the variation in the asset's random shock is sufficiently small, then as time gets sufficiently large, the proportion of time, that the asset price is arbitrarily close to the fundamental value, converges to one with probability one. This is established under a weak restriction regarding traders' behavior.

Chapter 7 uses an evolutionary approach to explain the origin of money as media of exchange in a primitive economy, where agents specialize in production for the purpose of trading for their own consumption goods. A general class of dynamics, which is consistent with Darwinian dynamics, is applied to the selection of strategies. The model produces many of the well-known results regarding the importance of intrinsic value and the proportion of agents specializing in different goods. In addition, the model also shows the importance of initial trading strategies and of the mutations of agents' strategies in selecting equilibria.

Chapter 8 concludes the book and points out some directions of future research in this area.

References

Alchian, A. 1950. Uncertainty, Evolution and Economic Theory. *Journal of Political Economy* 58:211–222.
Allen, B. 1981. "Generic Existence of Equilibria for Economies with Uncertainty When Prices Convey Information". *Econometrica* 49:1173–1199.
Bray, M. 1981. "Futures Trading, Rational Expectations, and the Efficient Markets Hypothesis". *Econometrica* 49:575–596.
Castro, L.I. de, Marialaura, P., and Yannelis, N. 2011. "A new perspective to rational expectations:maximin rational expectations equilibrium". Working paper, Department of Economics, University of Illinois at Urbana Champaign.
Enke, S. 1951. On Maximizing Profits: A Distinction Between Chamberlin and Robinson. *American Economic Review* 41:566–578.
Friedman, M. 1953. *Essays in Positive Economics*, Univ. of Chicago Press: Chicago.
Grossman, S.J. 1976. "On the Efficiency of Competitive Stock Markets where Traders Have Diverse Information". *Journal of Finance* 31:573–585.
Grossman, S.J. 1978. "Further Results On the Informational Efficiency of Competitive Stock Markets". *Journal of Economic Theory* 18:81–101.
Hart, O.D. 1985a. Monopolistic Competition in the Spirit of Chamberlin: A General Approach. *Review of Economic Studies* LII:529–546.
Hart, O.D. 1985b. Monopolistic Competition in the Spirit of Chamberlin: Special Results. *The Economic Journal* 95:889–908.
Hellwig, M.F. 1980. "On the Aggregation of Information in Competitive Markets". *Journal of Economic Theory* 22:477–498.
Penrose, E. T. 1952. "Biological analogies in the theory of the firm". *American Economic Review* 42:804–819.
Radner, R. 1979. "Rational Expectations Equilibrium: Generic Existence and the Information Revealed by Prices". *Econometrica* 47:655–678.
Spence, M. 1976. Product Selection, Fixed Costs, and Monopolistic Competition. *Review of Economic Studies* 43:217–235.

Chapter 2
Evolution, Irrationality, and Perfectly Competitive Equilibrium[1]

This chapter examines whether the concept of the perfectly competitive equilibrium would be valid if the firms are totally irrational in the industry in the sense that they cannot maximize or simply are not interested in maximizing their profits. This chapter begins with the motivation of the issue. Then an evolutionary model of an industry is constructed to prove analytically that the industry converges in probability to perfect competition as firms gets infinitesimally small relative to the market, as the fixed cost of entry gets sufficiently small and as time gets sufficiently large. Furthermore, in the long run, the only survivors are those who produce at the minimum efficient scale. No potential entrant can make a positive profit by entering the industry.

This chapter is organized into five sections. The next section provides the introduction. The framework of the model is described in the second section. The results of the model can be found in the third section. The fourth section provides some numerical examples to illustrate some of the results of the chapter. The last section concludes the chapter.

2.1 Introduction

One can find the standard perfectly competitive model in any microeconomic textbook. Although the perfectly competitive model is an ideal market structure, it plays a fundamental role in modern economic theory. It is commonly found in textbooks that, with free entry and exit and completely mobile resources, any industry arrives at a perfectly competitive equilibrium, provided that all firms are profit maximizers.

---

[1]This chapter is based on my article published in the *Journal of Economic Theory* 67: 223–250, 1995.

As we trace back historically through the development of modern microeconomics, it was not until Knight's (1921) meticulous discussion in "Risk, Uncertainty and Profit" that the concept of perfect competition as we know today received a complete formulation. Within his characterization of perfect competition is the fundamental premise of rationality: "the members of the society act with complete 'rationality'."They "know what they want" and "seek it intelligently."With respect to their actions "nothing is capricious or experimental, everything is deliberate"(Knight 1921, pp. 76–77). This is also very clear in the early writings of Robinson (1933) where the idea of marginalism is critical. "The fundamental assumption is that each individual acts in a sensible manner " (p. 15) and "any individual ... will always undertake an action which adds more to his gains than to his losses"(p. 6).

The conventional perfectly competitive model includes the following characteristics. A firm in a perfectly competitive market selects its output corresponding to where marginal cost equals the market price. As long as profit opportunities exist, firms continue to enter. Entry stops when all profit opportunities vanish. If firms see their profits becoming negative they leave. In the long run, the remaining firms produce at minimum efficient scale. There are three key "rationality " ingredients regarding choice in this conventional model. (1) Firms select a profit maximizing output in response to market conditions (i.e., where marginal cost equals market price), (2) firms choose whether to enter or stay out of the industry (in response to observed profit opportunities), and (3) firms can choose when to leave (i.e., when they see their potential profits becoming negative).

The profit maximization behavior, implied by "rationality", however, has been seriously attacked from several fronts.

One group of criticisms centers about alternative managerial goals. For example, Baumol (1967) suggests the possibility of firms maximizing sales revenue. Williamson (1963) suggests that firms maximize managers' utilities. Cyert and March (1963) suggest that when a firm faces conflicting objectives, it should proceed sequentially to satisfy one objective at a time before considering the fulfillment of others. Hence, in these criticisms profit maximization is replaced by other managerial objectives.

Another group of criticisms focuses on the organizational complexity of a firm and a business environment of continual dynamic uncertainty (e.g., Tintner 1941). Organizational complexity, often reflected by an elaborate vertical chain of command within firms, potentially can lead to a great distortion of information, both from the operator to the top manager and from the top management to the operating levels. Given such complexity, it may be very difficult for a firm to maximize profits. Furthermore, because at the operating level employees often see little correlation between their individual actions and the amount of profits in which they share, there may be little concern for profit maximization. In addition to organizational complexity the environment of uncertainty is another obstacle to profit maximization and rationality. Business decision making processes often require predictions about future events. However, the decision makers are often poorly informed about business conditions in general and most likely, they do

2.1 Introduction

not have a good knowledge about the probability of various departures from the firms' best guesses about the future. Decision makers are often restricted by their forecasting capabilities and limited computational capacities [e.g., see the work of Simon in (Simon 1976) and (1992)]. Consequently, it is not realistic to expect that firms could accurately maximize profits.(Also see Scherer (1980, pp. 28–34) for a further discussion of these issues.)

One reaction to such criticisms has been to abandon all rationality and motivation. Profit maximizing behavior no longer exists. Nevertheless, as Penrose (1952, p. 810) paraphrases Alchian (1950), "to survive, firms must make profits. Hence positive profits can be treated as the criterion of natural selection – the firms that make profits are selected or 'adopted' by the environment, others are rejected and disappear. This holds whether firms consciously try to make profits or not; even if the actions of firms were completely random and determined only by chance, the firms surviving, i.e., adopted by the environment, would be those that happened to act appropriately and thus made profits. Hence, 'individual motivation and foresight, while sufficient are not necessary,'(Alchian 1950, p. 217)." As Penrose (1952, p. 812) points out, "no matter what man's motives are, the outcome is determined not by the individual participants but by an environment beyond their control. Natural selection is substituted for purposive profit-maximizing behavior just as in biology natural selection replaced the concept of special creation of species."

The intention of this chapter is to prove analytically in a precise complete model that if firms' outputs are determined randomly by nature, instead of arising from profit maximization or the pursuit of any other goals, the industry will evolve into a perfectly competitive state under conditions of free entry and exit. Basically, this model begins with firms entering the industry exogenously. The behavior of firms is modeled over a discrete time horizon. After entry the firms' outputs are determined randomly by nature. As long as these firms' total profits are nonnegative the firms continue to produce the same output. The firms could produce a small amount or a large amount or an amount corresponding to the minimum efficient scale. Whether they are successful and make a profit in the market is a matter of chance. The firms' abilities are bounded in the extreme. They are not able to make profit maximization calculations and with the exception of exit, they do not respond to market conditions. The model allows one firm to enter each time period, no matter what the industry profits are. The exit flow is just the result of competition or "struggle for existence" (Penrose 1952, p. 812). The market selection criterion is that there must be nonnegative wealth in each period. Otherwise a firm exits.

Essentially, this chapter serves as a contrast to the conventional perfectly competitive model. The industry still evolves into perfect competition even though the profit maximizing behavior implied by rationality is replaced with (1) outputs being randomly determined, (2) firms entering regardless of profit opportunities, and (3) firms being involuntarily forced to exit as a result of market selection.

Two driving forces that produce the long-run perfectly competitive market outcome are economic natural selection and competition. Here, competition means continuous entry of various types of firms including firms that happen to produce at or near the minimum efficient scale. Economic natural selection alone is not sufficient to generate the long-run perfectly competitive market outcome where all the survivors are those who act as if they were profit maximizers. For example, Blume and Easley (1992) use a dynamic general equilibrium model of an asset market where wealth flows are permitted between traders. As time goes by, the flow of wealth constantly redistributes market power among traders. They discover that economic natural selection does not necessarily select for rational rules and does not necessarily select against irrational rules. Their results are partly due to the fact, that with no continuous entry of traders with all types of rules, not all traders' market power vanishes as time goes by; whereas, in this chapter, with continuous entry of various types of firms, perfect competition arises where no firm has market power. Competition among firms forces the market to select for firms that happen to produce at or near the minimum efficient scale and to select against firms that behave otherwise. The economic natural selection in conjunction with the characteristics associated with competition lead to an equilibrium which generates behavior observationally equivalent to profit maximization.

The results of this chapter indicate that, although each individual firm acts irrationally, with the market selection process competition will lead to a long-run perfectly competitive market outcome. This is much in the spirit of Gode and Sunder (1993), who with a simulated experiment of double auction bidding show that, by imposing a budget constraint (that all traders must settle their accounts), random strategies lead to an allocative competitive equilibrium. This is also consistent with the views of Patel, Zeckhauser, and Hendricks (1991) and Blume and Easley (1993) who discuss how rational aggregate market outcomes can be achieved in financial markets despite the irrational behavior of some participants.

2.2 The Model

Consider an industry in the economy where all the firms produce a single homogeneous good and the market prices for the input factors are constant. All the firms enter the industry sequentially over a discrete infinite time horizon. Only one firm is assumed to enter the industry in the beginning of time period t, where $t = 1, 2, \ldots$. This firm's output is determined by a random draw (q_t) in the beginning of its entry period t on the interval $A = [\underline{q}, \overline{q}]$, where $0 < \underline{q} < \overline{q} < \infty$, according to a continuous cumulative distribution function $F(\cdot)$. The output of the firm is αq_t, where the parameter $\alpha > 0$ (it will be seen in Lemma 2 that the shrinking of α is analogous to making the firm's output infintesimally small relative to the market). These random draws are independent across the time periods. In other words, $q_1, q_2, \ldots, q_t, \ldots, q_{t'}, \ldots$ (where $t' > t$) are independently and identically distributed according to the continuous distribution function $F(\cdot)$.

In other words, denote all possible states of the world at the time period t as $A = [\underline{q}, \overline{q}]$ with a typical element q_t, where q_t is the state of the world at time period t. Only one state occurs at time period t. $\{q_t\}_{t \geq 1}$ is independently and identically

2.2 The Model

distributed according to $F(\cdot)$. Denote $\Omega = \prod_{i=1}^{\infty} A$ with a typical element $\omega = q = (q_1, q_2, \ldots)$. Let $\Im$ denote the product σ-field on Ω and let $\Pr(\cdot)$ denote the product probability with marginal distribution $F(\cdot)$. Define $\Omega^t = \prod_{i=1}^{t} A$ with typical element $\omega^t = q^t = (q_1, q_2, \ldots, q_t)$ for each $t = 1, 2, \ldots$.

This model adopts an extreme assumption with respect to irrationality. The firm that enters at the time period t, producing αq_t, will continue to produce αq_t in all of the following periods as long as it is still in the industry. That is, the firm's output is not responsive to market conditions.

A fixed cost is incurred upon entry. It is paid once and only once during the period of entry. This cost of entry can be interpreted as including costs of building a plant and installing equipment and any registration fees. This cost of entry is assumed to be proportional to the firm's output. That is, the total cost of entry for a firm producing αq_t is $k\alpha q_t$, where $k > 0$, and therefore, this firm's average cost during the period of entry is k.

Each firm is assumed to have the same average variable cost function. The reference average variable cost function (AC) is defined over A with the following properties:

(a) $AC : A \to R_+$ and AC is continuous and differentiable
(b) There exists a q^* in A such that

$$AC'(q_t) \begin{cases} < 0 \text{ if } q_t < q^* \\ = 0 \text{ if } q_t = q^* \\ > 0 \text{ if } q_t > q^* \end{cases}.$$

(c) $AC(q^*) = c^*$.

To generate a family of average variable cost functions which shift in a parallel way toward the origin as α shrinks, the following scaled down cost function [see Novshek (1980) and Robson (1990)] is defined from the reference average cost according to

$$AC_\alpha(q_t) = AC\left(\frac{q_t}{\alpha}\right).$$

Every firm faces this same average variable cost function $AC_\alpha(\cdot)$. The scaled down cost function $AC_\alpha(\cdot)$ remains U-shaped like the reference average variable cost function $AC(\cdot)$ curve and both functions achieve the same minimum average variable cost (c^*) at output q^* and αq^* respectively, and more generally for $q_t \in [\underline{q}, \overline{q}]$ the average variable cost for a firm producing αq_t are the same for all α.

The industry is assumed to face the same inverse demand function each period. Let Q_t be the aggregate industry output produced in the time period t and P_t be the output price faced by all firms in the time period t. The inverse demand function $D : R_+ \to R_+$ is defined by $Q_t = D(P_t)$, $D(\cdot)$ is continuous and $D'(\cdot) < 0$.

The initial industry output and industry price satisfy $P_0 = D^{-1}(Q_0) > c^*$.[2] The determination of Q_t and P_t will be described in the following.

(a) The industry is assumed to begin with no firms. Hence, $Q_0 = 0$.[3]

(b) At the beginning of time period 1 a firm (called firm 1) enters producing αq_1. The industry output is $Q_1 = \alpha q_1$. Correspondingly the price is $P_1 = D^{-1}(Q_1)$. Firm 1 will survive and continue to produce αq_1 in time period 2 as long as it makes nonnegative profit during time period 1 $(((P_1 - AC_\alpha(\alpha q_1) - k)\alpha q_1) \geq 0)$ which is equivalent to $P_1 \geq AC_\alpha(\alpha q_1) + k$. To indicate this survival from time period 1 to time period 2, one can define an indicator function as

$$I_1^1 = \begin{cases} 1 \text{ if } P_1 - AC_\alpha(\alpha q_1) - k \geq 0 \\ 0 \text{ if } P_1 - AC_\alpha(\alpha q_1) - k < 0 \end{cases}.$$

The superscript (1) of I indicates that the firm entered in time period 1 and the subscript (1) indicates that the survival from time period 1 to period 2 is being examined. In other words, if $I_1^1 = 1$ then the firm survives from period 1 to period 2; otherwise, it exits at the end of period 1. In addition, firm 1's per unit wealth at the end of time period 1 is defined as $W_1^1 = P_1 - AC_\alpha(\alpha q_1) - k$. Therefore, the state of the industry at the end of time period 1 can be described as a vector $((I_1^1 \alpha q_1, I_1^1 W_1^1), (0, 0), \ldots)$, which is an element of $\prod_{t=1}^{\infty}((\{0\} \cup \alpha A) \times R)$.

(c) At the beginning of time period 2, another firm (called firm 2) enters, producing αq_2. The industry output is

$$Q_2 = I_1^1 \alpha q_1 + \alpha q_2$$

or

$$Q_2 = Q_1 - X_1 + \alpha q_2$$

where $X_1 = (1 - I_1^1)\alpha q_1$ represents the quantity of firm 1 exiting at the end of time period 1 and the price is $P_2 = D^{-1}(Q_2)$. Firm 1 survives at the end of time period 2 and continues to produce in the time period 3 as long as $I_2^1 I_1^1 = 1$ or $I_2^1 = I_1^1 = 1$ where

$$I_2^1 = \begin{cases} 1 \text{ if } \sum_{t=1}^{2}[P_t - AC_\alpha(\alpha q_1)] - k \geq 0 \\ 0 \text{ otherwise} \end{cases}.$$

---

[2] Given that the firm's average cost is at least c^*, if the industry price starts with a value of c^* or below c^* then any firm will exit at the end of its entry period. This scenario is of no interest in describing the evolution of an industry into perfect competition. That is, the industry price cannot possibly converge to c^*.

[3] In fact, the initial industry output will not affect the final results of this chapter. The initial value of industry output ($Q_0 = 0$) has been adopted merely for convenience.

2.2 The Model   11

If $I_2^1 I_1^1 = 0$ then firm 1 exits by the end of time period 2. Putting this in words, it says that firm 1 continues to produce αq_1 in time period 3 if both of the following two conditions hold : (a) at the end of time period 1 firm 1's profit made during period 1 is nonnegative (i.e., $((P_1 - AC_\alpha(\alpha q_1) - k)\alpha q_1) \geq 0$ or $I_1^1 = 1$) and (b) at the end of time period 2 firm 1's total profits made during the past two time periods are nonnegative (i.e., $(\sum_{t=1}^{2}[P_t - AC_\alpha(\alpha q_1)] - k)\alpha q_1 \geq 0$ or $I_2^1 = 1$). Let $W_2^1 = \sum_{t=1}^{2}[P_t - AC_\alpha(\alpha q_1)] - k$. Firm 1's per unit wealth at the end of time period 2 is W_2^1 if $I_2^1 I_1^1 = 1$. Firm 2 survives at the end of time period 2 and continues to produce in time period 3 as long as $I_2^2 = 1$ where

$$I_2^2 = \begin{cases} 1 \text{ if } P_2 - AC_\alpha(\alpha q_2) - k \geq 0 \\ 0 \text{ otherwise} \end{cases}.$$

That is, firm 2 continues to produce αq_2 in period 3 if firm 2's profit made during period 2 is nonnegative (i.e., $(P_2 - AC_\alpha(\alpha q_2) - k)\alpha q_2 \geq 0$ or $I_2^2 = 1$). If $I_2^2 = 0$ then firm 2 exits at the end of time period 2. Firm 2's per unit wealth at the end of time period 2 is $W_2^2 = P_2 - AC_\alpha(\alpha q_2) - k$. Therefore, the state of the industry at the end of time period 2 is now defined as $((I_2^1 I_1^1 \alpha q_1, I_2^1 I_1^1 W_2^1), (I_2^2 \alpha q_2, I_2^2 W_2^2), (0,0), \ldots)$, which is an element of $\prod_{t=1}^{\infty}((\{0\} \cup \alpha A) \times R)$.

This market selection process goes on. In general, at the beginning of time period t, a firm (called firm t) enters producing αq_t. The industry output is

$$Q_t = \sum_{i=1}^{t-1}\left[\left(\prod_{j=i}^{t-1} I_j^i\right)\alpha q_i\right] + \alpha q_t$$

or

$$Q_t = Q_{t-1} - X_{t-1} + \alpha q_t$$

where X_{t-1} represents the quantity of the firms exiting at the end of time period $t-1$[4] and the price is $P_t = D^{-1}(Q_t)$. Firm i (i=1,2,...,t) survives at the end of

---

[4] In fact, $X_{t-1} = \sum_{j=1}^{t-2}(1 - I_{t-1}^j)(\prod_{i=j}^{t-2} I_i^j)\alpha q_j + (1 - I_{t-1}^{t-1})\alpha q_{t-1}$, where $\prod_{i=j}^{t-2} I_i^j$ indicates whether the firm j , (where $j \leq t-2$.) remains in the industry by the end of time period $t-2$. If it does remain, then $\prod_{i=j}^{t-2} I_i^j = 1$. $1 - I_{t-1}^j$ indicates whether firm j exits at the end of time period $t-1$. If firm j exits at the end of time period $t-1$, then $1 - I_{t-1}^j = 1$. Therefore, $(1 - I_{t-1}^j)(\prod_{i=j}^{t-2} I_i^j)\alpha q_j$ represents the quantity of firm j exiting the industry at the end of time period $t-1$, and $\sum_{j=1}^{t-2}(1 - I_{t-1}^j)(\prod_{i=j}^{t-2} I_i^j)\alpha q_j$ represents the total quantity of firms 1,2,..., $t-2$ exiting at the end

time period t and continues to produce in time period t+1 as long as $\prod_{j=i}^{t} I_j^i = 1$
where

$$I_j^i = \begin{cases} 1 \text{ if } \sum_{s=i}^{j} [P_s - AC_\alpha(\alpha q_i)] - k \geq 0 \\ 0 \text{ otherwise} \end{cases}.$$

That is, firm i ($i = 1, 2, \ldots, t$) continues to produce αq_i in time period $t + 1$ if firm i's total profits made from period i to j, for all $j = i, i + 1, i + 2, \ldots, t$ are nonnegative (i.e., $(\sum_{s=i}^{j} [P_s - AC_\alpha(\alpha q_i)] - k)\alpha q_i \geq 0$ for all $j = i, i + 1, i + 2, \ldots, t$, or $I_j^i = 1$ for all $j = i, i + 1, i + 2, \ldots, t$). Firm i exits by the end of time period t if $\prod_{j=i}^{t} I_j^i = 0$. Let $W_t^i = \sum_{\tau=i}^{t} [P_\tau - AC_\alpha(\alpha q_i)] - k$. Firm i's (where $i = 1, 2, \ldots, t - 1$) per unit wealth at the end of time period t is W_t^i if $\prod_{j=i}^{t} I_j^i = 1$ and firm t's wealth at the end of time period t is W_t^t. Therefore, the state of the industry at the end of time period t is a vector
$\{((\prod_{j=1}^{t} I_j^1)\alpha q_1, (\prod_{j=1}^{t} I_j^1)W_t^1), ((\prod_{j=2}^{t} I_j^2)\alpha q_2, (\prod_{j=2}^{t} I_j^2)W_t^2), \ldots, (I_t^t \alpha q_t, I_t^t W_t^t), (0, 0),$
$\ldots\}$. The set of possible states of the industry at time period t is a subset of $\prod_{i=1}^{\infty} ((\{0\} \cup \alpha A) \times R)$. Clearly, the state of the industry at time period t depends only on the state of the industry at time period $t-1$, not on the state of the industry at time period $1, 2, \ldots, t - 2$.

As can be seen, the industry price at time t is a function of α, k and the realizations of $q_1, q_2, \ldots, q_t$. This chapter is interested in whether the industry evolves into perfect competition as time goes by, and as firm-size (α) and the entry cost (k) shrink. The perfectly competitive industry (see Novshek 1980) is characterized by (1) the perfectly competitive price $P^* = c^*$ and the corresponding competitive output is $Q^* = D(P^*)$, (2) all firms produce at minimum efficient scale and (3) no potential entrants can make strictly positive profits by entry.

2.3 The Results

In this section, the main result is the Theorem which proves rigorously that the industry converges in probability to perfect competition as firms gets infinitesimally small relative to the market, as the cost of entry gets sufficiently small and as time

---

of time period $t-1$. $(1 - I_{t-1}^{t-1})\alpha q_{t-1}$ represents the quantity of firm $t-1$ exiting at the end of time period $t-1$.

2.3 The Results

gets sufficiently large. The proof of the Theorem is directly established using the results of Lemma 1 and Lemma 2. Lemma 1 sets up the lowest bound for the industry price and Lemma 2 sets up a probabilistic upper bound for the industry price after some time period.

Now this chapter begins with Lemma 1 which establishes a lowest bound for the industry price. The intuition of Lemma 1 is straightforward. Essentially, it says the following: Any firm that drives the price below $c^* + k$ in its entry period would make per unit revenue below $c^* + k$, which is less than its entry period's per unit cost of at least $c^* + k$. Consequently, this firm makes a negative profit and exits the industry at the end of its entry period. Hence, the lowest price occurs when the price in the previous period is $c^* + k$ and when the firm with output $\alpha \bar{q}$ enters the industry. Therefore, the industry price cannot be lower than $D^{-1}(D(c^* + k) + \alpha \bar{q})$.

Lemma 1. *For any given positive numbers α and k,*

$$P_t \geq D^{-1}(D(c^* + k) + \alpha \bar{q}), \qquad \forall t.$$

Proof. Since $D'(\cdot) < 0$ then

$$P_t \geq D^{-1}(D(c^* + k) + \alpha \bar{q}), \qquad \forall \alpha > 0, k > 0, t.$$

is equivalent to

$$Q_t \leq D(c^* + k) + \alpha \bar{q}, \qquad \forall \alpha > 0, k > 0, t. \tag{2.1}$$

Therefore, it is sufficient to show (2.1).
The proof begins by showing inductively

$$Q_{t-1} - X_{t-1} \leq D(c^* + k), \qquad \forall t \geq 1, \alpha > 0, k > 0. \tag{2.2}$$

(1) The base step:

$$Q_0 - X_0 \leq D(c^* + k). \tag{2.3}$$

$$Q_1 - X_1 \leq D(c^* + k). \tag{2.4}$$

Given $Q_0 = 0$, and $X_0 = 0$, (2.3) is trivial.
To show (2.4), the following two cases are considered, case 1 : $Q_1 \leq D(c^* + k)$ and case 2 : $Q_1 > D(c^* + k)$.

Case 1: Since $Q_1 \leq D(c^* + k)$ and $X_1 \geq 0$, then it follows that

$$Q_1 - X_1 \leq D(c^* + k).$$

Case 2: Since $D(c^* + k) < Q_1$, and since $D'(\cdot) < 0$, then $P_1 < c^* + k$. This implies that the first firm with average cost of at least $c^* + k$ in the entry period would make strictly negative profit. Hence, it has to leave the industry at the end of period 1. That is, $X_1 = \alpha q_1$. Since $Q_0 = 0$, $Q_1 = \alpha q_1$ and $X_1 = \alpha q_1$. then $Q_1 - X_1 = \alpha q_1 - \alpha q_1 \leq D(c^* + k)$. That is,

$$Q_1 - X_1 \leq D(c^* + k).$$

(2) The induction step:
Suppose for any r,
$$Q_r - X_r \leq D(c^* + k). \tag{2.5}$$
then it needs to be shown that
$$Q_{r+1} - X_{r+1} \leq D(c^* + k). \tag{2.6}$$

To show (2.6), the following two cases are considered, case $1'$: $Q_{r+1} \leq D(c^* + k)$ and case $2'$: $Q_{r+1} > D(c^* + k)$.

Case $1'$: Since $X_{r+1} \geq 0$, then $Q_{r+1} \leq D(c^* + k)$ implies
$$Q_{r+1} - X_{r+1} \leq D(c^* + k).$$

Case $2'$: Since $D'(\cdot) < 0$, then $Q_{r+1} > D(c^* + k)$ is equivalent to $P_{r+1} < c^* + k$. This implies that the $(r+1)$st firm, with entry period's average cost of at least $c^* + k$, would make a strictly negative profit. Hence, the $(r + 1)st$ firm leaves at the end of time period $r + 1$. That is, $X_{r+1} \geq \alpha q_{r+1}$.
Therefore,
$$\begin{aligned} Q_{r+1} - X_{r+1} &= Q_r - X_r + \alpha q_{r+1} - X_{r+1} \\ &\leq Q_r - X_r, \text{ (since } \alpha q_{r+1} \leq X_{r+1}) \\ &\leq D(c^* + k), \text{ (by the inductive assumption (5))} \end{aligned}$$

That is,
$$Q_{r+1} - X_{r+1} \leq D(c^* + k).$$

(3) Conclusion: therefore,
$$Q_{t-1} - X_{t-1} \leq D(c^* + k), \qquad \forall t \geq 1, \alpha > 0, k > 0.$$

Now when αq_t is added to both sides of (2.2), (2.2) becomes
$$Q_{t-1} - X_{t-1} + \alpha q_t \leq D(c^* + k) + \alpha q_t. \tag{2.7}$$

Since $q_t \leq \overline{q}$, and $Q_t = Q_{t-1} - X_{t-1} + \alpha q_t$, then (2.7) becomes
$$Q_t \leq D(c^* + k) + \alpha \overline{q}.$$

The proof of Lemma 1 is complete. □

2.3 The Results

Thus, the lowest bound for the industry price has been established.

Now, the focus of the chapter turns to the determination of a probabilistic upper bound for the industry price after a certain number of time periods. The following Lemma specifically shows that for any given positive number $\epsilon' < k$ with probability 1 there exists a time period after which the industry price cannot be above $D^{-1}(D(c^* + k + \epsilon') - \alpha \bar{q})$ when the firms get infinitesimally small relative to the market. To identify precisely this upper bound in the following lemma, some further notation needs to be developed.

Definition 1. Denote a firm with average variable cost lying in the interval $[c^*, c^* + \epsilon']$ as an E-firm. Since $AC_\alpha(\cdot)$ is continuous, it therefore follows that E-firms' outputs must lie in a subinterval around αq^* in the interval αA. Define

$$e_t = \begin{cases} 1 & \text{if } AC_\alpha(\alpha q_t) \in [c^*, c^* + \epsilon'] \\ 0 & \text{otherwise} \end{cases}$$

for $t = 1, 2, \ldots$. Since $\{q_t\}_{t \geq 1}$ is independently and identically distributed according to $F(\cdot)$, $\{e_t\}_{t \geq 1}$ is independently and identically distributed. Denote

$$\Pr(e_t = 1) = \theta$$
$$\Pr(e_t = 0) = 1 - \theta.$$

Clearly, $\theta > 0$.[5]

Definition 2. Denote h_t, for $t = 1, 2, \ldots$, as

$$h_t = \begin{cases} 1 & \text{if } P_{t-1} \geq D^{-1}(D(c^* + k + \epsilon') - \alpha \bar{q}) \\ 0 & \text{otherwise} \end{cases}.$$

The proof of Lemma 2 focuses on showing that for any given $\epsilon' < k$ and for sufficiently small firm-size (α) there exists a time period after which the price stays below $D^{-1}(D(c^* + k + \epsilon') - \alpha \bar{q})$ with probability 1. The proof consists of two steps. Step 1 shows that with $\epsilon' < k$ and a sufficiently small firm-size (α) the price will always be greater than $c^* + \epsilon'$. This further implies that any E-firm which makes a nonnegative profit in its entry period will always be able to make nonnegative profits in all subsequent time periods. Consequently, this E-firm always stays in the industry. Step 2 shows that with probability 1 the price stays above $D^{-1}(D(c^* + k + \epsilon') - \alpha \bar{q})$ only a finite number of time periods. This is equivalent to showing that with probability 0 the number of time periods, after which the price stays above $D^{-1}(D(c^* + k + \epsilon') - \alpha \bar{q})$, tends to infinity. This step is shown by contradiction. Suppose that with some positive probability the number of time

---

[5]If the random draws $q_1, q_2, \ldots, q_t, \ldots$ are from a discrete subset of the interval A, then this discrete subset has to include the point q^* and the discrete probability distribution over the discrete subset has to place a strictly positive measure on q^* in order to achieve similar results to this paper.

periods, after which the price stays above $D^{-1}(D(c^*+k+\epsilon')-\alpha\bar{q})$, tends to infinity. Having this critical value $D^{-1}(D(c^*+k+\epsilon')-\alpha\bar{q})$ guarantees that if any E-firm enters in the time period, after which the price is above $D^{-1}(D(c^*+k+\epsilon')-\alpha\bar{q})$, this E-firm will make nonnegative profit in its entry period. Step 1 implies that this E-firm makes nonnegative profits in all subsequent periods. Therefore, this E-firm never exits the industry. Furthermore, with the independence of $\{e_t\}_{t\geq 1}$ it is shown that with a strictly positive probability the number of such E-firms that never exit the industry tends to infinity. Since all these E-firms produce a positive output, consequently, this would cause the price to go below the lowest bound established in Lemma 1, which is a contradiction.

Lemma 2. *For any positive k, for all positive $\epsilon' < k$, there exists a positive $\bar{\alpha}$ such that, for all $\alpha \leq \bar{\alpha}$,*

$$\Pr\{\exists \tau(\epsilon',\alpha,k,q) \text{ such that for } t \geq \tau(\cdot)\ P_t \leq D^{-1}(D(c^*+k+\epsilon')-\alpha\bar{q})\} = 1$$
$$\text{or } \Pr\left\{\lim_{t\to\infty} P_t \leq D^{-1}(D(c^*+k+\epsilon')-\alpha\bar{q})\right\} = 1.$$

Proof. To show Lemma 2 it is sufficient to show that for any positive k and for any $\epsilon' < k$, there exists a positive $\bar{\alpha}$ such that, for all $\alpha \leq \bar{\alpha}$, with probability 1 there exists only a finite number of time periods for which the price is greater than or equal to $D^{-1}(D(c^*+k+\epsilon')-\alpha\bar{q})$.

This is proved in the following two steps.

Step 1: This step shows the following claim.

Claim 1. *For any positive k and all positive $\epsilon' < k$, there exists a positive $\bar{\alpha}$ such that $\alpha \leq \bar{\alpha}$ implies that $P_t \geq c^* + \epsilon'$, for $t = 1, 2, \ldots$.*

Proof of Claim 1: For any $k > 0$ and all positive $\epsilon' < k$, pick a positive $\bar{\alpha}$ such that

$$D^{-1}(D(c^*+k)+\bar{\alpha}\bar{q}) = c^* + \epsilon'.^6$$

Since $D'(\cdot) < 0$, $\alpha \leq \bar{\alpha}$ implies that

$$D^{-1}(D(c^*+k)+\alpha\bar{q}) \geq c^* + \epsilon'. \tag{2.8}$$

Lemma 1 implies that

$$P_t \geq D^{-1}(D(c^*+k)+\alpha\bar{q}) \quad \forall \alpha, k, t. \tag{2.9}$$

Then (2.8) and (2.9) imply that

---

[6] Since $D'(\cdot) < 0$, if $k \leq \epsilon'$ then there does not exist a positive $\bar{\alpha}$ such that $D^{-1}(D(c^*+k)+\bar{\alpha}\bar{q}) = c^* + \epsilon'$. Therefore, it is necessary that $k > \epsilon'$.

2.3 The Results

$$P_t \geq c^* + \epsilon', \text{ for } t = 1, 2, \ldots.$$

That is, for any positive k and all positive $\epsilon' < k$, there exists a positive $\bar{\alpha}$ such that $\alpha \leq \bar{\alpha}$ implies that $P_t \geq c^* + \epsilon'$, for $t = 1, 2, \ldots.$

Step 2: Step 2 proves the following claim.

Claim 2. For any $k > 0$, for all positive ϵ' such that $0 < \epsilon' < k$, and for $\alpha \leq \bar{\alpha}$ (where $\bar{\alpha}$ is defined in Step 1)

$$\Pr\left\{\sum_{t=1}^{\infty} h_t < \infty\right\} = 1.$$

Proof of Claim 2: Since

$$\Pr\left\{\sum_{t=1}^{\infty} h_t < \infty\right\} + \Pr\left\{\sum_{t=1}^{\infty} h_t = \infty\right\} = 1,$$

to show Claim 2, it is sufficient to show that

$$\Pr\left\{\sum_{t=1}^{\infty} h_t = \infty\right\} = 0. \tag{2.10}$$

The following shows (2.10) by way of contradiction. Suppose that

$$\Pr\left\{\sum_{t=1}^{\infty} h_t = \infty\right\} = \lambda > 0.$$

This implies that for any integer M, there exists an integer $m \geq M$, such that

$$\Pr\left\{\sum_{t=1}^{m} h_t \geq M\right\} > \frac{\lambda}{2} > 0. \tag{2.11}$$

Denote $N(m) = \sum_{t=1}^{m} h_t$.

Now construct a collection of random variables $\{\widetilde{e}_{t_1}, \widetilde{e}_{t_2}, \ldots, \widetilde{e}_{t_M}, \ldots, \widetilde{e}_{t_{N(m)}}\}$, where $t_n = \min_{t}\{t : h_t = 1, t > t_{n-1}\}$, and the initial point $t_0 = 0$.

Define $\widetilde{e}_{t_n}$, for $n = 1, 2, \ldots, M, \ldots, N(m)$ as

$$\widetilde{e}_{t_n} = \begin{cases} 1 & \text{if } e_{t_n} = 1 \text{ at } t_n \\ 0 & \text{otherwise} \end{cases}.$$

Since e_t is independent of h_t (which is realized at time $t-1$) and $\{e_t\}_{t\geq 1}$ are independently and identically distributed, it follows that $\{\widetilde{e}_{t_i}\}_{i=1}^{N(m)}$ are independently and identically distributed and

$$\Pr\{\widetilde{e}_{t_n} = 1\} = \theta \text{ for } n = 1, 2, \ldots, N(m)$$
$$\Pr\{\widetilde{e}_{t_n} = 0\} = 1 - \theta \text{ for } n = 1, 2, \ldots, N(m)$$

Since $\{\widetilde{e}_{t_i}\}_{i=1}^{N(m)}$ are i.i.d., $\sum_{i=1}^{N(m)} \widetilde{e}_{t_i}$ has a binomial distribution with parameters $N(m)$ and θ, for any integer $E \leq N(m)$,

$$\Pr\left\{\sum_{i=1}^{N(m)} \widetilde{e}_{t_i} \geq E\right\} = \sum_{j=E}^{N(m)} \binom{N(m)}{j} \theta^j (1-\theta)^{N(m)-j}$$

Since $\sum_{i=1}^{N(m)} e_{t_i} = \sum_{i=1}^{N(m)} \widetilde{e}_{t_i}$, for $N(m) = M$

$$\Pr\left\{\sum_{i=1}^{N(m)} e_{t_i} \geq E | N(m) = M\right\} = \sum_{j=E}^{M} \binom{M}{j} \theta^j (1-\theta)^{M-j} \quad (2.12)$$

As shown in the Appendix, for any integer $E \leq M$

$$\Pr\left\{\sum_{i=1}^{N(m)} e_{t_i} \geq E | N(m) \geq M\right\} \geq \Pr\left\{\sum_{i=1}^{M} e_{t_i} \geq E | N(m) = M\right\}. \quad (2.13)$$

Equations (2.12) and (2.13) imply that

$$\Pr\left\{\sum_{i=1}^{N(m)} e_{t_i} \geq E | N(m) \geq M\right\} \geq \sum_{j=E}^{M} \binom{M}{j} \theta^j (1-\theta)^{M-j}. \quad (2.14)$$

Since $\sum_{j=E}^{M} \binom{M}{j} \theta^j (1-\theta)^{M-j} > 0$, it is possible to pick a positive number $\beta < \sum_{j=E}^{M} \binom{M}{j} \theta^j (1-\theta)^{M-j}$, and together with (2.14), this implies that for any given integer E there exist $M \geq E$ and m such that

$$\Pr\left\{\sum_{i=1}^{N(m)} e_{t_i} \geq E | N(m) \geq M\right\} \geq \sum_{j=E}^{M} \binom{M}{j} \theta^j (1-\theta)^{M-j} > \beta. \quad (2.15)$$

2.3 The Results

Finally, since $N(m) = \sum_{t=1}^{m} h_t$ and using (2.11) and (2.15)

$$\Pr\left\{\sum_{i=1}^{N(m)} e_{t_i} \geq E\right\} \geq \Pr\left\{\sum_{i=1}^{N(m)} e_{t_i} \geq E, \sum_{t=1}^{m} h_t \geq M\right\}$$

$$= \Pr\left(\sum_{i=1}^{N(m)} e_{t_i} \geq E \mid \sum_{t=1}^{m} h_t \geq M\right) \Pr\left(\sum_{t=1}^{m} h_t \geq M\right)$$

$$\geq \left\{\sum_{j=E}^{M} \binom{M}{j} \theta^j (1-\theta)^{M-j}\right\} \cdot \frac{\lambda}{2}$$

$$> \frac{\beta\lambda}{2}.$$

Then for any integer E there exists an integer m such that

$$\Pr\left\{\sum_{i=1}^{N(m)} e_{t_i} \geq E\right\} > \frac{\beta\lambda}{2} > 0.$$

This in turn implies that

$$\Pr\left\{\sum_{i=1}^{\infty} e_{t_i} = \infty\right\} > 0.$$

This means that, with positive probability, the number of E-firms entering over the time periods $\{t : P_{t-1} \geq D^{-1}(D(c^* + k + \epsilon') - \alpha\bar{q})\}$ tends to infinity.

Now consider an E-firm entering the industry in the time period t for which $P_{t-1} \geq D^{-1}(D(c^* + k + \epsilon') - \alpha\bar{q})$ or $h_t = 1$. This implies that $Q_{t-1} \leq D(c^* + k + \epsilon') - \alpha\bar{q}$ and since $Q_t = Q_{t-1} - X_{t-1} + \alpha q_t$, where $X_{t-1} \geq 0$ and $q_t \leq \bar{q}$,

$$Q_t \leq D(c^* + k + \epsilon')$$

or

$$P_t \geq c^* + k + \epsilon'$$

This E-firm makes per unit revenue P_t which is greater than or equal to its per unit cost which is no more than $c^* + k + \epsilon'$ in its entry period t. Hence this E-firm makes nonnegative profit in its entry period t. Claim 1 implies that $\forall k > 0$ and for all positive $\epsilon' < k$, there exists a $\bar{\alpha}$ such that $\alpha \leq \bar{\alpha}$ implies that $P_{t+1} \geq c^* + \epsilon'$, for $t = 0, 1, 2, \ldots$. This in turn implies that this E-firm makes per unit revenue, which is greater than its per unit costs ($P_{t+i} \geq c^* + \epsilon'$, $i = 1, 2, \ldots$), in all time periods after the entry period. Therefore, this E-firm always makes nonnegative profits after its entry and never exits the industry. Since all the E-firms have per unit costs no more than $c^* + k + \epsilon'$ in their entry periods and per unit costs no more than $c^* + \epsilon'$ in any time period after entry, the same argument implies that all the E-firms entering the industry over the time periods $\{t : P_{t-1} \geq D^{-1}(D(c^* + k + \epsilon') - \alpha\bar{q})\}$ or $\{t : h_t = 1\}$ make nonnegative profits in all the time periods and never exit the industry.

Therefore, the above has shown that with a positive probability the number of E-firms (that never exit the industry) in the industry tends to infinity. Since each of the E-firms produces a quantity of at least αq, with a positive probability the industry output quantity must be driven eventually to a quantity greater than $D(c^* + k) + \alpha\bar{q}$. Since $D'(\cdot) < 0$, then with a positive probability the price must be below the lowest bound $D^{-1}(D(c^* + k) + \alpha\bar{q})$. This is a contradiction of Lemma 1.

Therefore, Claim 2 has been proven. That is, for any $k > 0$, for all positive $\epsilon' < k$, and for $\alpha \leq \bar{\alpha}$ (where $\bar{\alpha}$ is defined in Step 1)

$$\Pr\left\{\sum_{t=1}^{\infty} h_t < \infty\right\} = 1.$$

Claims 1 and 2 imply that for any given positive k and all positive $\epsilon' < k$, there exists a positive $\bar{\alpha}$ such that for all $\alpha \leq \bar{\alpha}$, $\Pr\{\sum_{t=1}^{\infty} h_t < \infty\} = 1$. This means that with probability 1 there is only a finite number of time periods for which the price is greater than or equal to $D^{-1}(D(c^* + k + \epsilon') - \alpha\bar{q})$. This implies that eventually the price will stay below $D^{-1}(D(c^* + k + \epsilon')) - \alpha\bar{q}$ with probability 1.

Formally, for any given positive k and all positive $\epsilon' < k$, there exists a positive $\bar{\alpha}$ such that, for all $\alpha \leq \bar{\alpha}$,

$\Pr[\exists \tau(\epsilon', \alpha, k, q) \text{ such that for } t \geq \tau(\epsilon', \alpha, k, q) \ P_t \leq D^{-1}(D(c^* + k + \epsilon') - \alpha\bar{q})] = 1.$

The proof of Lemma 2 is complete. □

Remark. To make the firms' outputs become infinitesimally small relative to the market, the above proof shrinks α toward zero while fixing the market demand. Another equivalent way to achieve this is to keep the firms' outputs fixed but expand the market demand toward infinity. [For a further detailed discussion, see Novshek (1980).]

Having established the lowest bound and the probabilistic upper bound for the industry price, the chapter now presents the main results in Theorem 1. Theorem 1 has three parts. The first part of Theorem 1 proves that the industry price converges in probability to the perfectly competitive price P^* as the firms get infinitesimally small relative to the market, the cost of entry k gets sufficiently small and time gets sufficiently large. Furthermore, the second part of Theorem 1 shows that in the limit the only firms existing in the industry ($i \in \{\ell : \prod_{j=\ell}^{\infty} I_j^\ell = 1\}$) are those with average

2.3 The Results

cost equal to c^* and the last part shows that in the limit there are no potential entrants that can make strictly positive profits by entry.

Theorem 1. *For any positive numbers ϵ and $\eta \in (0,1)$, there exist positive numbers $\overline{\alpha}$ and $\overline{k}$ such that, for all $\alpha \le \overline{\alpha}$ and $\epsilon' < k \le \overline{k}$ (where $\epsilon' = D^{-1}(D(P^* + \epsilon) + \alpha\overline{q}) - c^* - \overline{k}$),*

(1) there exists a time period $\tau(\epsilon, \eta, \alpha, k)$ such that, for $t \ge \tau(\epsilon, \eta, \alpha, k)$,

$$\Pr\{P^* < P_t \le P^* + \epsilon\} > 1 - \eta$$

(2) Furthermore, there exists a time period $\tau'(\eta, \epsilon, \alpha, k)$ after which, with probability of at least $1 - \eta$ all the remaining firms are those with average variable cost lying in the interval $[c^*, c^* + \epsilon]$.

More precisely, there exists a time period $\tau'(\eta, \epsilon, \alpha, k)$ such that, for $t > \tau'(\eta, \epsilon, \alpha, k)$ and $i \in \{\ell : \prod_{j=\ell}^{t} I_j^\ell = 1\}$,

$$\Pr\{AC_\alpha(\alpha q_i) \in [c^*, c^* + \epsilon]\} > 1 - \eta.$$

(3) with probability of at least $1 - \eta$ no firm with average variable cost lying outside the interval $[c^*, c^* + \epsilon]$ can make positive profit by entering after time period $\tau(\eta, \epsilon, \alpha, k)$.

More precisely, for αq_t where $AC_\alpha(\alpha q_t) \notin [c^*, c^* + \epsilon]$,

$$\Pr\{P_t - (AC_\alpha(\alpha q_t) + k) < 0\} > 1 - \eta.$$

Proof. Lemma 2 implies that for any given positive k and all positive $\epsilon' < k$, there exists a positive $\overline{\alpha}$ such that for all $\alpha \le \overline{\alpha}$

$$\Pr[\exists \tau(\epsilon', \alpha, k, q) \text{ such that for } t \ge \tau(\epsilon', \alpha, k, q) \, P_t \le D^{-1}(D(c^* + k + \epsilon') - \alpha\overline{q})] = 1.$$

Pick a $\overline{k}$ such that $\overline{k} > \epsilon'$.
For $\epsilon' < k \le \overline{k}, \alpha \le \overline{\alpha}$,

$$D^{-1}(D(c^* + k + \epsilon') - \alpha\overline{q}) \le D^{-1}(D(c^* + \overline{k} + \epsilon') - \overline{\alpha}\,\overline{q}). \tag{2.16}$$

Define ϵ as the following,

$$P^* + \epsilon = D^{-1}(D(c^* + \overline{k} + \epsilon') - \overline{\alpha}\,\overline{q}) \tag{2.17}$$

Given the relationship between ϵ and ϵ' in (2.17), an arbitrarily small ϵ can always be produced by choosing an appropriately small ϵ'.[7] Therefore, (2.16) can be rewritten as the following:

---

[7] It can be easily shown that $\epsilon > \epsilon' + k$.

For $\epsilon' < k \leq \overline{k}, \alpha \leq \overline{\alpha}$,

$$D^{-1}(D(c^* + k + \epsilon') - \alpha \overline{q}) \leq P^* + \epsilon. \tag{2.18}$$

where

$$\epsilon' = D^{-1}(D(P^* + \epsilon) + \overline{\alpha} \, \overline{q}) - c^* - \overline{k} \text{ (from (2.17))}.$$

Using (2.18), Lemma 2 can be rewritten in the terms of ϵ and P^* as the following:

For any positive number ϵ there exist positive numbers $\overline{\alpha}$ and $\overline{k}$ such that for all $\alpha \leq \overline{\alpha}$ and $\epsilon' < k \leq \overline{k}$, (where $\epsilon' = D^{-1}(D(P^* + \epsilon) + \overline{\alpha} \, \overline{q}) - c^* - \overline{k}$),

$$\Pr\{\exists \tau(\epsilon, \alpha, k, q) \text{ such that for } t \geq \tau(\cdot) \; P_t < P^* + \epsilon\} = 1 \tag{2.19}$$

Clearly, the time period $\tau(\cdot)$ depends on the random variable q, not on the cumulative distribution function $F(\cdot)$. To be more practical and relevant to experimentation it is of more interest in an ex ante sense to determine from what time period and on, that the event $P_t > P^* + \epsilon$ occurs with a given probability. That is, for any given $\eta \in (0, 1)$, one can always construct a time period τ based on η (instead of q) such that from that time period and on

$$\Pr\{P_t > P^* + \epsilon\} < \eta.$$

Therefore, for any positive numbers ϵ and $\eta \in (0, 1)$, there exist positive numbers $\overline{\alpha}$ and $\overline{k}$ such that, for all $\alpha \leq \overline{\alpha}$ and $\epsilon' < k \leq \overline{k}$, (where $\epsilon' = D^{-1}(D(P^* + \epsilon) + \overline{\alpha} \, \overline{q}) - c^* - \overline{k}$), there exists a time period $\tau(\eta, \epsilon, \alpha, k)$ such that, for $t \geq \tau(\eta, \epsilon, \alpha, k)$,[8]

$$\Pr\{P_t \leq P^* + \epsilon\} > 1 - \eta. \tag{2.20}$$

Claim 1 of Lemma 2 implies that
$\forall k > 0, \forall \epsilon' < k$ and for all $\alpha \leq \overline{\alpha}$,

$$P_t \geq c^* + \epsilon' \text{ for } t = 1, 2, \ldots. \tag{2.21}$$

Since $P^* = c^*$, and $\epsilon' = D^{-1}(D(P^* + \epsilon) + \overline{\alpha} \, \overline{q}) - c^* - \overline{k}$, the above can be restated in terms of ϵ and P^* as the following.

$\forall \epsilon > 0$, for all $D^{-1}(D(P^* + \epsilon) + \overline{\alpha} \, \overline{q}) - c^* - \overline{k} < k$ and for all $\alpha \leq \overline{\alpha}$

$$P_t > P^* \text{ for } t = 1, 2, \ldots \tag{2.22}$$

Equations (2.20) and (2.22) imply that for any positive numbers ϵ and $\eta \in (0, 1)$, there exist positive numbers $\overline{\alpha}$ and $\overline{k}$ such that, for all $\alpha \leq \overline{\alpha}$ and $\epsilon' < k \leq \overline{k}$, (where

---

[8] The transition from (2.19) to (2.20) is due to the fact that almost sure convergence implies convergence in probability.

2.3 The Results

$\epsilon' = D^{-1}(D(P^* + \epsilon) + \overline{\alpha}\,\overline{q}) - c^* - \overline{k}$), there exists a time period $\tau(\eta, \epsilon, \alpha, k)$ such that, for $t \geq \tau(\eta, \epsilon, \alpha, k)$,

$$\Pr\{P^* < P_t \leq P^* + \epsilon\} > 1 - \eta$$

(2) First of all, the set $\{\ell : \prod_{j=\ell}^{t} I_j^\ell = 1\}$ is non-empty. This is true, because (2.21) implies that E-firms, which enter when $P_i \geq c^* + k + \epsilon'$, (where $i < t$), will make nonnegative profits all the time periods and will never exit the industry.

Second, (2.19) states that for any positive number ϵ there exist positive numbers $\overline{\alpha}$ and $\overline{k}$ such that for all $\alpha \leq \overline{\alpha}$ and $\epsilon' < k \leq \overline{k}$, (where $\epsilon' = D^{-1}(D(P^* + \epsilon) + \overline{\alpha}\,\overline{q}) - c^* - \overline{k}$),

$$\Pr\{\exists \tau(\epsilon, \alpha, k, q) \text{ such that for } t \geq \tau(\cdot) \ P_t \leq P^* + \epsilon\} = 1$$

This implies that for any firm i' entering the industry before time period $\tau(\epsilon', \alpha, k, q)$ and with average variable cost lying outside the interval $[c^*, c^* + \epsilon]$, where $i' \leq \tau(\cdot)$, with probability 1 there always exists a time period $\widetilde{t}_{i'}$, by the end of which, firm i' exits the industry (i.e., $\prod_{j=i'}^{\widetilde{t}_{i'}} I_j^{i'} = 0$). The reason is as follows: Since, with probability 1 P_t is less than or equal to $P^* + \epsilon$ after time period $\tau(\cdot)$, the firm i' with average cost lying outside the interval $[c^* + \epsilon]$ makes a negative profit after time period $\tau(\cdot)$. Since there is only a finite number of time periods before time period $\tau(\cdot)$, only a finite positive amount of wealth could have been accumulated up to period $\tau(\cdot)$. Therefore, there will exist a time period $\widetilde{t}_{i'} \geq \tau(\cdot)$ where the negative profits accumulated after time period $\tau(\cdot)$ will offset any positive profits accumulated before time period $\tau(\cdot)$. This causes the total wealth of firm i' to become negative. Therefore, firm i' exits the industry.

Of course, for any firm i'' entering the industry after time period $\tau(\cdot)$, where $\tau(\cdot) < i''$ and where $AC_\alpha(\alpha q_{i''}) \notin [c^*, c^* + \epsilon]$ it will exit at the end of its entry time period i''. That is, $I_{i''}^{i''} = 0$.

Define $t' = \max_{i' \leq \tau(\cdot)} \{\widetilde{t}_{i'}\}$. Therefore, with probability 1 for any $t > t'$ and for all $i \in \{\ell : \prod_{j=\ell}^{t} I_j^\ell = 1\}$, $AC_\alpha(\alpha q_i) \in [c^*, c^* + \epsilon]$. That is, for any positive number ϵ there exist positive numbers $\overline{\alpha}$ and $\overline{k}$ such that for all $\alpha \leq \overline{\alpha}$ and $\epsilon' < k \leq \overline{k}$, (where $\epsilon' = D^{-1}(D(P^* + \epsilon) + \overline{\alpha}\,\overline{q}) - c^* - \overline{k}$),

$$\Pr\{\exists t' \text{ such that for } t \geq t', i \in \{\ell : \prod_{j=\ell}^{t} I_j^\ell = 1\}, AC_\alpha(\alpha q_i) \in [c^*, c^* + \epsilon]\} = 1.$$

Which further implies that the results of part (2). That is, for any positive numbers ϵ and $\eta \in (0, 1)$, there exist positive numbers $\overline{\alpha}$ and $\overline{k}$ such that, for all $\alpha \leq \overline{\alpha}$ and ϵ'

$<k \leq \overline{k}$ (where $\epsilon' = D^{-1}(D(P^* + \epsilon) + \overline{\alpha}\,\overline{q}) - c^* - \overline{k}$), there exists a time period $\tau'(\eta, \epsilon, \alpha, k)$ such that, for $t > \tau'(\eta, \epsilon, \alpha, k)$ and $i \in \{\ell : \prod_{j=\ell}^{t} I_j^\ell = 1\}$,

$$\Pr\{AC_\alpha(\alpha q_i) \in [c^*, c^* + \epsilon]\} > 1 - \eta.$$

(3) Part (1) of Theorem 1 implies that $\forall \epsilon, \eta$, there exist positive numbers $\overline{\alpha}$ and $\overline{k}$ such that, for all $\alpha \leq \overline{\alpha}$ and $\epsilon' < k \leq \overline{k}$, there exists a time period $\tau(\epsilon, \eta, \alpha, k)$ such that, for $t \geq \tau(\epsilon, \eta, \alpha, k)$,

$$\Pr\{P_t \leq P^* + \epsilon\} > 1 - \eta.$$

Since $P^* + \epsilon < P^* + \epsilon + k$, $\Pr\{P_t \leq P^* + \epsilon\} < \Pr\{P_t < P^* + \epsilon + k\}$. Therefore,

$$\Pr\{P_t < P^* + \epsilon + k\} > 1 - \eta.$$

If $AC_\alpha(\alpha q_t) \notin [c^*, c^* + \epsilon]$, then $AC_\alpha(\alpha q_t) > c^* + \epsilon = P^* + \epsilon$ and $\Pr\{P_t < P^* + \epsilon + k\} < \Pr\{P_t < AC_\alpha(\alpha q_t) + k\}$. It then follows that, for αq_t where $AC_\alpha(\alpha q_t) \notin [c^*, c^* + \epsilon]$,

$$\Pr\{P_t < AC_\alpha(\alpha q_t) + k\} > 1 - \eta.$$

Therefore, part (3) has been proven.

The proof of the Theorem is complete. □

Remark. Since $D(\cdot)$ is a continuous function, one can similarly show that the industry quantity converges in probability to the perfectly competitive quantity Q^* as the firms get infinitesimally small relative to the market, the average fixed cost of entry k gets sufficiently small and time gets sufficiently large.

2.4 Numerical Illustration

The last section of the chapter has shown theoretically that, as time gets large and competition increases ($\alpha \to 0$ and the average cost of entry (k) gets small), the price converges to the competitive price and all of the remaining firms produce at minimum efficient scale. In practice, what would this convergence look like? In this section, some numerical examples are provided to help better understand the results of the chapter.

The following numerical illustrations examine an industry where

1. the consumer demand function is $Q_t = 4 - P_t$, $t = 1, 2, \ldots$,
2. the average variable cost function for all firms entering at time t (where $t = 1, 2, \ldots$) is

$$AC_\alpha(\alpha q_t) = \left(\frac{\alpha q_t}{\alpha} - 1\right)^2 + 2,$$

2.4 Numerical Illustration

3. the average entry cost is $k = 0.025$,
4. the q_t are drawn according to a uniform distribution from the interval [.5, 1.5], and
5. the level of competition and the size of the firm is represented by α. Firm t produces αq_t.

The first example illustrates how the distributions of price and surviving firms shift as time goes by for an industry with a sufficient amount of competition (reflected by small enough α and k). In this illustration $\alpha = 0.009$. For this model $P^* = c^* = 2$. The α and k are chosen to ensure the existence of E-firms. In this example E-firms have average variable costs lying in the interval $[c^*, c^* + \epsilon']$ where $c^* = 2$ and $\epsilon' = .01$. Based on Lemma 1, the lower bound of the price should be $D^{-1}(D(c^* + k) + \alpha \overline{q}) = 2.0115$ and based on Lemma 2, the upper bound of the price should be $D^{-1}(D(c^* + k + \epsilon') - \alpha \overline{q}) = 2.0485$.

Five hundred simulations are conducted with the above set of parameters. Each simulation consists of the following: At time period t ($t = 1, 2, \ldots$) q_t is drawn from the uniform distribution and firm t's output is αq_t as long as it remains in the industry. By summing up the supply of all surviving firms the market price is determined. At all time periods each firm's cumulative wealth is computed. As soon as a firm's wealth becomes negative it leaves the industry. Each simulation follows the industry from time period 1 to 10,000.

In Fig. 2.1, histograms are presented which illustrate the distribution of price and surviving firms' average variable costs at time periods 1,000 and 10,000. The price histogram (Fig. 2.1a) shows that at time 1,000 there is a small fraction of sample points (1.2%) which still lie outside the band [2.0115, 2.0485] (the interval predicted in the theory above). By time period 10,000 all sample points lie inside this band. Notice that at time 10,000 approximately 87% of the sample points fall in the [2.0115, 2.0254) interval while at time period 1,000 57% of the price sample points fall in the same interval. An analysis of the cost histogram (Fig. 2.1b) shows that after 10,000 time periods all of the remaining firms in the industry have average variable costs below the upper bound 2.0485. This is not true after 1,000 time periods (where about 20% of the firms still have average variable costs above 2.0485). By time period 10,000 approximately 83% of the firms are E-firms. This contrasts with 54% at time period 1,000.

The second example is designed to illustrate the instability in the distribution of price as time goes by for an industry without a sufficient amount of competition (represented by a sufficiently large α (=.03)). The second example conducts 500 simulations, where a sufficiently large α (=.03) is chosen such that no firm can make nonnegative profits in all time periods.[9] The price histograms are reported in Fig. 2.2 for time periods 500, 5,000, and 10,000. Evidence of the large variability in price movement is clear when a comparison is made between time periods 500

---

[9] With $\epsilon' = .01$ and $k = .025$, for the existence of E-firms with average variable costs in [2, 2.01] ,α must be less than or equal to $\overline{\alpha} = .01$.

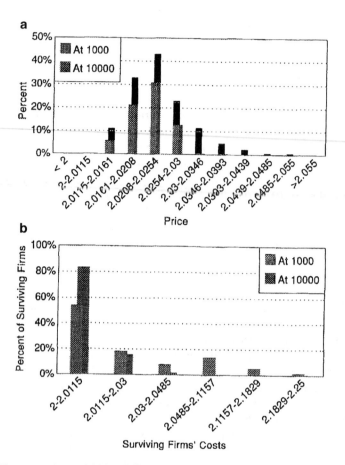

Fig. 2.1 Histograms ($\alpha = 0.009$ and $K = 0.025$), a comparison at times 1,000 and 10,000: (**a**) price, and (**b**) surviving firms' costs

and 5,000 and between time periods 500 and 10,000. Figure 2.2a shows that relative to time period 5,000 the mean value of price is much closer to 2 at time period 500. Interestingly, the dispersion of prices at 5,000 is very small but its mean is relatively large. Figure 2.2b shows that as time increases to 10,000 the distribution of price reverts to looking like the distribution at time period 500. Clearly, the price distribution does not appear to be very stable. Furthermore, at time periods 500 and 10,000 a sizeable percentage (approximately 10%) of sample price points fall below the long run competitive price, $P^* = 2$.

2.5 Conclusions

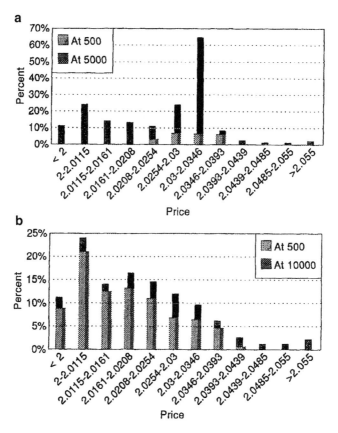

Fig. 2.2 Price histograms ($\alpha = 0.03$ and $K = 0.025$), a comparison at times (**a**) 500 and 5,000, and (**b**) 500 and 10,000

2.5 Conclusions

Although profit maximization is the usual prerequisite for achievement of a perfectly competitive equilibrium, this chapter has proven that even if the firms behave irrationally, the industry can arrive at the same perfectly competitive equilibrium. This was accomplished by following the evolution of an industry through an infinite time horizon model where firms randomly choose their outputs, continually enter the market and leave when their wealth becomes negative.

In this partial equilibrium model, all the firms' abilities are assumed to be bounded in the extreme. They cannot adapt their behavior to the environment. Presumably, if this assumption is relaxed, any amount of rationality which adds to their abilities should only lead to speeding up the convergence process to a perfectly competitive equilibrium. For example, if firms are allowed to adaptively adjust their outputs from period to period through learning, searching or imitating, eventually these firms will resemble those producing at minimum efficient scale. Consequently, the speed of convergence will be increased.

In conclusion, this chapter lends analytic support to earlier conjectures which have attempted to explain economic events in term of biological evolution and natural selection. That is, "the principle of conscious 'adaptation' by firms seeking more profits" can be "replaced by a principle of 'adoption' of successful firms by the environment. The survival of the 'viable' firms and the elimination of nonviable ones" are "the result of 'competition'." [paraphrase of Alchian (1950) by Machans (1978, p. 297)]. this chapter has proven that after abandoning the profit maximization assumption, the industry converges in probability to a perfectly competitive equilibrium as the firms get infinitesimally small relative to the market, as the entry cost gets sufficiently small and as time gets sufficiently large. Consequently, the surviving firms in the limit are those producing at minimum efficient scale and in the limit any potential entrants can never make strictly positive profits by entry.

Appendix

Proposition 1.

$$\Pr\left\{\sum_{i=1}^{N(m)} e_{t_i} \geq E | N(m) \geq M\right\} \geq \Pr\left\{\sum_{i=1}^{M} e_{t_i} \geq E | N(m) = M\right\}.$$

Claim 1.

$$\Pr\left\{\sum_{i=1}^{N(m)} e_{t_i} \geq E | N(m) \geq M\right\} \geq \min_{r} \Pr\left\{\sum_{i=1}^{r} e_{t_i} \geq E | N(m) = r\right\},$$

where $M \leq r \leq m$.

Proof.

$$\Pr\left\{\sum_{i=1}^{N(m)} e_{t_i} \geq E | N(m) \geq M\right\}$$

$$= \frac{\Pr\left\{\sum_{i=1}^{N(m)} e_{t_i} \geq E, \& \ (N(m) = M \text{ or } N(m) = M+1 \text{ or } \ldots \text{ or } N(m) = m)\right\}}{\Pr(N(m) = M \text{ or } N(m) = M+1 \text{ or } \ldots \text{ or } N(m) = m)}$$

Appendix

$$= \frac{\Pr\left\{\sum_{i=1}^{M} e_{t_i} \geq E, N(m) = M\right\}}{\Pr(N(m) = M) + \Pr(N(m) = M+1) + \cdots + \Pr(N(m) = m)}$$

$$+ \frac{\Pr\left\{\sum_{i=1}^{M+1} e_{t_i} \geq E, N(m) = M+1\right\}}{\Pr(N(m) = M) + \Pr(N(m) = M+1) + \cdots + \Pr(N(m) = m)} + \cdots$$

$$+ \frac{\Pr\left\{\sum_{i=1}^{m} e_{t_i} \geq E, N(m) = m\right\}}{\Pr(N(m) = M) + \Pr(N(m) = M+1) + \cdots + \Pr(N(m) = m)}$$

$$= \sum_{r=M}^{m} \left(\frac{\Pr\left(\sum_{i=1}^{r} e_{t_i} \geq E, N(m) = r\right)}{\Pr(N(m) = r)} \right.$$

$$\left. \frac{\Pr(N(m) = r)}{\Pr(N(m) = M) + \Pr(N(m) = M+1) + \cdots + \Pr(N(m) = m)} \right)$$

$$= \sum_{r=M}^{m} \left[\Pr\left(\sum_{i=1}^{r} e_{t_i} \geq E | N(m) = r\right) b_r \right],$$

where

$$b_r = \frac{\Pr(N(m) = r)}{\Pr(N(m) = M) + \Pr(N(m) = M+1) + \cdots + \Pr(N(m) = m)}$$

and $b_r \in [0, 1]$ and $\sum_{r=M}^{m} b_r = 1, \geq \min_{r} \Pr(\sum_{i=1}^{r} e_{t_i} \geq E | N(m) = r)$.

Claim 2.

$$\Pr\left\{\sum_{i=1}^{r} e_{t_i} \geq E | N(m) = r\right\} < \Pr\left\{\sum_{i=1}^{r+1} e_{t_i} \geq E | N(m) = r+1\right\}.$$

Proof. Since $e_{t_1}, e_{t_2}, \ldots, e_{t_{r+1}}$ are i.i.d,

$$\Pr\left\{\sum_{i=1}^{r+1} e_{t_i} \geq E | N(m) = r+1\right\} = \Pr\left\{(\sum_{i=1}^{r} e_{t_i} \geq E | N(m) = r), e_{t_{r+1}} = 1\right\}$$

$$+ \Pr\left\{\left(\sum_{i=1}^{r} e_{t_i} \geq E | N(m) = r\right), e_{t_{r+1}} = 0\right\}$$

$$+ \Pr\left\{\left(\sum_{i=1}^{r} e_{t_i} = E - 1 | N(m) = r\right), e_{t_{r+1}} = 1\right\}$$

$$= \Pr\left\{\sum_{i=1}^{r} e_{t_i} \geq E | N(m) = r\right\} \theta + \Pr\left\{\sum_{i=1}^{r} e_{t_i} \geq E | N(m) = r\right\}(1-\theta)$$

$$+ \Pr\left\{\sum_{i=1}^{r} e_{t_i} = E - 1 | N(m) = r\right\} \theta$$

$$= \Pr\left\{\sum_{i=1}^{r} e_{t_i} \geq E | N(m) = r\right\} + \binom{r}{E-1} \theta^{E-1}(1-\theta)^{r+1-E} \theta$$

$$> \Pr\left\{\sum_{i=1}^{r} e_{t_i} > E | N(m) = r\right\}.$$

Proof of Proposition : Using Claim 2,

$$\min_{r \geq M} \Pr\left\{\sum_{i=1}^{m} e_{t_i} \geq E | N(m) = r\right\} = \Pr\left\{\sum_{i=1}^{M} e_{t_i} \geq E | N(m) = M\right\}.$$

Therefore, the Proposition is directly established by using Claim 1.

References

Alchian, A. 1950. Uncertainty, evolution and economic theory. *Journal of Political Economy* 58:211–222.
Baumol, W.J. 1967. *Business behavior, value, and growth*. rev. ed. New York: Harcourt, Brace and World.
Blume, L., and D. Easley. 1992. Evolution and market behavior. *Journal of Economic Theory* 58:9–40.
L. Blume and D. Easley. 1993. Economic natural selection, *Economics Letters* 42:281–289.
R.M. Cyert and J.G. March. 1963. *A behavioral theory of the firm*. Englewood Cliffs: Prentice-Hall, Inc.
D.K. Gode and S. Sunder. 1993. Allocative efficiency of markets with zero-intelligence traders: market as a partial substitute for individual rationality. *Journal of Political Economy* 101:119–137.
F. Knight. 1921. *Risk, uncertainty, and profit*. Boston: Houghton Mifflin.
F. Machlup. 1978. *Methodology of economics and other social sciences*. New York: Academic.
W. Novshek. 1980. Cournot equilibrium with free entry. *Review of Economic Studies* 47:473–486.
J. Patel, R. Zeckhauser and D. Hendricks. 1991. The rationality struggle: illustrations from financial markets. *American Economic Review* 81:232–236.
E.T. Penrose. 1952. Biological analogies in the theory of the firm, *American Economic Review* 42:804–819.
J. Robinson. 1933. *The economics of imperfect competition*. London: Macmillan and Company Ltd.
A. Robson. 1990. Stackelberg and Marshall. *American Economic Review* 80: 69–82.
F.M. Scherer. 1980. *Industrial market structure and economic performance*. 2nd ed. Chicago: Rand McNally College Publishing Company.

References

H. Simon. 1976. From substantive to procedural rationality. In *Method and appraisal in economics*, ed. S.J. Latsis, Cambridge: Cambridge University Press.

H. Simon, M. Egidi, R. Marris and R. Viale. 1992. *Economics, bounded rationality and the cognitive revolution*. Aldershot: Edward Elgar Publishing Limited.

G. Tintner. 1941. The pure theory of production under technological risk and uncertainty. *Econometrica* 9:305–311.

O.E. Williamson. 1963. Managerial discretion and business behavior. *American Economic Review* 53:1032–1057.

Chapter 3
Evolution, Irrationality, and Monopolistically Competitive Equilibrium[1]

The chapter presents an evolutionary model of a product differentiated industry and proves that the monopolistically competitive equilibrium will arrive as a long run outcome even though firms are totally irrational. In this evolutionary model, firms are totally irrational in the sense that firms enter the industry regardless of the existence of profits; firms' outputs are randomly determined rather than generated from profit maximization problems; and firms exit the industry if their wealth is negative. The model concludes that the industry converges in probability to the monopolistically competitive equilibrium as the size of each firm becomes sufficiently small, as entry costs become sufficiently small and as time gets sufficiently large. The firms that remain in the industry in the long run are those producing output at the tangency of the demand curve to the average cost curve. Furthermore, in the long run, no potential entrant can make a positive profit by entry.

This chapter is organized into five sections. The introduction is provided in the next section. The second section describes the model. The results can be found in the third section. The fourth section presents numerical illustrations. The last section concludes the chapter.

3.1 Introduction

In the late 1920s and early 1930s it became apparent that there were severe limitations in conducting economic analysis using a framework of either pure competition or pure monopoly. Consequently, economists began shifting their attention to middle ground between monopoly and perfect competition. One of the most notable

---

[1]This chapter is based on my article published in *European Economic Review* 53(5): 512–526, 2009.

achievements was Chamberlin's (1933) blending of elements of perfect competition and pure monopoly in a notion of "large group" monopolistic competition where there are many competing firms producing similar but different commodities which are not perfect substitutes. Because of the product differentiation each firm has a certain degree of monopoly power (i.e., faces a downward-sloping demand curve). The presence of a product group with free entry leads the industry to a long-run zero profit situation of active firms. The corresponding output is where the firms' demand curves are tangent to their respective average cost curves. This same equilibrium corresponds to where firms are long run profit maximizers. Furthermore, due to the lack of perfect substitution among all products the equilibrium output is less than the minimum efficient scale.

Coincident with Chamberlin's publication was Robinson's (1933) presentation of this same equilibrium tangency. Although it may be argued [e.g., see Kaldor (1938) and Triffin (1940)] that Chamberlin and Robinson arrive at this equilibrium with different techniques, both of their original arguments for deriving this equilibrium rely heavily on rationality and purposive profit maximization. Robinson (1933, p. v) attempted to place monopolistic competition within the context of a general theory of monopoly where "the individual firm will always arrange its affairs in such a way as to make the largest profits that can be made" (Robinson 1933, p. 6,). Chamberlin similarly characterizes individual firms as setting a price and quantity "which will render the total profit a maximum" (Chamberlin 1933, p. 71). Generally, the notion of firms maximizing profits within a monopolistic context has also remained in modern analyses of monopolistic competition [e.g., Spence (1976) and Hart (1985a,1985b).

The objection to firms behaving as profit maximizers comes from several sources. First, there may be other maximization objectives such as maximizing sales subject to a minimum profit constraint [see Baumol (1959)], or padding expenses in order to increase managers' utility [see Williamson (1964)]. Second, it is questionable that the managers of firms have the information and computational ability to correctly maximize profits [e.g., see Simon (1979)]. This is further compounded when firms have some monopoly power. To properly optimize profits firms must have complete knowledge of not only their own cost structures but also their demand curve; and in the case of monopolistic competition the relevant demand curve must take account of the constantly changing output of competitors [see Arrow[2] (1986, p. s391)]. An individual firm's demand curve is influenced by the production of other firms and other firms' production are in turn affected by its production. A third objection to optimizing models is that firms just do not make any attempts to optimize [e.g., Andrews (1949), and Cyert and March (1963)]. Rather, rules-of-thumb are used for production targets and price setting.

---

[2]As noted by Arrow (1986, p. s391), the knowledge requirements under a monopoly are very demanding. "The demand curve is more complex than a price. It involves knowing about the behavior of others. Measuring a demand curve is usually thought of as a job for an econometrician. We have the curious situation that scientific analysis imputes scientific behavior to its subjects."

3.1 Introduction

Hence, the underlying presumption of firms deliberately maximizing profits remains questionable. However, it has been thought that the monopolistically competitive result should not be so dependent on the assumption of rational profit maximizing behavior. For example, with respect to the treatment of entry of new firms, Chamberlin and Robinson both do not claim as much rationality. Robinson (1933) did not necessarily see positive profits as a signal for entry of new firms. "The abnormal profits are a symptom rather than a cause of situation in which new firms will find it profitable to enter the trade" (Robinson, p. 92–93). Although originally Chamberlin (1933) insisted that "entry profit will attract new competition to the field" (Chamberlin, p. 96), later he (1957, p. 290) argued that the monopolistically competitive equilibrium could occur when entrants flooded in irrationally, even when profits disappear. And also Chamberlin, himself, later in justifying the theory of monopolistic competition played down the role of his original marginal revenue and marginal cost curves and the idea that profit maximizing was an exclusive motive of the firm (see Kuenne (1987)).

Nevertheless, there remains the concern of how analytically robust are the equilibrium results of monopolistic competition if the firms are not rational and are not purposive profit maximizers.

This chapter, by using the evolutionary approach, is interested in showing that even if firms' output levels are determined at random, a monopolistically competitive equilibrium can still evolve. Certainly, it has been shown [see Luo (1995)] that for firms producing a homogeneous good, a perfectly competitive equilibrium evolves regardless of the degree of rationality in choice of outputs. However, it remains to be proven whether in the much more complex industrial structure of product differentiation among firms who face interdependent but firm-specific demand curves, irrational choices of outputs by firms lead to a stable equilibrium.

In the spirit of Nelson and Winter (1982), with respect to their evolutionary treatment of the firm, in this chapter, it is assumed that firms select their output levels randomly on entry and routinize their own output levels at the fixed levels thereafter. Using biological language, one may interpret the fixed level of each firm's output as its genotype. As in biology, success is rewarded and failure is punished. Here, whether a firm succeeds or fails is indicated by whether that firm passes the survival test of making nonnegative wealth in the market. In other words, if a firm makes a nonnegative wealth, it survives; otherwise it disappears. Darwinian "survival of the fittest" applies. However, for the selection of the fittest firms, just as in biology, the theory of natural selection requires competition [e.g., see Enke (1951) and Penrose (1952)]. In this chapter, competition takes the form of continuous entry of new firms across time. Thus, whatever routines are adopted by firms, competition among monopolistic competitors drives prices down, causing all but the fittest firms to make negative wealth and to exit the market, and leaving in the market only surviving firms that are lucky enough to produce at the tangency output. The surviving firms are the ones that act like long-run profit-maximizers.

In contrast to earlier discussions of monopolistic competition, the evolutionary approach focuses on the dynamics in arriving at the equilibrium. Whether it is in the early work of Chamberlin (1933) and Robinson (1933) or in the modern treatment of monopolistic competition [e.g., Hart (1985a,1985b)], the concept of time and the dynamics of arriving at an equilibrium are imprecisely described. But, as noted by O'Brien (1985, p. 31) and Shackle (1967, p. 59), it is precisely the dimension of time that is required to account for the competing away of profits as entry occurs. In this chapter, as time goes by, new firms keep entering, and firms exit whenever their wealth is negative. As a result, as time goes by the remaining firms' demand curves are always shifting up and down. It is the evolutionary dynamic process of natural selection leads to the equilibrium. Using the selection criterion of nonnegative wealth, a monopolistically competitive market selects firms, whose actions happen to be consistent with long-run profit maximization.[3]

In the literature there are oligopolistic dynamic models that allow for entry and exit of firms. Some allow for full rationality on the part of firms in a non-competitive setting and others allow for growth on the part of the firm relative to the market. For example, Jovanovic (1982) in explaining the relative growth rates of small versus large firms, describes a learning by firms about their own efficiency as they maximize expected profits conditional on information received each period. Amir and Lambson (2003) presented an infinite-horizon, stochastic model of entry and exit with sunk costs and imperfect competition. In its subgame perfect Nash equilibrium there is excessive entry and insufficient exit relative to a social optimum. Ericson and Pakes (1995) provides a model of firm and industry dynamics that allows for entry, exit, and firm-specific uncertainty arising from investment in research and exploration-type processes. The chapter shows the existence of a rational expectations, Markov-perfect equilibrium which can generate various industry structures. Herings et al. (2005) presents an equilibrium with market dominance in a simple two-firm model with neither entry barriers nor sophisticated punishment strategies. The equilibrium induces an intertemporal market division in which the two firms alternate as monopolists. In an evolutionary context, allowing for technological heterogeneity, differential growth of individual firms and turnover, Winter et al. (2003) analyses some general dynamic properties of industries characterized by heterogeneous firms and continuing stochastic entry. In contrast to the above oligopolistic dynamic models, this chapter examines firms producing differentiated products in a competitive setting - that is, monopolistic competition. Firms are atomistic relative to the market and there is unlimited entry of non-rational firms with routinized production levels.

---

[3]Certainly, there are two possible extreme assumptions with respect to firms' behavior. One is complete rationality and the other is no rationality. Other behavioral traits such as adaptive behavior would lie in between. The chapter abandons all rationality on the firms' part to illustrate and highlight the impact of a very irrational world on the long run aggregate market. Even when we remove the plank of rationality and replace this with total irrationality, the traditional monopolistic competition equilibrium emerges. This is very compelling and reinforces the idea that even without rationality, natural selection forces lead to a monopolistically competitive equilibrium. Purposive maximization of profits is not required. Undoubtedly, allowing adaptive behavior on the firm side will also lead to convergence; however, the speed of convergence is faster.

3.2 The Model

Consider monopolistic competition in a market, where firms produce nonhomogeneous products. These nonhomogeneous products are similar but not perfect substitutes for one another. To characterize the dynamic process of monopolistic competition, a discrete dynamic model is used and time is indexed by t, where $t = 1, 2, \ldots$. It is assumed that all firms enter the market sequentially over time. For simplicity, only one firm is assumed to enter the market at time t, where $t = 1, 2, \ldots$. The firm that enters at time t is labeled as firm t and produces good t at a production level αq^t, where α is a positive parameter and q^t is randomly taken from an interval $[\underline{q}, \overline{q}]$, where $0 < \underline{q} < \overline{q} < \infty$, according to a distribution function $F(\cdot)$, where $F(\cdot)$ has full support on $[\underline{q}, \overline{q}]$. As long as firm t remains in the market, it always produces αq^t. The α parameter is a scale parameter, which reflects the size of the firm relative to the overall market. This random selection of q^t and fixity of αq^t as long as the firm remains in the market, illustrates an irrationality with respect to firms' responses to market conditions. The firm is not purposively adjusting its output each time period in response to changing market conditions (e.g., such as prices).

There is an entry barrier in the industry. An entry cost must be incurred to overcome this entry barrier upon each firm's entry period. There is no such cost in any subsequent time period. An example of the entry barrier is some fixed costs associated with setting up the plant. The total entry cost for each firm is assumed to be proportional to this firm's output. The average entry cost for each firm is assumed to be k, where $k > 0$. For example, firm t, producing good t at the production level αq^t, incurs a total entry cost of $k\alpha q^t$ at its entry period t and incurs no such cost in any period afterward.

3.2.1 The Demand and Average Cost Functions

The market demand function for each product is assumed to be the same in each time period. Specifically, consider firm i, where $i = 1, 2, \ldots$, at time t, where $t \geq i$. Denote the price for firm i's product i at time t as $P_t^i(\alpha q^i)$. The inverse market demand function for product i at time t is defined as

$$P_t^i(\alpha q^i) = A\left(1 - b \sum_{\substack{j \in S_{t-1} \\ j \neq i}} (\alpha q^j)\right) - a\alpha q^i, \tag{3.1}$$

where $A > 0$, $a > 0$, $b > 0$, and S_{t-1} is a set of firms, that have entered before or in time period $t - 1$ and are producing in the market at time period t and $S_0 = \phi$.

Notice that the intercept of the demand function is reduced as a result of more firms competing for the market. And also notice that the parameter b is the same across all firms, which means that the presence of each firm's product has equal effect on the intercepts of the demand functions for all other firms' products. This is basically the symmetric demand curve used in the standard microeconomic textbook.

In addition, all firms are assumed to have the same average cost function. Define a reference average cost function for all firms as $C : [\underline{q}, \overline{q}] \to \Re_+$, where $C(\cdot)$ is assumed to be continuous and $C(\cdot)$ has a negative first derivative and a positive second derivative, i.e., $C'(\cdot) < 0$ and $C''(\cdot) > 0$;[4] furthermore, it is also assumed that there exists a $q^* \in [\underline{q}, \overline{q}]$ such that

$$C'(q^*) = -a. \tag{3.2}$$

Denote

$$c^* = C(q^*). \tag{3.3}$$

Since the purpose of this chapter is to show the convergence of the industry to a monopolistically competitive equilibrium where the size of each firm is infinitesimally small relative to the market demand, it is necessary to transform the reference average cost function of each firm as a function of the scale parameter (α) while preserving the relevant properties of the original average cost function. This $\alpha-$ transformation is an effective way of shrinking the scale of the firm relative to the aggregate market demand (keeping the firms atomistic). This technique has been used in chapters such as Novshek (1985), Robson (1990), and Luo (1995). The shrinking of the scale parameter α toward zero represents increased competition among firms.

Specifically, to generate a family of average cost functions, which shifts toward the Y-axis as α shrinks toward zero and to preserve the same slope and the same magnitude of the reference average cost function at the output level q^* as α shrinks, a scaled down average cost function is defined from the reference average cost function as

$$C_\alpha(q^i) = C\left(\frac{q^i}{\alpha}\right) + a\left(\frac{q^i}{\alpha} - q^*\right) - a(q^i - \alpha q^*). \tag{3.4}$$

Equation (3.4) can also be rewritten as

$$C_\alpha(\alpha q^i) = C(q^i) + a(q^i - q^*) - a(\alpha q^i - \alpha q^*). \tag{3.5}$$

If $\alpha = 1$, the scaled down average cost function is the reference average cost function. The following Proposition 1 formally states the property that at the point

---

[4]The average cost function could be U-shaped but the relevant part of the average cost curve for this model is the downward sloping part of the average cost curve.

3.2 The Model

of tangency between the firm's average cost function and the slope of the firm's demand function, the average cost (c^*) and its slope ($-a$) remain invariant with respect to α. As well, it states that the convex average cost at output αq_i lies above the value corresponding to the point on the tangent line going through the point of tangency ($\alpha q^*, c^*$).

Proposition 1. *(1) For any given α, $C_\alpha(\alpha q^*) = C(q^*) = c^*$.*
(2) For any given α, $\frac{\partial C_\alpha(\alpha q^i)}{\partial(\alpha q^i)}\Big|_{\alpha q^i = \alpha q^*} = \frac{\partial C(q^i)}{\partial q^i}\Big|_{q^i = q^*} = -a$.
(3) $C_\alpha(\alpha q^i) \geq c^* + a\alpha(q^* - q^i)$.

Proof. (1) Property (1) can be obtained by replacing q^i with q^* in the definition of $C_\alpha(\alpha q^i)$ and then applying (3.3).
(2) Totally differentiating both side of (3.5) results in the following equation,

$$\frac{\partial C_\alpha(\alpha q^i)}{\partial(\alpha q^i)}\Big|_{\alpha q^i = \alpha q^*} = \frac{1}{\alpha}\frac{\partial C(q^i)}{\partial q^i}\Big|_{q^i = q^*} + \frac{a}{\alpha} - a.$$

This together with (3.2) implies Property (2).
(3) Since $C_\alpha(\alpha q^*) = c^*$, $\frac{\partial C_\alpha(\alpha q^i)}{\partial(\alpha q^i)}\Big|_{\alpha q^i = \alpha q^*} = -a$ and $\frac{\partial^2 C_\alpha(\alpha q^i)}{\partial(\alpha q^i)^2} > 0$ it follows that $C_\alpha(\alpha q^i) \geq c^* + a\alpha(q^* - q^i)$. □

Furthermore, the above α-transformation preserves relative per unit profits (or relative profitability) across firms. This is demonstrated below. For $i \geq 1$, firm i's per unit profit at time period t, where $t \geq i$, denoted as $\Pi_t^i(\alpha q^i)$, is calculated as

$$\Pi_t^i(\alpha q^i) = \begin{cases} P_t^i(\alpha q^i) - C_\alpha(\alpha q^i) - k, & \text{if } i = t, \\ P_t^i(\alpha q^i) - C_\alpha(\alpha q^i), & \text{if } i > t. \end{cases} \quad (3.6)$$

Then, the following is true.

Proposition 2. *For any firm i, where $i = 1, 2, ...$, producing at time t, where $t \geq i$,*

(1) the per unit profit for a firm producing at αq^* is maximized, i.e.,

$$\Pi_t^i(\alpha q^i)\Big|_{q^i = q^*} \geq \max_{q^i \in [\underline{q}, \overline{q}]} \Pi_t^i(\alpha q^i); \quad (3.7)$$

and furthermore,
(2) the difference between the per unit profit of firm i and the per unit profit of the firm producing at αq^* is independent of α, specifically,

$$\Pi_t^i(\alpha q^i) - \Pi_t^i(\alpha q^i)\Big|_{q^i = q^*} = \Pi_t^i(q^i) - \Pi_t^i(q^i)\Big|_{q^i = q^*} \text{ for all } \alpha. \quad (3.8)$$

Proof. (1) Substitute (3.1) and (3.4) into (3.6). Then use the resulting equation and take the first order and second order derivative of firm i's per unit profit with respect to its output αq^i. Finally, apply property (2) and the assumption $C''(\cdot) > 0$ to obtain (3.7).

(2) Consider the following two cases:

Case 1: $i > t$. Since

$$\Pi_t^i(\alpha q^i) - \Pi_t^i(\alpha q^i)\Big|_{q^i=q^*} = [P_t^i(\alpha q^i) - C_\alpha(\alpha q^i)] - \left[P_t^i(\alpha q^i)\Big|_{q^i=q^*} - C_\alpha(\alpha q^*)\right],$$

and since $P_t^i(\alpha q^i)\Big|_{q^i=q^*} = P_t^i(\alpha q^i) + a\alpha(q^i - q^*)$, it follows that

$$\Pi_t^i(\alpha q^i) - \Pi_t^i(\alpha q^i)\Big|_{q^i=q^*} = -C_\alpha(\alpha q^i) + c^* - a\alpha(q^i - q^*). \tag{3.9}$$

Using the definition of $C_\alpha(\alpha q^i)$ and the equation

$$P_t^i(q^i)\Big|_{q^i=q^*} = P_t^i(q^i) + a(q^i - q^*),$$

Equation (3.9) implies that

$$\Pi_t^i(\alpha q^i) - \Pi_t^i(\alpha q^i)\Big|_{q^i=q^*} = -C(q^i) + c^* - a(q^i - q^*)$$

$$= P_t^i(q^i) - C(q^i) - \left[P_t^i(q^i)\Big|_{q^i=q^*} - c^*\right]$$

$$= \Pi_t^i(q^i) - \Pi_t^i(q^i)\Big|_{q^i=q^*}.$$

Case 2: $i = t$. The only difference from Case 1 is that firm i must pay a per unit entry cost of k. However, the value α does not affect the per unit entry cost (k). Therefore, the result can be obtained easily by following a similar approach to the above. □

The above suggests that firms producing at αq^* have the largest per unit profits at any time period. In fact, if the demand curve is tangent to the average cost curve, firms producing at αq^* also have the largest profit among all firms. The theory of monopolistic competition predicts that the tangent position for the demand curve eventually occurs in the long run and all the remaining firms produce at αq^*. Therefore, in this chapter, firms, producing at αq^*, are mimicking the profit maximizing behavior in the long run.

3.2.2 The Dynamic Process of Monopolistic Competition

Firms enter the industry sequentially over time. A firm is forced to exit the industry if its wealth is negative. This assumption serves as a market selection criterion.[5] Now, the following describes the evolution of each firm's product price along with the entry and exit process in the industry.

1. At the initial time period, the industry is assumed to begin with no firms. This assumption is used merely for convenience. It does not matter how many and what types of firms are in the industry in the beginning of this evolutionary process.
2. At the beginning of time period 1, only one firm (labeled as firm 1) enters the industry, producing αq^1 of product 1. The price of product 1 at time 1 is $P_1^1(\alpha q^1) = A(1 - \sum_{i \in S_0}(\alpha q^i)) - a\alpha q^1$, where S_0 is a set of firms that have entered before time period 1 and are producing in time period 1. By the assumption in part (i), $S_0 = \phi$. Hence, the price for product 1 of firm 1 is $P_1^1(\alpha q^1) = A - a\alpha q^1$. The parameter A is assumed to be greater than or equal to $c^* + k$. This assumption is used to prevent all prices from originally being below $c^* + k$. Since if $A < c^* + k$, then no as-if profit maximizing firm is able to enter the industry and survive in any time period. Firm 1's total entry cost is $k\alpha q^1$ and its average cost is $C_\alpha(\alpha q^1)$. It follows that firm 1's profit at time 1 is $(P_1^1(\alpha q^1) - C_\alpha(\alpha q^1) - k)\alpha q^1$. Firm 1's wealth at the end of time period 1 is defined as $W_1^1 = (P_1^1(\alpha q^1) - C_\alpha(\alpha q^1) - k)\alpha q^1$. Firm 1 continues to produce αq^1 of product 1 at time 2 if $W_1^1 \geq 0$ and otherwise exits the industry at the end of time 1.
3. At the beginning of time period 2, another firm (labeled as firm 2) enters the industry, producing αq^2 of product 2. The price for product 2 at time 2 is $P_2^2(\alpha q^2) = A(1 - b\sum_{i \in S_1}(\alpha q^i)) - a\alpha q^2$, where S_1 is a set of firms, which entered in time period 1 and are continuing to produce at time 2. Specifically, $S_1 = \{1 : W_1^1 \geq 0\}$. Firm 2's total entry cost is $k\alpha q^2$ and its average cost is $C_\alpha(\alpha q^2)$; hence, firm 2's profit at time 2 is $(P_2^2(\alpha q^2) - C_\alpha(\alpha q^2) - k)\alpha q^2$. Firm 2's wealth at the end of time period 2 is defined as $W_2^2 = (P_2^2(\alpha q^2) - C_\alpha(\alpha q^2) - k)\alpha q^2$. Firm 2 continues to produce αq^2 of product 2 at time 3 if $W_2^2 \geq 0$ and otherwise exits at the end of its entry period 2.

    If firm 1 is producing αq^1 of product 1 at time 2 (i.e., firm 1 has had a nonnegative wealth at time 1), then firm 1 has survived period 1 and continues

---

[5]Using wealth as the selection criterion means that for a firm to survive, the firm upon entry must cover its entry cost in addition to its variable costs. However, this condition could be relaxed to allow for a firm to continue its operations as long as it recovers some part (say dk for some $d < 1$)) of its entry costs in addition to its variable cost, upon entry. This relaxation of the survival condition on entry does not change the results of the chapter (as the only change in the proofs would be that the wealth at the end of entry period would be modified to subtract off dk rather than k).

producing αq^1 of product 1 in the industry in time period 2. Firm 1's wealth at the end of time period 2 is defined as an accumulative profits up to the end of time period 2. That is, $W_2^1 = W_1^1 + (P_2^1(\alpha q^1) - C_\alpha(\alpha q^1))\alpha q^1$. Furthermore, firm 1 continues to produce αq^1 of product 1 at time 3 if firm 1's wealth is nonnegative at time 2 (i.e., $W_2^1 \geq 0$) and otherwise, firm 1 exits at the end of time period 2.

4. This process goes on and on. In general, at the beginning of time t, one firm (labeled as firm t) enters the industry, producing αq^t of product t. The price of product t at time t is $P_t^t(\alpha q^t) = A(1 - b \sum_{i \in S_{t-1}} (\alpha q^i)) - a\alpha q^t$, where S_{t-1} is a set of firms, which entered before and in time period $t - 1$ and are still producing at time t, i.e., $S_{t-1} = \{i \leq t - 1 : W_i^i \geq 0, W_{t'}^i \geq 0 \text{ for all } t' \in (i, t-1]\}$, where $W_i^i = (P_i^i(\alpha q^i) - C_\alpha(\alpha q^i) - k)\alpha q^i$ and $W_{t'}^i = W_{t'-1}^i + (P_{t'-1}^i(\alpha q^i) - C_\alpha(\alpha q^i))\alpha q^i$ for all $t' \in (i, t-1]$. In other words, S_{t-1} is a set of firms that have survived all time periods up to the end of time period $t - 1$ and remain in the market at time t. Firm t's total entry cost is $k\alpha q^t$ and its average cost is $C_\alpha(\alpha q^t)$; hence, firm t's profit at time t is $(P_t^t(\alpha q^t) - C_\alpha(\alpha q^t) - k)\alpha q^t$. Firm t's wealth is $W_t^t = (P_t^t(\alpha q^t) - C_\alpha(\alpha q^t) - k)\alpha q^t$. Firm t continues to produce αq^t of product t at time $t + 1$, if firm t's wealth is nonnegative and otherwise firm t exits at the end of time period t.

If firm i, where $i < t$, has nonnegative wealth in all time periods before time t, (i.e., $W_i^i \geq 0$, $W_{t'}^i \geq 0$ for all $t' \in (i, t-1]$), then firm i has survived all time periods up to the end of time $t - 1$ and remains producing αq^i of product i in the industry in time period t. Furthermore, firm i continues to produce αq^i of product i at time period $t + 1$ if firm i also has nonnegative wealth at time t and otherwise, firm i exits at the end of time period t.

As can be seen, at time period t the price for any one of the surviving firms in that time period is a function of k, α and $q^1, q^2, ..., q^t$.

This chapter is interested in showing the convergence of the industry to the monopolistically competitive equilibrium even without purposive profit maximization. The monopolistically competitive equilibrium is characterized by

1. all prices for all firms' products are equal to c^*,
2. all firms produce profit maximizing outputs, and
3. no potential entrant can make a positive profit by entry.

3.3 The Results

For the monopolistic competitive equilibrium to emerge, it needs competition in terms of an infinite number of firms, which is satisfied by letting the scale of each firm relative to the market shrink to zero; and furthermore, it also needs the entry barrier to be reduced to zero. This section shows that as the size of each firm gets infinitesimally small relative to the market, as the entry cost gets sufficiently small and as time gets sufficiently large, all prices for all remaining firms converge to

3.3 The Results

c^*; and consequently, in the limit, the only remaining firms are those that produce at αq^* and furthermore, in the limit, no potential entrant firm can make a positive profit by entry. This result is established in Theorem 1. Before showing the result in Theorem 1, two lemmas are first proven. Lemma 1 establishes the lower bound for all prices of all producing firms in all time periods and Lemma 2 establishes the probabilistic upper bound for all prices of all producing firms after some time period. Then Theorem 1 follows from the results in the two lemmas.

Lemma 1. *For any given k, for any given positive $\epsilon' < \frac{k}{2}$, there exists an $\overline{\alpha}$ such that, for $\alpha < \overline{\alpha}$, at any time period t, where $t = 1, 2, ...$, for any firm i in the set $\overline{S}_t = \{t\} \cup S_{t-1}$,*

$$P_t^i(\alpha q^i) > c^* + a\alpha \left(q^* - q^i\right) + \epsilon'.$$

Proof. See Appendix A for the proof.

After establishing the lower bound for the price of each producing firm, the following lemma establishes a probabilistic upper bound for the price of each producing firm.

Lemma 2. *With probability 1 the following occurs: for any given k and for any given positive $\epsilon' < \frac{k}{2}$, there exists an $\overline{\alpha}$, such that, for any $\alpha < \overline{\alpha}$, there exists a time period $\tau(\epsilon', q, k, \alpha)$ such that, for $t > \tau(\epsilon', q, k, \alpha)$, for all $i \in \overline{S}_t = \{t\} \cup S_{t-1}$,*

$$P_t^i(\alpha q^i) < c^* + a\alpha \left(q^* - q^i\right) + k + 2\epsilon'.$$

Proof. See Appendix A for the proof.

By bringing together the results in Lemma 1 and 2, Theorem 1 shows that the industry converges to the monopolistically competitive equilibrium. Specifically, it shows that as the size of each firm relative to the market gets infinitesimally small, as the entry cost gets sufficiently small, and as time gets sufficiently large, all prices for all remaining firms in the industry converge to c^*; consequently, in the limit, all the surviving firms are those that happen to produce at the profit-maximizing output αq^*, and furthermore, no potential entrant firm can make a positive profit by entry.

Theorem 1. *For any given positive numbers ϵ and $\eta \in (0, 1)$, there exist positive numbers $\overline{\alpha}$ and $\overline{k}$ such that, for any $\alpha < \overline{\alpha}$ and for $\frac{2}{5}\epsilon < k < \overline{k}$, there exists a time period $\tau(\epsilon, \eta, \alpha, k)$ such that, for all $t > \tau(\epsilon, \eta, \alpha, k)$,*
(i)

$$\Pr\left(c^* + a\alpha \left(q^* - q^i\right) < P_t^i(\alpha q^i) < c^* + a\alpha \left(q^* - q^i\right) + \epsilon, \text{ for all } i \in \overline{S}_t\right)$$
$$> 1 - \eta;$$

(ii) *with probability of at least $1 - \eta$, each of the remaining firms, say firm i, is the one with the average cost lying in the interval $[c^* + a\alpha(q^* - q^i), c^* + a\alpha(q^* - q^i) + \epsilon)$, i.e.,*

$$\Pr\left(C_\alpha(\alpha q^i) \in \left[c^* + a\alpha\left(q^* - q^i\right), c^* + a\alpha\left(q^* - q^i\right) + \epsilon\right), \text{ for all } i \in S_t\right)$$
$$> 1 - \eta;$$

(iii) with probability of at least $1 - \eta$, no new entrant firm, say firm t, with the average cost lying outside the interval $[c^* + a\alpha(q^* - q^i), c^* + a\alpha(q^* - q^i) + \epsilon)$ can make positive profit by entry. That is, for firm t, producing αq^t, where $C_\alpha(\alpha q^t) \notin [c^* + a\alpha(q^* - q^t), c^* + a\alpha(q^* - q^t) + \epsilon)$,

$$\Pr\left(P_t^i(\alpha q^t) - C_\alpha(\alpha q^t) - k < 0\right) > 1 - \eta.$$

Proof. See Appendix A for the proof.

Remark. Under monopolistic competition, firms are atomistic and produce similar but different commodities which are not perfect substitutes. In this industry, with market selection criterion of nonnegative wealth, the firms that happen to produce at the profit maximizing output survive and others disappear. The long run monopolistically competitive equilibrium evolves at a price corresponding to the tangency of the demand curve and the average cost curve. In the model's dynamic framework shrinking α and k are merely ways of shrinking the scale of the firms relative to the market (keeping the firms atomistic) and shrinking entry costs to zero, respectively. As α and k get smaller and as time goes longer, the industry moves closer to the monopolistic competitive equilibrium.

It should be mentioned that k and α have no time dimension. That is, as time goes to infinity, firms continually enter the industry. The parameters k and α, however small, are fixed. Another way of reading Theorem 1, is to say that for some given k and α, however small, the firms' prices eventually fall within a particular range of monopolistically competitive price. And as α and k shrinks (making firms more atomistic and reduce entry costs), the firms prices eventually move closer to the point of tangency of the demand curve and the average cost function. The speed of convergence and the range of the long run price are influenced by the size of k and α. In addition, it is worth mentioning that in the process of shrinking α and k, k must be maintained to be sufficiently high relative to the scale parameter α. (This is reflected in the lower bound, $\frac{2}{5}\epsilon$, for k.) Otherwise, the entry cost loses its role of creating entry barriers to the industry.

3.4 Numerical Illustration

This section provides a numerical example to help better understand the results of the chapter.

Let $A = 4$, $b = 0.05$, $a = 0.1$, and $q^i = Un[0.25, 1.24]$. The cost function is chosen to be $C(q^i) = 0.2(q^i - 1.25)^2 + 1.9875$. This produces $c^* = 2$ and $q^* = 1$. Moreover, let $\alpha = 0.005$ and $k = 0.02$. For $\epsilon' = 0.005$, the lower and upper bounds for the firms' prices are 2.00488 and 2.030375, respectively.

3.4 Numerical Illustration

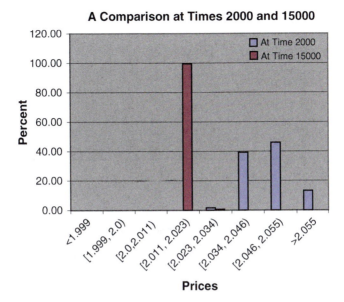

Fig. 3.1 Price histogram. A comparison at times 2,000 and 15,000

With these parameters, the first set of five-hundred simulations are conducted to illustrate how the distributions of prices and the average variable costs of surviving firms shift as time goes by for an industry with a sufficient amount of competition (reflected by small enough α and k). Each simulation follows the industry from time period 1 to 15,000. The histograms are presented in Figs. 3.1 and 3.2, which illustrate the distributions of prices and the surviving firms' average variable costs at time periods 2,000 and 15,000. The price histogram of Fig. 3.1 shows that at time 2,000, there is almost zero percent firms' prices lying in the interval of [2.011, 2.023). But, by the time period of 15,000, 99.4 percent firms' prices lie in this interval. At the same time, from Fig. 3.2, the percentage of surviving firms' average costs in the interval of [2.0, 2.011) increases from 31.87 at time 2,000 to 59.12 at time period 15,000. All of this shows that the surviving firms are those whose prices and average costs are closer to the tangency point with $c^* = 2$.[6]

A second set of simulations are done to illustrate that as k and α are reduced (entry costs are reduced and firms are more atomistic relative to the market demand), the surviving firms' prices concentrate more on an interval closer to the point of tangency of the demand curve and the average cost function (at $c^* = 2$). Another five hundred simulations are conducted now with a slightly bigger α and k, where

---

[6]It should be noted that a part of the distribution of surviving firms' average costs at time 15,000 lies to the right of the corresponding price distribution. With wealth being used as the selection criterion, it may take a while for firms with higher average costs than current prices to leave the industry.

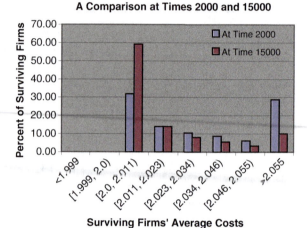

Fig. 3.2 Surviving firms' average cost histogram. A comparison at times 2,000 and 15,000

Table 3.1 Percentage of prices in each interval

	$\alpha = 0.005, k = 0.02$			$\alpha = 0.009, k = 0.025$		
	Time period			Time period		
Price	1,000	2,000	15,000	1,000	2,000	15,000
<1.999	0.00	0.00	0.00	0.00	0.00	0.00
[1.999, 2.0)	0.00	0.00	0.00	0.00	0.00	0.00
[2.0, 2.011)	0.00	0.00	0.00	0.00	0.00	0.00
[2.011, 2.023)	0.00	0.00	99.40	0.00	1.84	2.85
[2.023, 2.034)	0.00	1.56	0.60	0.00	97.79	97.15
[2.034, 2.046)	0.00	39.25	0.00	0.00	0.04	0.00
[2.046, 2.055)	0.00	46.02	0.00	0.00	0.00	0.00
>2.055	100.00	13.17	0.00	100.00	0.00	0.00

$\alpha = 0.009$ and $k = 0.025$. The results are summarized in Table 3.1. Table 3.1 shows that the percentage of firms' prices lying in the interval [2.011, 2.023) increases to 2.85 at time 15,000 from 1.84 at time 2,000. This compares with the percentage of firms' prices lying in the same interval being 99.4 by the time period of 15,000 in the simulations with a smaller α and k, where $\alpha = 0.005$ and $k = 0.02$. As can be seen that for a smaller α and k, the surviving firms' prices concentrate more on an interval closer to the tangency point.

However, it is also true that, for the convergence to occur, there must be a sufficient amount of competition. Firms' output sizes must be sufficiently small relative to the entry cost. This is implied from the statement of Theorem 1 where the k is bounded from below by $\frac{2}{5}\epsilon$. To verify this, another set of five hundred simulations are conducted with a sufficiently large α relative to the entry cost, where

Table 3.2 Percentage of prices in each interval for a sufficiently large α relative to the k ($\alpha = 0.25$, $k = 0.025$)

Price	Time period			
	500	1,000	5,000	15,000
<1.999	25.41	24.86	20.98	23.95
[1.999, 2.0)	0.62	0.76	0.78	0.70
[2.0, 2.011)	11.25	11.82	14.60	12.86
[2.011, 2.023)	14.53	14.37	15.11	14.17
[2.023, 2.034)	14.56	13.40	14.77	14.62
[2.034, 2.046)	12.20	12.84	12.55	12.01
[2.046, 2.055)	7.97	9.11	9.02	9.04
>2.055	13.46	12.84	12.19	12.65

$\alpha = 0.25$ and $k = 0.025$.[7] The resulting distribution of prices is summarized in Table 3.2. As can be seen, the firms' prices do not converge to a single price nor an interval near the tangency point.[8]

3.5 Conclusions

From the earliest to the modern analyses of monopolistic competition, the underlying operating principle has been that firms are purposive profit maximizers and, as long as profits are positive, firms deliberately enter and eventually all surviving firms produce below minimum efficient scale where the demand curve is tangent to the average cost function.

In keeping with the philosophy of Alchian (1950) this chapter has abandoned "all individual rationality, motivation and foresight ... in order to concentrate upon the ability of the environment to adopt 'appropriate' survivors, even in the absence of any adaptive behavior" [(Alchian (1950, p. 214)]. A dynamic model has been proposed which describes the evolution of a monopolistically competitive equilibrium through time to the traditional long-run tangency equilibrium, where the surviving firms happen to mimic the long-run profit maximizing behavior. Although the result is consistent with that arrived at by Robinson (1933) and Chamberlin (1933) on the basis of rational profit maximizing producers, the evolutionary dynamics in this chapter are built on firms' total irrationality in the sense that they randomly choose their output levels, continually enter the market without motive and are forced out of the market as a result of making negative wealth. This stands in contrast with the traditional treatment of the dynamics of monopolistic competition,

---

[7] Since (3.25) suggests that $\alpha < \frac{k - 2\epsilon'}{Ab\bar{q}}$, with $\epsilon' = 0.005$, $k = 0.025$ and with $A = 4$, $b = 0.05$ and $\bar{q} = 1.75$, this would mean that for convergence, $\alpha < 0.043$.

[8] Due to the nonconvergence of price, many more firms with a greater variation of average costs, are surviving at time period 15,000.

where the discussion of dynamics is imprecise. (e.g., Robinson (1933), Chamberlin (1933), and Hart 1985b). A further benefit of the evolutionary approach, as noted by Alchian (1950) and Penrose (1952), is that it provides knowledge of what conditions are required for survival and what characteristics of firms will be required for these conditions of survival. The market environment, in which surviving firms exist, is essential in determining which firms are the ultimate survivors. This assessment of survival requisites can be done without understanding firms' motivations.

In conclusion, this chapter has formulated a complete analytic model where firms' outputs levels are randomly determined and routinized, with sufficient competition the monopolistically competitive equilibrium still evolves, where all the surviving firms are those that act as if they were profit maximizers in the long run. More precisely, the industry converges in probability to the monopolistically competitive equilibrium as the size of each firm becomes sufficiently small, as entry costs become sufficiently small and as time gets sufficiently large. The firms that remain in the industry in the long run are those producing output at the tangency of the demand curve to the average cost curve. Furthermore, in the long run, no potential entrant can make a positive profit by entry.

In this chapter, the firms have the same average cost function and have symmetrical demand functions. Although these are the standard textbook assumptions used in the discussion of monopolistic competition, one may wonder if the same conclusion could be reached in a more general assumption setting, where the firms are assumed to have their own and different demand and average cost functions. Luo (2009) reexamines the evolutionary process of the industry where firms produce differentiated products under these general assumptions. In her chapter, firms are assumed to be totally irrational in the sense that firms enter the industry regardless of the existence of profits; firms' outputs are randomly determined rather than generated from profit maximization problems; and firms exit the industry if their wealth is negative. Luo (2009) concludes that without purposive profit maximization assumption, monopolistic competition still evolves in the long run. The only long run survivors are those that possess the most efficient technology, face the most favorable market conditions, and produce at their profit maximizing outputs. Luo (2009) along with the model presented in this chapter modifies and supports the classic argument for the derivation of monopolistic competition.

Appendix A

Before proving Lemma 1, the following definition is first stated. This definition is used in the proofs of Lemma 1 as well as Lemma 2.

Definition 1. For $t = 1, 2, ...$,

$$I_t^t = \begin{cases} 1 \text{ if } P_t^t(\alpha q^t) \geq C_\alpha(\alpha q^t) + k \\ 0 \text{ otherwise.} \end{cases}$$

Appendix A

Proof of Lemma 1: Before pursuing the proof, the following notation must be introduced. Denote

$$\widehat{P}_t = A\left(1 - b\sum_{i \in S_t}(\alpha q^i)\right), \text{ for } t = 1, 2, \ldots \quad (3.10)$$

The following claim is first proven:

Claim. For any given k and for any given positive $\epsilon' < \frac{k}{2}$, there exists an α_1 such that for $\alpha < \alpha_1$,

$$\widehat{P}_t \geq c^* + a\alpha q^* + k - \epsilon', \text{ for all } t = 1, 2, \ldots. \quad (3.11)$$

This claim is shown by induction.

1. The base step: The claim is true for $t = 1$. For any given positive k and for any given positive $\epsilon' < \frac{k}{2}$, define α_1 such that

$$-Ab\alpha_1\overline{q} = a\alpha_1 q^* - \epsilon', \text{ or } \alpha_1 = \frac{\epsilon'}{Ab\overline{q} + aq^*}. \quad (3.12)$$

Since $\widehat{P}_1 = A(1 - b\alpha q^1 I_1^1)$. This together with (3.12) and $q^1 \leq \overline{q}$ and $A > c^* + k$ implies that $\widehat{P}_1 \geq A - Ab\alpha\overline{q} > c^* + a\alpha q^* + k - \epsilon'$, for $\alpha < \alpha_1$.

2. The induction step: Suppose that the claim is true for $t = r$, i.e., for any given k and for any given positive $\epsilon' < \frac{k}{2}$, there exists an α_1 such that for $\alpha < \alpha_1$, at time period r,

$$\widehat{P}_r \geq c^* + a\alpha q^* + k - \epsilon'. \quad (3.13)$$

Now it needs to be shown that the claim is also true for $t = r + 1$, i.e., for the given k, for the given $\epsilon' < \frac{k}{2}$, if $\alpha < \alpha_1$, then at time period $r + 1$,

$$\widehat{P}_{r+1} \geq c^* + a\alpha q^* + k - \epsilon'. \quad (3.14)$$

Using (3.10),

$$\widehat{P}_r = A\left(1 - b\sum_{i \in S_r}(\alpha q^i)\right). \quad (3.15)$$

This further implies that

$$\widehat{P}_{r+1} = \widehat{P}_r - Ab\alpha q^{r+1} I_{r+1}^{r+1} + Ab \sum_{\substack{i \in X_{r+1} \\ i \neq r+1}} (\alpha q^i), \quad (3.16)$$

where X_{r+1} represents a set of firms that exit the industry at the end of time period $r + 1$. Equation (3.16) further implies that

$$\widehat{P}_{r+1} \geq \widehat{P}_r - Ab\alpha q^{r+1} I_{r+1}^{r+1}. \quad (3.17)$$

Now consider the following two cases:

Case 1: Suppose that $\widehat{P}_r - Ab\alpha q^{r+1} I_{r+1}^{r+1} - a\alpha q^{r+1} \geq c^* + a\alpha \left(q^* - q^{r+1}\right) + k - \epsilon'$. Then, (3.17) implies that

$$\widehat{P}_{r+1} \geq c^* + a\alpha q^* + k - \epsilon'.$$

That is, (3.14) holds.

Case 2: Suppose that

$$\widehat{P}_r - Ab\alpha q^{r+1} I_{r+1}^{r+1} - a\alpha q^{r+1} < c^* + a\alpha \left(q^* - q^{r+1}\right) + k - \epsilon'. \quad (3.18)$$

Notice that

$$P_{r+1}^{r+1}(\alpha q^{r+1}) = A\left(1 - b\sum_{i \in S_r}(\alpha q^i)\right) - a\alpha q^{r+1}. \quad (3.19)$$

Using (3.15),

$$\widehat{P}_r - Ab\alpha q^{r+1} I_{r+1}^{r+1} - a\alpha q^{r+1} = A\left(1 - b\sum_{i \in S_r}(\alpha q^i)\right) - Ab\alpha q^{r+1} I_{r+1}^{r+1} - a\alpha q^{r+1}.$$
$$(3.20)$$

Equations (3.19) and (3.20) imply that

$$P_{r+1}^{r+1}(\alpha q^{r+1}) - \left(\widehat{P}_r - Ab\alpha q^{r+1} I_{r+1}^{r+1} - a\alpha q^{r+1}\right) = Ab\alpha q^{r+1} I_{r+1}^{r+1} < Ab\alpha \bar{q}.$$
$$(3.21)$$

Since, using the definition of α_1 in (3.12), $Ab\alpha_1 \bar{q} < \epsilon'$, it follows that for any $\alpha < \alpha_1$,

$$Ab\alpha \bar{q} < \epsilon'.$$

This further implies that for $\alpha < \alpha_1$,

$$P_{r+1}^{r+1}(\alpha q^{r+1}) < \widehat{P}_r - Ab\alpha q^{r+1} I_{r+1}^{r+1} - a\alpha q^{r+1} + \epsilon'. \quad (3.22)$$

Using (3.18) and (3.22) and since any price on the demand curve which is tangent to the average cost curve at αq^* is no higher than $C_\alpha(\alpha q^{r+1})$, it follows that for $\alpha < \alpha_1$,

$$P_{r+1}^{r+1}(\alpha q^{r+1}) < c^* + a\alpha \left(q^* - q^{r+1}\right) + k \leq C_\alpha(\alpha q^{r+1}) + k. \quad (3.23)$$

Equation (3.23) implies that firm $r + 1$ makes a negative profit in its entry period. Therefore, firm $r + 1$ must exit the industry at the end of its entry period $r + 1$. That is, using Definition 1,

Appendix A

$$I_{r+1}^{r+1} = 0.$$

This together with (3.17) implies that

$$\widehat{P}_{r+1} \geq \widehat{P}_r,$$

which together with (3.13) further implies that for any $\alpha < \alpha_1$,

$$\widehat{P}_{r+1} \geq c^* + a\alpha q^* + k - \epsilon'.$$

Therefore, the claim holds.

Now, at time period $t = 1, 2, ...$, for any firm $i \in \overline{S}_t = \{t\} \cup S_{t-1}$,

$$P_t^i(\alpha q^i) = \widehat{P}_{t-1} - (a - Ab)\alpha q^i - Ab\alpha q^t.$$

This together with the claim implies that for any $\alpha < \alpha_1$,

$$\begin{aligned} P_t^i(\alpha q^i) &\geq c^* + a\alpha q^* + k - \epsilon' - (a - Ab)\alpha q^i - Ab\alpha q^t \\ &> c^* + a\alpha \left(q^* - q^i\right) + k - \epsilon' - Ab\alpha \overline{q}. \end{aligned} \quad (3.24)$$

Furthermore, with $\epsilon' < \frac{k}{2}$, there exists an $\overline{\alpha} < \alpha_1$ such that for $\alpha < \overline{\alpha}$,

$$k - \epsilon' - Ab\alpha \overline{q} > \epsilon'. \quad (3.25)$$

Therefore, (3.24) implies that for any $\alpha < \overline{\alpha}$, at time period t, where $t = 1, 2, ...$, for any firm $i \in \overline{S}_t = \{t\} \cup S_{t-1}$,

$$P_t^i(\alpha q^i) > c^* + a\alpha \left(q^* - q^i\right) + \epsilon'$$

Therefore, Lemma 1 follows. $\square$

The following two definitions are used in the proof of Lemma 2.

Definition 2. Denote $q = (q^1, q^2, ...)$.

Definition 3. For α and ϵ' as defined in Lemma 1, define M_t for $t = 1, 2, ...$, as

$$M_t = \begin{cases} 1 & \text{if } C_\alpha(\alpha q^t) \in [c^*, c^* + \epsilon') \\ 0 & \text{otherwise.} \end{cases}$$

Notice that when $M_t = 1$, $q_t \leq q^*$ (due to $\frac{\partial C_\alpha(\alpha q^t)}{\partial (\alpha q^t)} < 0$). Since $\{q^t\}_{t \geq 1}$ are independently and identically distributed according to the function $F(\cdot)$, $\{M_t\}_{t \geq 1}$ are also independently and identically distributed. Furthermore, since the distribution function has support at q^* and since $C_\alpha(\cdot)$ is continuous, there must exist a positive number, say $\theta \in (0, 1)$, such that for $t = 1, 2, ...$,

$\Pr(M_t = 1) = \theta$ and $\Pr(M_t = 0) = 1 - \theta$.

In addition, a firm with its average cost lying the interval $[c^*, c^* + \epsilon')$ is referred to as a M-firm. For simplicity, denote a M-firm's output as αq^M.

Proof of Lemma 2: The proof begins by first proving the following Claim. The result in Lemma 2 directly follows from the claim.

Claim. With probability 1, there are only a finite number of time periods, in which $\widehat{P}_t$ is above $c^* + a\alpha q^* + k + \epsilon'$. Specifically,

$$\Pr\left(\sum_{t=2}^{\infty} h_t < \infty\right) = 1, \tag{3.26}$$

where for any $t > 1$, the random variable h_t is defined to be 1 if at time $t-1$, $\widehat{P}_{t-1}$ is above $c^* + a\alpha q^* + k + \epsilon'$ for $\alpha < \overline{\alpha}$, where $\overline{\alpha}$ is defined in Lemma 1.

Proof of Claim: Since

$$\Pr\left(\sum_{t=2}^{\infty} h_t < \infty\right) + \Pr\left(\sum_{t=2}^{\infty} h_t = \infty\right) = 1, \tag{3.27}$$

to show (3.26), it is sufficient to show that

$$\Pr\left(\sum_{t=2}^{\infty} h_t = \infty\right) = 0. \tag{3.28}$$

Equation (3.28) is shown by way of contradiction. Suppose (3.28) is not true, then for some $\delta > 0$,

$$\Pr\left(\sum_{t=2}^{\infty} h_t = \infty\right) > \delta.$$

This implies that for any given integer $J > 0$, there exists a positive integer $m' \geq J$ such that for $m > m'$, and, for $N(m) = \sum_{t=2}^{m} h_t$,

$$\Pr(N(m) \geq J) > \frac{\delta}{2}. \tag{3.29}$$

Now, construct a collection of random variables $\{\widetilde{M}_{t_1}, \widetilde{M}_{t_2}, ..., \widetilde{M}_{t_{N(m)}}\}$, where, for $i = 1, 2, ..., N(m)$, $t_i = \min_t\{t : h_t = 1, t > t_{i-1}, t_0 = 0\}$ according to

$$\widetilde{M}_{t_i} = \begin{cases} 1 & \text{if } M_{t_i} = 1 \\ 0 & \text{otherwise.} \end{cases}$$

Appendix A

Since for $i = 1, 2, ..., N(m)$, M_{t_i} is independent of h_{t_i} (which is realized at $t_i - 1$) and since $\{M_t\}_{t \geq 1}$ is independently and identically distributed, it follows that $\{\widetilde{M}_{t_i}\}_{i \geq 1}^{N(m)}$ is independently and identically distributed and furthermore, in each time period, M_t and $\widetilde{M}_t$ have the same distribution function. This together with Definition 3 further implies that,

$$\Pr(\widetilde{M}_{t_i} = 1) = \theta \text{ and } \Pr(\widetilde{M}_{t_i} = 0) = 1 - \theta \text{ for } i = 1, 2, ..., N(m).$$

Since $E(\widetilde{M}_{t_i}) = \theta$, $Var(\widetilde{M}_{t_i}) = \theta(1 - \theta)$ and since $\theta \in (0, 1)$, it follows that

$$Var\left(\sum_{i=1}^{N(m)} \widetilde{M}_{t_i}\right) < E\left(\sum_{i=1}^{N(m)} \widetilde{M}_{t_i}\right). \tag{3.30}$$

Denote $Z_{N(m)} = E\left(\sum_{i=1}^{N(m)} \widetilde{M}_{t_i}\right)$. Using Chebyshev's inequality, for any given positive integer $x < Z_{N(m)}$,

$$\Pr\left(\sum_{i=1}^{N(m)} \widetilde{M}_{t_i} \leq x\right) \leq \Pr\left(\left|\sum_{i=1}^{N(m)} \widetilde{M}_{t_i} - Z_{N(m)}\right| \geq Z_{N(m)} - x\right)$$

$$\leq \frac{Var\left(\sum_{i=1}^{N(m)} \widetilde{M}_{t_i}\right)}{(Z_{N(m)} - x)^2}$$

$$< \frac{Z_{N(m)}}{(Z_{N(m)} - x)^2} \text{ (using (3.30))}$$

This together with the fact that $\Pr\left(\sum_{i=1}^{N(m)} \widetilde{M}_{t_i} \leq x\right) = 1 - \Pr\left(\sum_{i=1}^{N(m)} \widetilde{M}_{t_i} > x\right)$ implies that

$$\Pr\left(\sum_{i=1}^{N(m)} \widetilde{M}_{t_i} > x\right) > 1 - \frac{Z_{N(m)}}{(Z_{N(m)} - x)^2}.$$

Notice that as $N(m) \to \infty$, $Z_{N(m)} \to \infty$ and $\frac{Z_{N(m)}}{(Z_{N(m)}-x)^2} \to 0$. Hence, for any given positive integer x and for any given positive $y < 1$, there exists a positive integer $\overline{N}$, such that for $N(m) \geq \overline{N}$,

$$\Pr\left(\sum_{i=1}^{N(m)} \widetilde{M}_{t_i} > x\right) > 1 - y > 0. \tag{3.31}$$

Define $\overline{m}$, such that $N(\overline{m}) = \overline{N}$. Since $\sum_{i=1}^{N(m)} M_{t_i} = \sum_{i=1}^{N(m)} \widetilde{M}_{t_i}$, using (3.31), it follows that for $m > \overline{m}$,

$$\Pr\left(\sum_{i=1}^{N(m)} M_{t_i} > x \,|\, N(m) = r\right) > 1 - y, \text{ for } r \geq \overline{N}. \tag{3.32}$$

Using Proposition 3 in Appendix B, (3.32) also implies that

$$\Pr\left(\sum_{i=1}^{N(m)} M_{t_i} > x \,|\, N(m) \geq \overline{N}\right) > 1 - y > 0. \tag{3.33}$$

Set $J = \overline{N}$ in (3.29). Equation (3.29) means that for this given $\overline{N}$, there exists a positive $m' \geq \overline{N}$, such that for $m > m'$,

$$\Pr\left(N(m) \geq \overline{N}\right) > \frac{\delta}{2}. \tag{3.34}$$

Since for $m > \max(m', \overline{m})$,

$$\Pr\left(\sum_{i=1}^{N(m)} M_{t_i} > x\right) \geq \Pr\left(\sum_{i=1}^{N(m)} M_{t_i} > x, N(m) \geq \overline{N}\right)$$

$$= \Pr\left(\sum_{i=1}^{N(m)} M_{t_i} > x \,|\, N(m) \geq \overline{N}\right) \Pr\left(N(m) \geq \overline{N}\right)$$

$$> (1 - y)\frac{\delta}{2}, \text{ (using (3.33) and (3.34))}.$$

The above means that for any given positive integer x and for any given positive $y < 1$, there exists an integer $\overline{m}' = \max(m', \overline{m})$ such that for $m > \overline{m}'$,

$$\Pr\left(\sum_{i=1}^{N(m)} M_{t_i} > x\right) > (1 - y)\frac{\delta}{2} > 0.$$

This further implies that

$$\Pr\left(\sum_{i=1}^{\infty} M_{t_i} = \infty\right) > 0. \tag{3.35}$$

This means that with a strictly positive probability the number of M-firms goes to infinity.

Appendix A

Now, if $M_{t_i} = 1$, then the firm that enters at time t_i, where $h_{t_i} = 1$, is a M-firm. Consider this M-firm. When $h_{t_i} = 1$, this implies that, at time $t_i - 1$, $\widehat{P}_{t_i-1} > c^* + a\alpha q^* + k + \epsilon'$. This together with the property that for an M firm $q^M \leq q^*$, implies that

$$P_{t_i}^{t_i}(\alpha q^{t_i})\Big|_{q^{t_i}=q^M} = \widehat{P}_{t_i-1} - a\alpha q^M > c^* + a\alpha(q^* - q^M) + k + \epsilon' \geq c^* + k + \epsilon'. \tag{3.36}$$

This means that this M-firm's per unit revenue at its entry period $P_{t_i}^{t_i}(\alpha q^{t_i})\Big|_{q^{t_i}=q^M}$ exceeds its per unit cost at its entry period, which is no more than $c^* + k + \epsilon'$. Hence, this M-firm makes a strictly positive profit in its entry time period and it continues to produce in time period $t_i + 1$. Lemma 1 implies that for this k and ϵ' and for any $\alpha < \overline{\alpha}$, this M-firm in any subsequent time periods has its product price greater than per unit cost, which is no more than $c^* + \epsilon'$. In other words, this M-firm makes a strictly positive profit in any subsequent time period after its entry. Therefore, this M-firm never exits the economy. Equation (3.35) implies that with a strictly positive probability there is an infinite number of such M-firms in the economy. Since those M-firms never exit the economy and since each individual M-firm produces at least $\alpha \underline{q}$, the presence of the infinite number of such M-firms would drive the price for each of all producing firms, say firm i, below $c^* + a\alpha(q^* - q^i) + \epsilon'$ with a strictly positive probability. This contradicts the result in Lemma 1. Therefore, the Claim of Lemma 2 must be true.

Since $P_t^i(\alpha q^i) = \widehat{P}_{t-1} - (a - Ab)\alpha q^i - Ab\alpha q^t$ and since from the proof of Lemma 1, $Ab\alpha q^i \leq Ab\alpha \overline{q} < \epsilon'$, (3.26) further implies that with probability 1 the following occurs: for any given positive k and $\epsilon' < \frac{k}{2}$ and for any $\alpha < \overline{\alpha}$, there must exist a time period, say $\tau(\epsilon', q, k, \alpha)$, such that for all $t > \tau(\epsilon', q, k, \alpha)$, for all firms $i \in \overline{S}_t$,

$$\begin{aligned} P_t^i(\alpha q^i) &\leq c^* + a\alpha q^* + k + \epsilon' - (a - Ab)\alpha q^i - Ab\alpha q^t \\ &< c^* + a\alpha(q^* - q^i) + k + \epsilon' + Ab\alpha \overline{q} \\ &< c^* + a\alpha(q^* - q^i) + k + 2\epsilon'. \quad \Box \end{aligned}$$

Proof of Theorem 1: (i) Using Lemma 1 and Lemma 2, it follows that with probability 1, the following occurs: for any given k, for any given positive $\epsilon' < \frac{k}{2}$, there exists an $\overline{\alpha}$ such that, for $\alpha < \overline{\alpha}$, there exists a time period $\tau(\epsilon, q, \alpha, k)$ such that, for $t > \tau(\epsilon, q, \alpha, k)$,

$$c^* + a\alpha(q^* - q^i) + \epsilon' < P_t^i(\alpha q^i) < c^* + a\alpha(q^* - q^i) + k + 2\epsilon', \text{ for all } i \in \overline{S}_t. \tag{3.37}$$

Define $\overline{k} = 3\epsilon'$ and $\epsilon = 5\epsilon'$. Restate (3.37) in terms of ϵ and reduce the lower bound to $c^* + a\alpha(q^* - q^i)$. That is, with probability 1, the following occurs: for any given positive ϵ, there exist positive numbers $\overline{k}$ and $\overline{\alpha}$ such that, for $\frac{2}{5}\epsilon < k < \overline{k}$ and for $\alpha < \overline{\alpha}$, there exists a time period $\tau(\epsilon, q, \alpha, k)$ such that, for $t > \tau(\epsilon, q, \alpha, k)$,

$$c^* + a\alpha \left(q^* - q^i\right) < P_t^i(\alpha q^i) < c^* + a\alpha \left(q^* - q^i\right) + \epsilon, \text{ for all } i \in \overline{S}_t. \quad (3.38)$$

Since $\tau(\epsilon, q, \alpha, k)$ depends on the entire sample path $q = (q^1, q^2, ...)$, and not on the distribution function $F(\cdot)$, from which the $q^1, q^2, ...$, are drawn, perhaps, for experimentation purposes, it is of more interest to know from what time period and on that all the price for each of all the remaining firms, say firm i, is lying outside the interval $(c^* + a\alpha(q^* - q^i), c^* + a\alpha(q^* - q^i) + \epsilon)$ with a certain given probability. This can be done by applying the fact that almost sure convergence implies convergence in probability. In other words, using (3.38), it follows that for any positive numbers ϵ and $\eta \in (0, 1)$, there exist positive numbers $\overline{\alpha}$ and $\overline{k}$ such that, for any $\alpha < \overline{\alpha}$ and for $\frac{2}{5}\epsilon < k < \overline{k}$, there exists a time period $\tau(\epsilon, \eta, \alpha, k)$ such that, for all $t > \tau(\epsilon, \eta, \alpha, k)$,

$$\Pr\left(c^* + a\alpha \left(q^* - q^i\right) < P_t^i(\alpha q^i) < c^* + a\alpha \left(q^* - q^i\right) + \epsilon, \text{ for all } i \in \overline{S}_t\right) > 1 - \eta.$$

Hence, the result in Part (i) is proven.

(ii) Consider any firm $j \in S_t$, where firm j's average cost $C_\alpha(\alpha q^j) \notin [c^* + a\alpha(q^* - q^j), c^* + a\alpha(q^* - q^j) + \epsilon)$. Since $C_\alpha(\alpha q^j) \geq c^* + a\alpha(q^* - q^j)$ (due to Property (3) of the average cost function), this means that $C_\alpha(\alpha q^j) \geq c^* + a\alpha \left(q^* - q^j\right) + \epsilon$. Given that for firm $j \in S_t \subset \overline{S}_t$, $P_t^j(\alpha q^j) < c^* + a\alpha \left(q^* - q^j\right) + \epsilon$, then firm j's per unit profit $P_t^j(\alpha q^j) - C_\alpha(\alpha q^j) < 0$ and as a result, firm j would exit the industry at the end of time period t. This together with the result in Part (i) implies that for any positive numbers ϵ and $\eta \in (0, 1)$, there exist positive numbers $\overline{\alpha}$ and $\overline{k}$ such that, for any $\alpha < \overline{\alpha}$ and for $\frac{2}{5}\epsilon < k < \overline{k}$, there exists a time period $\tau(\epsilon, \eta, \alpha, k)$ such that, for all $t > \tau(\epsilon, \eta, \alpha, k)$, with probability of at least $1 - \eta$, at time period t, all the remaining firms, say firm i, must be the one with its average cost lying in the interval $[c^* + a\alpha(q^* - q^i), c^* + a\alpha(q^* - q^i) + \epsilon)$. Hence, the result in part (ii) is proven.

(iii) Consider an entrant firm t, where its average cost $C_\alpha(\alpha q^t)$ lies outside the interval $[c^* + a\alpha(q^* - q^t), c^* + a\alpha(q^* - q^t) + \epsilon)$. Since $c^* + a\alpha \left(q^* - q^t\right) + \epsilon < c^* + a\alpha \left(q^* - q^t\right) + k + \epsilon$ and furthermore since $\Pr(c^* + a\alpha(q^* - q^t) < P_t^t(\alpha q^t) < c^* + a\alpha(q^* - q^t) + \epsilon) \leq \Pr(c^* + a\alpha(q^* - q^t) < P_t^t(\alpha q^t) < c^* + a\alpha(q^* - q^t) + k + \epsilon)$, using the result in Part (i), it follows that for any positive numbers ϵ and $\eta \in (0, 1)$, there exist positive numbers $\overline{\alpha}$ and $\overline{k}$ such that, for any $\alpha < \overline{\alpha}$ and for $\frac{2}{5}\epsilon < k < \overline{k}$, there exists a time period $\tau(\epsilon, \eta, \alpha, k)$ such that, for all $t > \tau(\epsilon, \eta, \alpha, k)$,

$$\Pr\left(c^* + a\alpha \left(q^* - q^t\right) < P_t^t(\alpha q^t) < c^* + a\alpha \left(q^* - q^t\right) + k + \epsilon\right) > 1 - \eta. \quad (3.39)$$

Since $C_\alpha(\alpha q^t) \notin [c^* + a\alpha \left(q^* - q^j\right), c^* + a\alpha \left(q^* - q^j\right) + \epsilon)$ and since by Proposition 1 $C_\alpha(\alpha q^t) \geq c^* + a\alpha \left(q^* - q^t\right)$ implies that $C_\alpha(\alpha q^t) \geq c^* + a\alpha \left(q^* - q^t\right) + \epsilon$, (3.39) further implies that for any positive numbers ϵ and $\eta \in (0, 1)$, there exist positive numbers $\overline{\alpha}$ and $\overline{k}$ such that, for any $\alpha < \overline{\alpha}$ and for $\frac{2}{5}\epsilon < k < \overline{k}$, there exists a time period $\tau(\epsilon, \eta, \alpha, k)$ such that, for all

Appendix B

$t > \tau(\epsilon, \eta, \alpha, k)$,

$$\Pr\left(P_t^t(\alpha q^t) - C_\alpha(\alpha q^t) - k < 0\right) > 1 - \eta.$$

The result in Part (iii) is proven. □

Appendix B

Proposition 3. *If*

$$\Pr\left(\sum_{i=1}^{N(m)} M_{t_i} > x \,\Big|\, N(m) = r\right) > 1 - y, \text{ for } r \geq \overline{N}, \tag{3.40}$$

then

$$\Pr\left(\sum_{i=1}^{N(m)} M_{t_i} > x \,\Big|\, N(m) \geq \overline{N}\right) > 1 - y.$$

Proof.

$$\Pr\left(\sum_{i=1}^{N(m)} M_{t_i} > x \,\Big|\, N(m) \geq \overline{N}\right)$$

$$= \frac{\Pr\left(\sum_{i=1}^{N(m)} M_{t_i} > x, \left(N(m) = \overline{N}, \text{ or, } N(m) = \overline{N}+1, \text{ or, } ..., \text{ or, } N(m) = m\right)\right)}{\Pr\left(N(m) = \overline{N}, \text{ or, } N(m) = \overline{N}+1, \text{ or, } ..., \text{ or, } N(m) = m\right)}$$

$$= \sum_{r=\overline{N}}^{m} \frac{\Pr\left(\sum_{i=1}^{N(m)} M_{t_i} > x, N(m) = r\right)}{\Pr\left(N(m) = \overline{N}, \text{ or, } N(m) = \overline{N}+1, \text{ or, } ..., \text{ or, } N(m) = m\right)}$$

$$= \sum_{r=\overline{N}}^{m} \left(\frac{\Pr\left(\sum_{i=1}^{N(m)} M_{t_i} > x, N(m) = r\right)}{\Pr(N(m) = r)} \right.$$

$$\left. \frac{\Pr(N(m) = r)}{\Pr\left(N(m) = \overline{N}, \text{ or, } N(m) = \overline{N}+1, \text{ or, } ..., \text{ or, } N(m) = m\right)} \right)$$

$$> (1-y) \sum_{r=\overline{N}}^{m} \frac{\Pr(N(m) = r)}{\Pr\left(N(m) = \overline{N}, \text{ or, } N(m) = \overline{N} + 1, \text{ or, ..., or, } N(m) = m\right)}$$
× (using (3.40)) > $(1 - y)$.

References

Alchian, A. (1950). Uncertainty, evolution and economic theory, *Journal of Political Economy* 58:211–2??

Amir, R. and V.E. Lambson. (2003). Entry, exit, and imperfect competition in the long run. *Journal of Economic Theory* 110:191–203.

Andrews, P.W.S. (1949). *Manufacturing business*. London: Macmillan.

Arrow, K.J. (1986). Rationality of self and others in an economic system. *Journal of Business* 59(4, pt. 2):s385–s399.

Baumol, W.J. (1959) *Business behavior, value and growth*. New York: Macmillan.

Chamberlin, E.H. (1933). *The theory of monopolistic competition*, 8th ed. Cambridge: Harvard University Press (1969).

Chamberlin, E.H. (1957). *Towards a more general theory of value*. New York: Oxford University Press.

Cyert, R.M. and J.G. March. (1963). *A behavioral theory of the firm*. Englewood Cliffs: Prentice-Hall.

Enke, S. (1951). On maximizing profits: a distinction between Chamberlin and Robinson. *American Economic Review* 41:566–578.

Ericson, R., and A. Pakes. (1995). Markov-perfect industry dynamics: a framework for empirical work. *Review of Economic Studies* 62:53–82.

Hart, O.D. (1985a). Monopolistic competition in the spirit of Chamberlin: a general approach. *Review of Economic Studies* LII:529–546.

Hart, O.D. (1985b). Monopolistic competition in the spirit of Chamberlin: special results. *The Economic Journal* 95:889–908.

Herings, P.J.J., R. Peeters, and M.P. Schinkel. (2005). Intertemporal market division: a case of alternating monopoly. *European Economic Review* 49:1207–1223.

Jovanovic, B. (1982). Selection and the evolution of industry. *Econometrica* 50: 649–670.

Kaldor, N. (1938). Professor Chamberlin on monopolistic and imperfect competition. *Quarterly Journal of Economics* May, 52(3):513–529.

Kuenne, R.E., (1987) Chamberlin, Edward Hastings In *The new palgrave: a dictionary of economics*, eds. J. Eatwell et al. London: Pinter, 398–401.

Luo, G. (1995). Evolution and market competition. *Journal of Economic Theory* 67:223–250.

Luo, G. (2009). Natural selection, irrationality and monopolistic competition: the case of firms producing differentiated products with firm-specific technologies, working paper, McMaster University.

Nelson, R. and S. Winter. (1982). *An evolutionary theory of economic change*. Cambridge, MA: Harvard University Press.

Novshek, W. (1985) On the existence of cournot equilibrium. *Review of Economic Studies* 52:85–98.

O'Brien, D. (1985). Research programmes in competitive structure. *Journal of Economic Studies* 10:29–51.

Penrose, E.T. (1952). Biological analogies in the theory of the firm. *American Economic Review* 42:804-819.

Robinson, J. (1933). *The economics of imperfect competition*. London: Macmillan.

Robson, A. (1990). Stackleberg and Marshall, *American Economic Review* 80:69–82.

References

Shackle, G. (1967). *The years of high theory*. Cambridge: Cambridge University Press.
Simon, H. (1979). Rational decision making in business organizations. *American Economic Review* 69:493–513.
Spence, M. (1976) Product selection, fixed costs, and monopolistic competition. *Review of Economic Studies* 43:217–235.
Triffin, R. (1940). *Monopolistic competition and general equilibrium theory*. Boston: Harvard University Press.
Williamson, O.E. (1964) *The economics of discretionary behavior: managerial objectives in a theory of the firm*. Englewood Cliffs: Prentice-Hall.
Winter, S.G., Y.M. Kaniovski, and G. Dosi. (2003). A baseline model of industry evolution. *Journal of Evolutionary Economics* 13:355–383.

Chapter 4
Evolution and Informationally Efficient Equilibrium in a Commodity Futures Market[1]

This chapter presents an evolutionary model of a futures market to justify the eventual occurrence of an informationally efficient equilibrium. While the literature usually justifies informational efficiency in the context of rationality, here, in this dynamic futures market, traders do not maximize their profits or utilities nor do they form rational expectation about spot prices. Instead, they are preprogramed with some predetermined behavioral traits (such as trading types (buyer or seller), traders' inherent abilities to predict the spot price). With the markets serving as a selection process of information, it can be shown that the proportion of time that the futures price equal to the spot price converges to one with probability one.

This chapter is organized into four sections. The framework of the model is described in Sect. 4.2. Section 7.3 provides the results of the model. Section 7.4 concludes the chapter.

4.1 Introduction

Much financial economic theory has been developed to examine the informational efficiency of markets. If traders are rational, in the sense that they maximize expected utility and form rational expectations, then informational efficiency can be achieved in the Bayesian Rational Expectation Equilibrium framework, as shown by Grossman (1976, 1978), Radner (1979), Hellwig (1980), Allen (1981), and Bray (1981). A new alternative approach to Bayesian Rational Expectation Equilibrium framework is Maximin Rational Expectation Equilibrium [see Castro et al. (2011)]. This approach can be used to examine market efficiency if market individual participants are rational and able to solve the complex problem set up

---

[1]This chapter is based on my article published in *The Review of Financial Studies* 11(3): 647–674, 1998.

by MREE framework. Instead of relying on rationality to justify market efficiency, this chapter takes an evolutionary approach. An evolutionary model of natural selection is offered. It produces a unique long run outcome: market efficiency. The evolutionary approach abandons any rationality assumption by adopting a framework where it is not possible for agents to learn about other traders or the market environment; nor is it possible for agents to maximize particular objectives. Agents' behaviors are exogenously preprogramed.[2] (Economic justifications for moving away from assuming rationality on the part of agents (speculators) can be found in Alchian (1950) and Tversky and Kahneman (1974)). By adopting this extreme framework with such mechanical rules, we can emphasize the market's ability to promote market efficiency through the selection process. The market rewards the speculator whose behavior happens to fit the market environment the most, and takes wealth away from the speculator whose behavior happens to not fit well with the market. Economic natural selection drives the market to a state where informational efficiency arises.

The following economic modeling approach is analogous to the biological approach where a variety of animals compete under a common environment for food (or resources) and where natural selection selects only those who are most fit. Here, there are speculators, with a variety of abilities to predict the future spot price, who compete in the futures and spot market for wealth and where market selection rewards only those who are most fit.

Consider an economy with a commodity spot and a futures market. The futures market consists of both speculators and producers. Producers sell contracts in the futures market to hedge against the risk in the spot market. Speculators enter the futures market sequentially with an initial endowment of wealth V_0. Speculators either buy futures contracts with the hope of selling at a higher spot market price (acting as a buyer) or short sell futures contracts with the hope of buying at a lower spot market price (acting as a seller). In addition, the fraction of wealth allocated for speculative activity differs across speculators. Furthermore, the abilities to predict the future spot price also differ across speculators. A speculator's ability to predict the future spot price is modeled as inherent and is characterized by the distribution of his or her prediction error with respect to the future spot price. A speculator's prediction error represents the amount by which this speculator overpredicts or underpredicts the spot price at that time period. Each speculator is labeled according to his or her trading type (buyer or seller), his or her fraction of wealth allocated for speculative activities, and his or her inherent probability distribution of prediction error with respect to the spot price, which are all randomly determined upon his or her entry period and are fixed thereafter.[3] In this chapter

---

[2] In the traditional rationality models agents make choices to maximize certain objectives. Here, in this chapter, the evolutionary approach is deployed for the purpose of abandoning the rationality of making choices. Instead the choice variables are exogenously prespecified.

[3] Analogous to the biological term of genotype, the economic agent's type is characterized by his or her choice variable. The choice variable could be interpreted as arising from an agent maximizing

4.1 Introduction

the speculators are modeled as unsophisticated and they merely act upon their predetermined trading type (buyer or seller), and a predetermined fraction of wealth that they allocate on speculative activities, and their predetermined abilities to predict the future spot price. All speculators are noise traders in the sense that the distribution of each speculator's prediction error generates a strictly positive probability of overpredicting or underpredicting the spot price. In other words, each trader has a strictly positive probability of acting upon noise as if it were information. Nevertheless, some speculators have a higher probability of predicting the future spot price than others. That is, some speculators are less noisy than others.

As more and more speculators enter the economy, at any point in time, whoever acts upon better predictions makes profit at the expense of his or her trading counterparts who act on less reliable predictions. For those buyers (sellers), who predict exactly right the spot price with a low probability and overpredict (underpredict) the spot price with a high probability, their wealth will be frequently reduced. Consequently, their ability to influence the futures price will be overshadowed by buyers (sellers) with a high probability of predicting exactly right the spot price and a low probability of overpredicting (underpredicting) the spot price. Therefore, as time goes by, with this natural selection of information caused by the reallocation of wealth away from more noisy traders to less noisy traders and with an ongoing flow of entering speculators, some of whom have better predictive ability than others, the convergence of the futures price to the spot price eventually occurs.

This chapter is not alone in applying natural selection to examine market behavior. Early papers which use the idea of natural selection to examine market efficiency are Figlewski (1978) and Figlewski (1982). In Figlewski (1978), in a pure speculation market with two representative traders with different quality of information, traders with better information make profits at the expense of those with less information. Figlewski (1982) extends the discussion to N traders. However, efficiency cannot be obtained in the long run.[4] A fundamental reason for the difference in results is that, unlike Figlewski (1978) and Figlewski (1982), this chapter allows for sequential entry of traders with a wide diversity of predictive abilities. This ongoing arrival of new agents, some of whom have better predictive ability, prevents the economy from being stuck in an inefficient market equilibrium.

Among the few recent papers that have analytically explored this issue are Blume and Easley (1992), Biais and Shadur (2000), and Luo (1995a). These papers illustrate that market selection will not necessarily lead to the elimination of noise or inefficiency. For example, Blume and Easley (1992), in a dynamic market with wealth flows between traders, find that economic natural selection does not necessarily lead to efficient markets. Similarly, Biais and Shadur (2000) arrive at the same conclu-

---

his or her own objective within his or her resource constraints, information constraints and his or her ability constraints.

[4]In Figlewski (1982), informational efficiency is obtained in the long run only in the special case when all traders have independent information. In contrast, this is not a required assumption in the evolutionary model of this chapter.

sions using Darwinian dynamics in a non-overlapping generations model of a risky asset. In the above two papers the reason for the market's departure from efficiency is that, aside from not allowing traders to enter with better predictive abilities than existing traders, traders' behavior rules are modeled as being linked to their utility functions. Since utility maximizing rules do not guarantee that traders have accurate predictions, it follows that wealth may not be maximized. Therefore, traders with rational rules do not necessarily dominate the market in the long run. On the contrary, traders with irrational rules may come to dominate the market. On the other hand, Luo's (1995a) examination of competition among firms shows that with sequential entry of various types of firms over time, including those that happen to produce at or near the minimum efficient scale, the market selects the most efficient firms.

4.2 The Model

Consider a dynamic economy with an industry producing one commodity. Discrete time is indexed by t, $t = 1, 2, \ldots$. It is assumed that the commodity is nonstorable and cannot be carried to the next time period. There is a commodity futures market and there is a spot market. The futures market opens at the beginning of each time period and the spot market opens at the end of each time period. The participants in the futures market consist of speculators and producers. It is assumed that the spot price is determined at the beginning of each time period[5]. Nevertheless, the realized spot price is unknown to each producer and to each speculator at the beginning of each time period, and the spot price is only revealed to all producers and all speculators at the end of each time period when the output is delivered to the spot market. Therefore, the spot price is independent of the futures price in the futures market.

At the beginning of each time period, each producer contracts a percentage of their production in the futures market to hedge against the risk associated with an unknown spot price. Producers' aggregate contracts brought to the futures market at the beginning of each time period are assumed to be drawn from an interval $U = (0, \overline{S}]$ according to an arbitrarily given distribution, where $0 < \overline{S} < \infty$.[6] Denote

---

[5]The justification for this assumption is as follows. For each of a large number of independent producers the output level is randomly determined at the beginning of each time period. Since the commodity is nonstorable, the total output of all producers must be delivered to the spot market at the end of each time period and sold at a market clearing spot price. Since the individual output levels of producers are determined in the beginning of each time period, the industry's aggregate output is also determined at the beginning of each time period. Given any exogenously specified continuous demand schedule in the spot market, the spot price is determined at the beginning of each time period.

[6]A more elaborate production model, which characterizes the costs of individual producers, could be specified. This adds very little to the issues examined in this chapter, which focuses on the effect of various speculators' behavior on the futures market.

4.2 The Model

producers' aggregate contracts brought to the futures market at the beginning of time period t as S_t^f.

Since the commodity is nonstorable and cannot be carried to the next period, the futures contract is a one-period contract. All payments among all futures market participants are settled at the end of each time period after both the futures and the spot markets close.[7] Each speculator's wealth at the end of a time period is defined as accumulated profits up to the end of that time period.

The futures contract size is perfectly divisible. The price of the commodity in the spot market p_t and the price of a futures contract p_t^f at time t (where $t = 1, 2, \ldots$) are always quoted as nonnegative multiples (m) of a unit size d (> 0). The spot price p_t is randomly drawn at the beginning of time period t (before the futures market opens) from the set $\{d, d+1, \ldots, (\overline{m}-1)d, \overline{m}d\}$, where $\overline{m} \geq 1$ is a positive integer, according to a distribution function. The futures price p_t^f is merely the market clearing price in the commodity futures market and for any t, p_t^f is constrained to be greater than or equal to d. The determination of p_t^f is described in Subsect. 4.2.3.

The following subsections provide further detailed descriptions of the model.

4.2.1 Speculators' Types

Speculators enter the commodity futures and spot markets sequentially over time. At the beginning of the time period t, where $t = 1, 2, \ldots$, only one speculator (called speculator t) is allowed to enter the futures and spot markets. The spot price at time t is determined at the beginning of time period t, but it is unknown to all speculators and all producers. At time s, where $s \geq t$, speculator t's prediction or belief about the spot price, denoted as b_s^t, consists of the summation of the spot price p_s and a noise term v_s^t which characterizes the prediction error of speculator t at time s. That is,

$$b_s^t = p_s + v_s^t, \qquad (4.1)$$

as in Grossman (1976, 1978) and Hellwig (1980). It is assumed that $v_s^t \in \{-\underline{N}d, -(\underline{N}-1)d, \ldots -2d, -d, 0, d, 2d, \ldots (\overline{N}-1)d, \overline{N}d\}$,[8] where $\underline{N}$ and $\overline{N}$ are both positive whole numbers. The smaller a prediction error is, the more accurate is the information reflected in the prediction. It is assumed that v_s^t is independent of

---

[7]The producers honor their futures contracts sold at the beginning of each time period, by transferring, at the end of the time period, to the buyers of the futures contracts the corresponding revenue received in the spot market and in return the producers receive from the buyers the value of these same contracts at the futures price previously agreed upon. The short sellers deliver to the buyers their short sales valued at the spot price and receive from the buyers the value of the same contracts at the previously agreed upon futures price.

[8]To prevent unrealistic negative predictions, the range of predictions sometimes may have to be truncated if $p_s + v_s^t < d$. More precisely, $b_s^t = \max[p_s + v_s^t, d]$.

p_s at time s. For a fixed t, the v_s^t are assumed to be independently and identically distributed across time $s = t, t+1, \ldots$.[9] Therefore, denote

$$\theta_1^t = \Pr(v_s^t > 0), \quad \theta_2^t = \Pr(v_s^t = 0) \text{ and } \theta_3^t = \Pr(v_s^t < 0)$$

where superscript t indicates speculator t. It is assumed that the vector $(\theta_1^t, \theta_2^t, \theta_3^t)$ is randomly taken in the beginning of time period t from a set $\Theta = \{(\theta_1, \theta_2, \theta_3) \in (0,1)^3 : \theta_1 + \theta_2 + \theta_3 = 1\}$ according to an arbitrarily given distribution with its support being Θ. And furthermore, the vector $(\theta_1^t, \theta_2^t, \theta_3^t)$ is independent of p_t. The vector $(\theta_1^t, \theta_2^t, \theta_3^t)$ describes the probability distribution of speculator $t's$ overprediction, exact prediction, and underprediction. This probability distribution characterizes speculator $t's$ predictive ability. Once speculator $t's$ predictive ability $(\theta_1^t, \theta_2^t, \theta_3^t)$ is determined in the beginning of his or her entry time period t, it is fixed thereafter. One justification for modeling a speculator's probability distribution of prediction error being fixed through time is that speculators display systematic biases due to cognitive errors (e.g., Tversky and Kahneman (1974)).

If the speculator is buying (short selling) at time s, b_s^t indicates the highest (lowest) price that a speculator is willing to pay for (supply) a contract at time s. Essentially, b_s^t is speculator t's reservation price at time s. The terms prediction, belief, bid, and reservation bid are used interchangeably in the remainder of the chapter. This way of modeling the speculator's predictions reflects diverse information among the speculators, diverse abilities to process the same information among the speculators or diverse bidding strategies.[10]

There are two further characterizations of speculators. First, speculator t on entry is endowed with one of the following two trading types:

1. Speculator t participates only as a buyer at all times $s \geq t$. That is, speculator t only buys contracts at a price no higher than his or her reservation bid b_s^t at all times $s \geq t$. Denote this type of speculator as $z_t = 1$, where subscript t indicates speculator t.
2. Speculator t participates only as a short seller at all times $s \geq t$. That is, speculator t only sells contracts at a price no lower than his or her reservation bid b_s^t at all times $s \geq t$. Denote this type of speculator as $z_t = -1$, where subscript t indicates speculator t.

---

[9] This reflects the impossibility of speculators learning from other traders and learning from their past experiences.

[10] One can interpret the b_s^t as a signal that speculator t receives at time s. The prediction error v_s^t is the noise that speculator t brings into the market at time s. As long as b_s^t is not equal to p_s speculator t is acting upon noise. Of course, given the differences in the distribution of speculators' prediction errors, different speculators have different probabilities of acting upon noise. In this paper no assumptions are made with respect to the type of the distribution of the prediction error. (This stands in contrast to most papers including recent papers by Kyle and Wang (1997) and Fischer and Verrecchia (1997).)

4.2 The Model

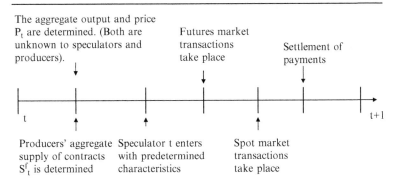

Fig. 4.1 The timing of events

Therefore, speculator t's trading type, represented by a random variable z_t, is randomly taken from a set $\{-1, 1\}$ in the beginning of time period t according to an arbitrarily given discrete probability distribution with its support being $\{-1, 1\}$. And furthermore, z_t is independent of p_t for $t = 1, 2, \ldots$.

The second further characterization is that each speculator spends a fraction of his or her total wealth on speculative activity. This fraction could be viewed as a reflection of a speculator's inherent attitude toward risk. A smaller fraction indicates more risk aversion. The remaining fraction of total wealth can be viewed as risk-free and earns no return. This fraction is randomly determined in the beginning of his or her entry period and fixed thereafter. Denote f_t as speculator t's fraction of wealth allocated for speculative activities. f_t is randomly taken from an interval $(0, 1]$ according to a distribution with its support being $(0, 1]$ in the beginning of time period t. And furthermore, f_t is independent of p_t for $t = 1, 2, \ldots$.

It is assumed that the random vectors $(\theta_1^t, \theta_2^t, \theta_3^t)$, (z_t) and (f_t) are mutually independent for a fixed t and the random vector $(\theta_1^t, \theta_2^t, \theta_3^t, z_t, f_t)$ is independently and identically distributed across speculators $t = 1, 2, \ldots$.

To summarize, on entry speculator t is characterized by random draws, represented by the ordered vector $(\theta_1^t, \theta_2^t, \theta_3^t, z_t, f_t)$, where the first three elements characterize the distribution of speculator t's prediction error, the fourth element describes speculator t's trading type, and the last element describes the fraction of wealth spent by speculator t on speculative activity. Figure 4.1 shows the timing of the above events. Since there is an ongoing entry of speculators with characteristics $(\theta_1^t, \theta_2^t, \theta_3^t, z_t, f_t)$ randomly drawn from the supports of their distributions, collectively the speculators can be described as having a continuous spectrum of characteristics. Since θ_1^t, θ_2^t, and θ_3^t for all t are strictly between 0 and 1, all speculators are noise traders. Nevertheless, some speculators with a higher probability of predicting the spot price are less noisy than others with a lower probability of predicting the spot price.

4.2.2 Speculators in the Market Selection Process

Each speculator is assumed to be endowed with initial wealth V_0, where $0 < V_0 < \infty$, in the entry time period. The futures market is assumed to have no speculators at time 0. After time 0 speculators enter sequentially. Denote speculator t's wealth at the end of time period s (where $s \geq t$) as V_s^t and $V_{t-1}^t = V_0$. The futures market will not open if there are only sellers in the futures market.

Speculator t's prediction about the spot price (where $t = 1, 2, \ldots$) at time s (where $s \geq t$) is characterized by b_s^t. If speculator t is a buyer, speculator t is willing to buy contracts up to what his or her speculative wealth permits at a price no higher than his or her prediction b_s^t, at time s, where $s > t$. Therefore, for $z_t = 1$, speculator t's demand for futures contracts in time period s, denoted as $q_s^t(p_s^f)$, is[11]

$$q_s^t(p_s^f) = \begin{cases} \left(\dfrac{f_t V_{s-1}^t}{p_s^f + d}, \dfrac{f_t V_{s-1}^t}{p_s^f} \right] & \text{if } p_s^f = b_s^t - rd, \text{ where } r = 1, 2, \ldots, \widehat{R}, \\ \left[0, \dfrac{f_t V_{s-1}^t}{p_s^f} \right] & \text{if } p_s^f = b_s^t, \\ 0 & \text{if } p_s^f > b_s^t. \end{cases}$$

where $\widehat{R}$ is characterized by $\begin{cases} b_s^t - (\widehat{R}+1)d < 0 \\ b_s^t - \widehat{R}d \geq 0. \end{cases}$

Figure 4.2 provides an example of this type of demand curve. If speculator t is a short seller, at time s, where $s \geq t$, speculator t is willing to sell contracts up to what his or her speculative wealth permits at a price no lower than his or her prediction b_s^t. To ensure that short sellers honor their contracts, short sellers are constrained to invest $\dfrac{f_t}{\overline{m}-1}$ of their total wealth.[12] The reason is that if short sellers are allowed to invest f_t of their wealth and if the spot price exceeds twice the futures price then short sellers would not be able to honor their contracts. Since the maximum loss that a short seller would incur is when the spot price takes the highest value $\overline{m}d$ and the futures price takes the lowest value d, the constraints for investing $\dfrac{f_t}{\overline{m}-1}$ of the total wealth by the short seller ensures no defaults on any contract.[13] Therefore, for

---

[11] Because of the discreteness of prices, when $p_s^f < b_s^t$ a buyer may not be able to spend all of his or her speculative wealth ($f_t V_{s-1}^t$) if the supply of futures contracts lies between $\dfrac{f_t V_{s-1}^t}{p_s^f + d}$ and $\dfrac{f_t V_{s-1}^t}{p_s^f}$. Thus, a step-like demand curve is used for any buyer.

[12] Ensuring no defaults can also be accomplished if the spot price is constrained such that it cannot exceed twice that of the futures price. This latter assumption is similar to that used by Feiger (1978). Either assumption leads to the same conclusions.

[13] More precisely, consider $q_s^t = -k \dfrac{f_t V_{s-1}^t}{p_s^f}$, $(k > 0)$ (1') where $p_s \leq \overline{m}d$ (2') and $p_s^f \geq d$ (3'). To ensure that short sellers honor their transactions it is assumed that the speculative wealth

4.2 The Model

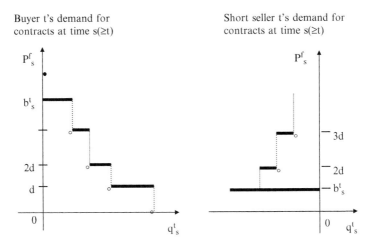

Fig. 4.2 Speculators demands for contracts

$z_t = -1$ speculator t's demand for futures contracts in time period s, denoted as $q_s^t(p_s^f)$, is[14]

$$q_s^t(p_s^f) = \begin{cases} 0 & \text{if } p_s^f < b_s^t, \\ \frac{1}{m-1}\left[-\frac{f_t V_{s-1}^t}{p_s^f}, 0\right] & \text{if } p_s^f = b_s^t, \\ \frac{1}{m-1}\left[-\frac{f_t V_{s-1}^t}{p_s^f}, -\frac{f_t V_{s-1}^t}{p_s^f + d}\right) & \text{if } p_s^f = b_s^t + rd, \text{ where } r = 1, 2, \ldots. \end{cases}$$

A negative number of futures contracts indicates the quantity of short sales. See Fig. 4.2 for a plot of such a demand curve. The above demand functions are similar to those used by Feiger (1978).

Obviously, if a speculator's wealth is zero then this speculator will not be able to continue to participate in the markets in any of the future time periods, since this speculator is not able to buy or sell any contracts in any of the future time periods. In other words, if a speculator's wealth is zero in one time period then this speculator is considered to exit the economy at the end of that time period.

$f_t V_s^t = (p_s - p_s^f)q_s^t + f_t V_{s-1}^t \geq 0$ (4'). Therefore, with equations (1'), (2'), and (3'), equation (4') is ensured when $k \leq \frac{1}{m-1}$. Suppose this constraint is not imposed for short sellers and suppose that k is set equal to one. Then in the extreme case of $p_s^f = d$ and $p_s = \overline{m}d$ it would follow that $f_t V_s^t = (p_s - p_s^f)q_s^t + f_t V_{s-1}^t < 0$ for $\overline{m} > 2$. This implies that the short seller is not able to honor his or her contracts.

[14] For similar reasons described in footnote 10, a step-like demand curve is used for any seller.

Therefore, at the end of time period s, where $s \geq t$, the wealth of speculator t is

$$V_s^t = (p_s - p_s^f)q_s^t + V_{s-1}^t.$$

4.2.3 The Futures Market Equilibrium

The futures market structure is the standard Walrasian mechanism. Denote the net aggregate demand at time s as $Q_s^f\left(p_s^f\right)$. Hence,

$$Q_s^f\left(p_s^f\right) = \sum_{t=1}^{s-1} q_s^t(p_s^f) + q_s^s(p_s^f).$$

Since, the spot price is at least d, to be consistent, the futures price is assumed to be greater than or equal to d. Furthermore, this regulation prevents short-selling at zero price which could cause unlimited defaults. Under the Walrasian market structure, the futures market clearing price p_s^f is set to fulfill the condition that the net aggregate demand is greater than or equal to the aggregate number of contracts offered for sale by producers. That is,

$$p_s^f = \max\left[\max\left\{p_s^f : Q_s^f\left(p_s^f\right) \geq S_s^f\right\}, d\right].$$

There may be multiple solutions to $\left\{p_s^f : Q_s^f\left(p_s^f\right) \geq S_s^f\right\}$. Choosing the equilibrium solution with the highest futures price is arbitrary. Nevertheless, whatever equilibrium is chosen, the results of the chapter are unchanged. Notice that in the early time periods of the market process, if a buyer has not yet entered, then no futures market transaction takes place. If a buyer has entered and if the producers' supply in the futures market exceeds the speculators' net demand at all positive prices (usually occurring in the earlier time periods) then the futures market price is regulated to be d, and the futures market demand is delivered to the buyer at price d and the excess of the producers' supply is returned to the producers (to be sold at the end of the time period at the spot price).

The demand and supply orders made by speculators are executed as follows. At time period s, at the futures market clearing price p_s^f, $Q_s^f\left(p_s^f\right) \geq S_s^f$ or $p_s^f = d$. For the short sellers with reservation bids below or equal to the market clearing price p_s^f, their supply orders at the market clearing price p_s^f are executed at the market clearing price p_s^f and their wealth is exhausted; for the buyers with reservation bids above the market clearing price, their demand orders at a price of d above the market-clearing p_s^f are filled at p_s^f; and the remaining supply in the market is allocated to buyers with reservation bids greater than the market clearing price p_s^f

4.3 Convergence of Futures Market to Efficiency

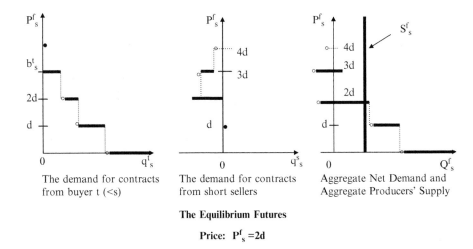

Fig. 4.3 An example of future market equilibrium price. Two speculators in the futures market

and to all speculators with reservation bids equal to the market clearing price p_s^f.[15] One example of a futures market equilibrium is shown in Fig. 4.3.

As can be seen, the futures price p_s^f will be a function of the realizations of $z_1, z_2, \ldots, z_s$; and $f_1, f_2, \ldots, f_s$; and v_k^t for all $t \leq s$ and all $k \in [t, s]$; and $p_1, p_2, \ldots, p_s$; and producers' supplies $S_1^f, S_2^f, \ldots S_s^f$.

The purpose of this chapter is to show that with probability 1, the proportion of time that the futures price equals the fundamental value (the spot price) converges to one as time goes to infinity. In the limit, the futures price reflects only accurate information about the spot price and ignores noise. Consequently, no individual speculator can cause the futures price to systematically deviate away from the spot price in the limit.

4.3 Convergence of Futures Market to Efficiency

This section shows that with the above market selection process, with probability 1, the proportion of time that the futures price equals the fundamental value (the spot price) converges to one as time goes to infinity. This is established in Theorem 3. To show Theorem 3, first of all, the chapter shows that with probability 1, the proportion of time that the futures price is below the spot price converges to zero as time goes to infinity. This is proven in Theorem 1. Second, Theorem 2 shows that with probability 1, the proportion of time that the futures price is above the spot

---

[15] The precise way that the remaining supply is allocated has no effect on the results of the chapter.

price converges to zero as time goes to infinity. Finally, Theorem 3 is established by using Theorems 1 and 2.[16]

The chapter begins by proving Theorem 1, which shows that with probability 1, the proportion of time that the futures price is below the spot price converges to zero as time goes to infinity. The intuition goes as follows. Suppose Theorem 1 is not true, then with a strictly positive probability, there must exist a subsequence such that up to any point of time on this subsequence, the proportion of time that the futures price is below the spot price is bounded away from zero. Given the continuous spectrum of speculators' all possible characteristics, with probability one there is one buyer, say buyer I, who enters the market with a fraction of wealth allocated for speculation of at least $\frac{\overline{m}}{\overline{m}+1}$ and who predicts exactly right the spot price with a probability (θ_2^I) sufficiently larger than the probability (θ_1^I) of predicting above the spot price every time period. That is, over an infinite period of time, eventually there will be entry into the market by some buyer I who has a rather large probability of predicting the spot price accurately and a rather low probability of overpredicting it. Since short sellers always honor their contracts and since the spot price never goes below d, buyer $I's$ wealth is always positive. This prevents buyer $I's$ wealth from being stuck at zero. Since buyer I makes gains if he or she predicts exactly right the spot price at a time period when the futures price is below the spot price and potentially makes a loss if he or she overpredicts the spot price at a time period when the futures price is above the spot price, the relative magnitudes of θ_2^I and θ_1^I, together with the existence of the aforementioned subsequence, ensure that buyer $I's$ wealth grows at least exponentially. (This growth of wealth comes from a constant redistribution of wealth away from producers and relatively noisy traders. In other words, there is a natural selection of information leading to this wealth redistribution, which in turn causes exponential growth of buyer $I's$ wealth.) However, the total wealth injected into the market and shared by all speculators in the market can only be from producers' losses or new entrants' injections of new wealth. Producers' losses in each time period can be no more than $(\overline{m} - 1)d\overline{S}$. The new entrant's injection of wealth is V_0 in each time period. Therefore, the total wealth of all speculators in the market grows at most arithmetically. This contradicts the fact that buyer $I's$ wealth grows at least exponentially with a strictly positive probability.

Before proving Theorem 1, an indicator variable for describing whether at time t the futures price is below the spot price is defined.

Definition 1. Define random variables I_t, where $t = 1, 2, \ldots$, as

---

[16] Although the model of this chapter is formulated in a particular manner, the conclusions do not rely on the range of trading types. The proof can be modified to provide the same conclusions if all speculators are buying contracts in some time periods and in other time periods selling contracts (see Luo 1995b). Furthermore, the results of the model would also hold with continuous rather than discrete futures and spot prices.

4.3 Convergence of Futures Market to Efficiency

$$l_t = \begin{cases} 1 \text{ if } p_t^f < p_t \\ 0 \text{ otherwise.} \end{cases}$$

Theorem 1. *With probability 1, the proportion of time that the futures price is below the spot price converges to zero as time goes to infinity. That is,*

$$\Pr\left\{\lim_{T\to\infty}\left(\frac{\#\{t \leq T : p_t^f < p_t\}}{T}\right) = 0\right\} = 1.$$

Proof. Using the l_t notation, Theorem 1 can be restated as

$$\Pr\left(\lim_{T\to\infty}\left(\frac{\sum_{t=1}^T l_t}{T}\right) = 0\right) = 1. \quad (4.2)$$

This is shown by way of contradiction. Suppose (4.2) is not true, then with a strictly positive probability, there exists an $\epsilon_0 \in \left(0, \frac{1}{2}\right]$ and there exists a subsequence $T_1, T_2, \ldots, T_s, \ldots$ such that for any s, $\frac{\sum_{k=1}^{T_s} l_k}{T_s} \geq 2\epsilon_0$. This together with Proposition 1 in Appendix A implies that

$$\lim_{s\to\infty} \Pr\left(\exists \text{ a buyer } I < s \text{ s.t. } \left\{z_I = 1, (\theta_1^I, \theta_2^I) \in \Theta(\epsilon_0), f_I \geq \underline{f}\right\} | G\right) > 0, \quad (4.3)$$

where $\frac{\overline{m}}{\overline{m}+1} < \underline{f} < 1$, $\Theta(\epsilon_0) = \{(\theta_1, \theta_2) : \theta_2 \geq 1 - \epsilon_0, \theta_1 < \frac{\ln\left(\frac{f(\overline{m}+1)}{\overline{m}}\right)}{\ln\left(\frac{\overline{N}+1}{\underline{L}}\right)}(\theta_2 - (1 - \epsilon_0))\}$ and G represents the event that there exists an $\epsilon_0 \in \left(0, \frac{1}{2}\right]$ and there exists a subsequence $T_1, T_2, \ldots, T_s, \ldots$ such that for any s, $\frac{\sum_{k=1}^{T_s} l_k}{T_s} \geq 2\epsilon_0$.

Notice that since short sellers always honor their contracts and since the spot price never goes below d, the wealth of buyer I is always positive. (The importance of buyer I's wealth remaining positive in any time period is that if buyer I's wealth is zero in one time period, then buyer I will not be able to buy futures contracts in any subsequent time period and his or her wealth will be zero in all subsequent time periods.)

Proposition 2 in Appendix A uses the characteristics of buyer I, $(\theta_1^I, \theta_2^I, \theta_3^I, z_I, f_I)$, and uses (4.3) to show that the probability, that buyer I's average wealth over time on a subsequence $T_1, T_2, \ldots, T_s, \ldots$ is unbounded, is bounded away from zero. That is, for any $F > 0$,

$$\lim_{s\to\infty} \Pr\left(\frac{V_{T_s}^I}{T_s} \geq F\right) > 0.$$

However, this contradicts the fact that the average wealth of any individual speculator over time, including buyer I, must be strictly bounded from above by a constant $(\overline{m} - 1)d\overline{S} + V_0$. The reason is as follows. The new wealth at time t, which could be injected into the futures market and which is potentially shared by all speculators including buyer I, must be transferred from the producer or brought in by the new entrant at time t. The wealth which could come from the producers at time t is $(p_t - p_t^f)S_t^f$, which is bounded from above by $(\overline{m} - 1)d\overline{S}$. The wealth that a new entrant brings in is V_0. Therefore, at time t the total wealth that could be injected into the futures market and is shared by existing speculators in the market must be bounded from above by $(\overline{m} - 1)d\overline{S} + V_0$. It follows that the aggregate wealth of all speculators in the market at the end of time period T_s, where $s = 1, 2, \ldots$, must be bounded from above by $T_s((\overline{m} - 1)d\overline{S} + V_0)$. This further implies that the average total wealth of all speculators over time at the end of time period T_s, where $s = 1, 2, \ldots$, must be bounded from above by $(\overline{m} - 1)d\overline{S} + V_0$. Hence, the average wealth of any individual speculator over time, including buyer I, at the end of time period T_s, where $s = 1, 2, \ldots$, must be bounded from above by $(\overline{m} - 1)d\overline{S} + V_0$. □

The following will show that with probability 1, the proportion of time that the futures price equals the spot price converges to one as time goes to infinity. To show that, given the result in Theorem 1, it needs to be shown that with probability 1, the proportion of time that the futures price is above the spot price converges to zero as time goes to infinity. This is proven in Theorem 2. The proof of Theorem 2 follows exactly the same logic as the proof of Theorem 1.

Theorem 2, like Theorem 1, is shown by way of contradiction. Assuming that the result of Theorem 2 is not true, one can show that with a strictly positive probability, there exists an entering seller with certain characteristics. This seller never exits the economy. Following the same logic, one can show that this seller's average wealth over time is unbounded with a positive probability, which produces a contradiction.

Theorem 2. *With probability 1, the proportion of time that the futures price is above the spot price converges to zero as time goes to infinity. That is,*

$$\Pr\left(\lim_{T \to \infty} \left(\frac{\#\{t \leq T : p_t^f > p_t\}}{T}\right) = 0\right) = 1.$$

Proof. See Appendix C for proof.

Finally, using Theorem 1 and Theorem 2, Theorem 3 can be established as follows.

Theorem 3. *With probability 1, the proportion of time that the futures price equals the spot price converges to one as time goes to infinity. That is,*

4.4 Conclusions

$$\Pr\left(\lim_{T\to\infty}\left(\frac{\#\{t \leq T : p_t^f = p_t\}}{T}\right) = 1\right) = 1.$$

Proof. Noticing that for any $T \geq 1$,

$$\frac{\#\{t \leq T : p_t^f < p_t\}}{T} + \frac{\#\{t \leq T : p_t^f = p_t\}}{T} + \frac{\#\{t \leq T : p_t^f > p_t\}}{T} = 1,$$

and using Theorem 1 and Theorem 2, Theorem 3 follows. □

The result of Theorem 3 suggests that in the limit, the futures price fully reflects accurate information in the futures market. In the short run, the futures price reflects all the beliefs of speculators, but in the long run, the futures price reflects only accurate information and eliminates noise.

Furthermore, one can also show that each individual speculator's logarithm of wealth is infinitesimally small relative to the market aggregate of logarithms of wealth. This is formally stated in Corollary 1.

Corollary 1. *With probability 1, the ratio between the logarithm of wealth of speculator t, $t \geq 1$, at the end of time period T ($\ln V_T^t$) and the aggregate of logarithms of wealth of all speculators at the end of time period T ($\sum_{k=1}^{T} \ln V_T^k$) converges to zero as $T \to \infty$. That is,*

$$\Pr\left(\lim_{T\to\infty}\left(\frac{\ln V_T^t}{\sum_{k=1}^{T} \ln V_T^k}\right) = 0\right) = 1.$$

Proof. See Appendix D for the proof.

4.4 Conclusions

This chapter shows that, due to natural selection, information efficiency can be achieved even if the agents are not assumed to be rational. In the long run, the impact of irrational traders on market prices becomes negligible. This is consistent with the conjecture made by Friedman (1953) and in contrast with the assumptions posited by Kyle and Wang (1997) or Fischer and Verrecchia (1997) (who appeal to the psychology literature, e.g., Kahneman et al. (1982)). In this chapter each speculator is assumed to be randomly endowed with its own trading type, its own fraction of wealth allocated for speculation and its own inherent distribution of prediction error with respect to the spot price. Those who act upon better predictions accumulate wealth at the expense of trading counterparts acting on less reliable predictions. With ongoing entry of such speculators into the economy over time, the market selection process redistributes wealth constantly among the speculators.

Consequently, this constant redistribution process causes the futures price to reflect more accurate predictions with higher and higher weights as time goes by. In the short run, the futures price merely aggregates all noise speculators' beliefs or predictions. In the long run, with probability 1, the proportion of time that the futures price equals the spot price converges to one as time goes to infinity. In the limit, the futures price reflects only accurate information and ignores noise. Furthermore, the logarithm of each individual speculator's wealth is infinitesimally small relative to the market aggregate of logarithms of all speculators' wealth.

Appendix A

Proposition 1. *If, with a strictly positive probability, there exists an $\epsilon_0 \in \left(0, \frac{1}{2}\right]$ and a subsequence $T_1, T_2, \ldots, T_s, \ldots$ such that for all s, $\frac{\sum_{k=1}^{T_s} l_k}{T_s} \geq 2\epsilon_0$, then*

$$\lim_{s \to \infty} \Pr\left(\exists \, a \, buyer \, I < s \, \text{ s.t. } \left\{z_t = 1, (\theta_1^t, \theta_2^t) \in \Theta(\epsilon_0), f_t \geq \underline{f}\right\} | G \right) > 0,$$

where $\frac{\overline{m}}{\overline{m}+1} < \underline{f} < 1, \Theta(\epsilon_0) = \{(\theta_1, \theta_2) : \theta_2 \geq 1 - \epsilon_0, \theta_1 < \frac{\ln\left(\frac{f(\overline{m}+1)}{\overline{m}}\right)}{\ln\left(\frac{\overline{N}+1}{\overline{L}}\right)} (\theta_2 - (1 - \epsilon_0))\}$, and G represents the event, that there exists an $\epsilon_0 \in \left(0, \frac{1}{2}\right]$ and a subsequence $T_1, T_2, \ldots, T_s, \ldots$ such that for all s, $\frac{\sum_{k=1}^{T_s} l_k}{T_s} \geq 2\epsilon_0$.

Proof. If, with a strictly positive probability, there exists an $\epsilon_0 \in \left(0, \frac{1}{2}\right]$ and a subsequence $T_1, T_2, \ldots, T_s, \ldots$ such that for all s,

$$\frac{\sum_{k=1}^{T_s} l_k}{T_s} \geq 2\epsilon_0, \tag{4.4}$$

then, define a random variable R_t for $t = 1, 2, \ldots$, as

$$R_t = \begin{cases} 1 \text{ if } z_t = 1, (\theta_1^t, \theta_2^t) \in \Theta(\epsilon_0), f_t \geq \underline{f} \\ 0 \text{ otherwise,} \end{cases}$$

where $\frac{\overline{m}}{\overline{m}+1} < \underline{f} < 1$ and $\Theta(\epsilon_0) = \{(\theta_1, \theta_2) : \theta_2 \geq 1 - \epsilon_0, \theta_1 < \frac{\ln\left(\frac{f(\overline{m}+1)}{\overline{m}}\right)}{\ln\left(\frac{\overline{N}+1}{\overline{L}}\right)} (\theta_2 - (1 - \epsilon_0))\}$.

Appendix A

Since the random vectors $(\theta_1^t, \theta_2^t, \theta_3^t)$, (z_t), and (f_t) are mutually independent for a fixed t and the random vector $(\theta_1^t, \theta_2^t, \theta_3^t, z_t, f_t)$ is independently and identically distributed across speculators $t = 1, 2, \ldots$, it follows that $\{R_t\}_{t \geq 1}$ is independently and identically distributed. Therefore, $\Pr(R_t = 1) = \Pr(z_t = 1, (\theta_1^t, \theta_2^t) \in \Theta(\epsilon_0), f_t \geq \underline{f}) = \Pr(z_t = 1) \Pr((\theta_1^t, \theta_2^t) \in \Theta(\epsilon_0)) \Pr(f_t \geq \underline{f})$. Notice that since z_t has support at 1, (θ_1^t, θ_2^t) has support over $\Theta(\epsilon_0)$ and f_t has support over the interval $(0, 1]$, it follows that $\Pr(R_t = 1) > 0$, for all t. This further implies that

$$\sum_{t=1}^{\infty} \Pr(R_t = 1) = \infty,$$

and using The Second Borel Cantelli Lemma (see Billingsley (1986, p. 83)),

$$\Pr\left(\sum_{t=1}^{\infty} R_t = \infty\right) = 1.$$

This further implies that

$$\lim_{s \to \infty} \Pr(\text{there exists a buyer, say buyer } I, \ I < s, \text{ s.t. } R_I = 1) = 1. \quad (4.5)$$

Equations (4.4) and (4.5) imply that

$$\lim_{s \to \infty} \Pr(\exists \text{ buyer } I, I < s, \text{s.t. } R_I = 1 \,|\, G) > 0,$$

where G represents the event, that there exists an $\epsilon_0 \in \left(0, \frac{1}{2}\right]$ and a subsequence $T_1, T_2, \ldots, T_s, \ldots$ such that for all s, $\frac{\sum_{k=1}^{T_s} l_k}{T_s} \geq 2\epsilon_0$.
Proposition 1 follows. $\square$

The following definitions are used in all the following propositions.
Define m_k and a_k, for $k = 1, 2, \ldots$, as

$$m_k = \begin{cases} 1 \text{ if } p_k^f = p_k \\ 0 \text{ otherwise} \end{cases} ; \quad a_k = \begin{cases} 1 \text{ if } p_k^f > p_k \\ 0 \text{ otherwise.} \end{cases}$$

Proposition 2. *If*

$$\lim_{s \to \infty} \Pr\left(\exists \text{ a buyer } I < s \text{ s.t. } \left\{z_I = 1, (\theta_1^I, \theta_2^I) \in \Theta(\epsilon_0), f_I \geq \underline{f}\right\} \,\Big|\, G\right) > 0, \quad (4.6)$$

where $\frac{\overline{m}}{\overline{m}+1} < \underline{f} < 1$, $\Theta(\epsilon_0) = \{(\theta_1, \theta_2) : \theta_2 \geq 1 - \epsilon_0, \theta_1 < \frac{\ln\left(\frac{f(\overline{m}+1)}{\overline{m}}\right)}{\ln\left(\frac{\overline{N}+1}{\overline{L}}\right)} (\theta_2 - (1 - \epsilon_0))\}$ *and G represents the event that there exists an $\epsilon_0 \in \left(0, \frac{1}{2}\right]$ and there exists* a subsequence $T_1, T_2, \ldots, T_s, \ldots$ such that for any s, $\frac{\sum_{k=1}^{T_s} l_k}{T_s} \geq 2\epsilon_0$, then for any $F > 0$,

$$\lim_{s \to \infty} \Pr\left(\frac{V_{T_s}^I}{T_s} \geq F\right) > 0.$$

Proof. Before the proof begins, some notation is needed. Define another two indicator variables x_k^I and g_k^I, where $k \geq I$, for buyer I as

$$x_k^I = \begin{cases} 1 & \text{if } v_k^I > 0 \\ 0 & \text{otherwise;} \end{cases} \quad g_k^I = \begin{cases} 1 & \text{if } v_k^I = 0 \\ 0 & \text{otherwise.} \end{cases}$$

Consider buyer I. Buyer I's wealth at the end of time period T_s is $V_{T_s}^I$ and

$$\theta_2^I \geq 1 - \epsilon_0 \text{ and } \theta_1^I < \frac{\ln\left(\frac{f(\overline{m}+1)}{\overline{m}}\right)}{\ln\left(\frac{N+1}{\underline{f}}\right)} \left(\theta_2^I - (1 - \epsilon_0)\right). \quad (4.7)$$

Since the prediction error v_k^I are independently and identically distributed across time (k), x_k^I are independently and identically distributed across time periods (k) and g_k^I are independently and identically distributed across time periods (k), using the strong law of large numbers, it follows that

$$\frac{\sum_{k=I}^{T_s} x_k^I}{T_s - I + 1} \to \theta_1^I \text{ a.s. and } \frac{\sum_{k=I}^{T_s} g_k^I}{T_s - I + 1} \to \theta_2^I \text{ a.s. and } \frac{\ln V_0}{T_s - I + 1} \to 0.$$

This together with (4.7) implies that if

$$\lim_{s \to \infty} \Pr\left(\exists \text{ a buyer } I < s \text{ s.t. } \left\{z_I = 1, (\theta_1^I, \theta_2^I) \in \Theta(\epsilon_0), f_I \geq \underline{f}\right\} | G\right) > 0,$$

where $\frac{\overline{m}}{\overline{m}+1} < \underline{f} < 1$, $\Theta(\epsilon_0) = \{(\theta_1, \theta_2) : \theta_2 \geq 1 - \epsilon_0, \theta_1 < \frac{\ln\left(\frac{f(\overline{m}+1)}{\overline{m}}\right)}{\ln\left(\frac{N+1}{\underline{f}}\right)} (\theta_2 - (1 - \epsilon_0))\}$ and G represents the event that there exists an $\epsilon_0 \in (0, \frac{1}{2}]$ and there exists a subsequence $T_1, T_2, \ldots, T_s, \ldots$ such that for any s, $\frac{\sum_{k=1}^{T_s} l_k}{T_s} \geq 2\epsilon_0$, then for some positive $\lambda > 0$,

for $E = \left(\exists \text{ a buyer } I < s \text{ s.t. } \left\{z_I = 1, (\theta_1^I, \theta_2^I) \in \Theta(\epsilon_0), f_I \geq \underline{f}\right\} \cap G\right)$,

Appendix A

$$\lim_{s\to\infty} \Pr\left(\left(\frac{\sum_{k=I}^{T_s} g_k^I}{T_s - I + 1} - (1 - \epsilon_0)\right)\ln\left(\frac{f(\overline{m}+1)}{\overline{m}}\right) + \frac{\ln V_0}{T_s - I + 1} \right.$$

$$\left. + \frac{\sum_{k=I}^{T_s} x_k^I}{T_s - I + 1}\ln\left(\frac{\overline{f}}{\overline{N}+1}\right) \geq \lambda \,\bigg|\, E \right) = 1. \qquad (4.8)$$

Now, Notice that

$$\sum_{k=I}^{T_s} x_k^I \geq \sum_{k=I}^{T_s} (a_k x_k^I). \qquad (4.9)$$

In addition, since

$$\sum_{k=I}^{T_s} (l_k g_k^I) = \sum_{k=I}^{T_s} g_k^I - \sum_{k=I}^{T_s} (m_k g_k^I) - \sum_{k=I}^{T_s} (a_k g_k^I)$$

$$\geq \sum_{k=I}^{T_s} g_k^I - \sum_{k=I}^{T_s} m_k - \sum_{k=I}^{T_s} a_k$$

$$= \sum_{k=I}^{T_s} g_k^I - (T_s - I + 1) + \sum_{k=I}^{T_s} l_k$$

$$= \left(\frac{\sum_{k=I}^{T_s} g_k^I}{T_s - I + 1} + \frac{\sum_{k=I}^{T_s} l_k}{T_s - I + 1} - 1\right)(T_s - I + 1),$$

if $\frac{\sum_{k=1}^{T_s} l_k}{T_s} \geq 2\epsilon_0$ then it follows that $\frac{\sum_{k=I}^{T_s} l_k}{T_s-I+1} = \left(\frac{\sum_{k=1}^{T_s} l_k}{T_s} - \frac{\sum_{k=1}^{I-1} l_k}{T_s}\right)\left(\frac{T_s}{T_s-I+1}\right) >$

$\left(2\epsilon_0 - \frac{\sum_{k=1}^{I-1} l_k}{T_s}\right)\left(\frac{T_s}{T_s-I+1}\right) > \epsilon_0$ (for a sufficiently large s). Therefore, for a sufficiently large s,

$$\sum_{k=I}^{T_s} (l_k g_k^I) \geq \left(\frac{\sum_{k=I}^{T_s} g_k^I}{T_s - I + 1} + \epsilon_0 - 1\right)(T_s - I + 1). \qquad (4.10)$$

Notice that $\ln\left(\frac{f}{\overline{N}+1}\right) < 0$ and $\ln\left(\frac{f(\overline{m}+1)}{\overline{m}}\right) > 0$. Hence, (4.8), (4.9) and (4.10) imply that

$$\lim_{s\to\infty} \Pr\left(\frac{\sum_{k=I}^{T_s}(a_k x_k^I)}{T_s - I + 1} \ln\left(\frac{f}{\overline{N}+1}\right) + \frac{\sum_{k=I}^{T_s}(l_k g_k^I)}{T_s - I + 1} \ln\left(\frac{f(\overline{m}+1)}{\overline{m}}\right)\right.$$

$$\left. + \frac{\ln V_0}{T_s - I + 1} \geq \lambda \middle| E\right) = 1.$$

This together with (4.6) imply that

$$\lim_{s\to\infty} \Pr\left(\frac{\sum_{k=I}^{T_s}(a_k x_k^I)}{T_s - I + 1} \ln\left(\frac{f}{\overline{N}+1}\right) + \frac{\sum_{k=I}^{T_s}(l_k g_k^I)}{T_s - I + 1} \ln\left(\frac{f(\overline{m}+1)}{\overline{m}}\right)\right.$$

$$\left. + \frac{\ln V_0}{T_s - I + 1} \geq \lambda\right) > 0. \tag{4.11}$$

Now, the following uses (4.11) to show that for any $F > 0$,

$$\lim_{s\to\infty} \Pr\left(\frac{V_{T_s}^I}{T_s} > F\right) > 0.$$

Consider buyer I's wealth at time period k. If $a_k = 1$ and $x_k^I = 1$ then $p_k^f > p_k$ and $b_k^I > p_k$, which further implies that $q_k^I \leq \frac{f_I V_{k-1}^I}{p_k^f}$. Hence, buyer I potentially makes a loss (a negative profit) at time period k. At the end of time period k buyer I's wealth is

$$V_k^I = V_{k-1}^I + q_k^I\left(p_k - p_k^f\right) \geq V_{k-1}^I\left(1 + \left(p_k - p_k^f\right)\frac{f_I}{p_k^f}\right)$$

$$\geq \left(\frac{p_k}{p_k^f}\right) f_I V_{k-1}^I \geq \left(\frac{f}{\overline{N}+1}\right) V_{k-1}^I. \tag{4.12}$$

If $l_k = 1$ and $g_k^I = 1$ then $p_k^f < p_k$ and $b_k^I = p_k$, which further implies that $q_k^I \in \left(\frac{f_I V_{k-1}^I}{p_k^f + d}, \frac{f_I V_{k-1}^I}{p_k^f}\right]$. Hence, buyer I makes a gain (a positive profit) at time

Appendix A

period k. At the end of time period k buyer I's wealth is

$$V_k^I = V_{k-1}^I + \left(p_k - p_k^f\right) q_k^I > V_{k-1}^I + \left(p_k - p_k^f\right) \frac{f_I V_{k-1}^I}{p_k^f + d}$$

$$\geq V_{k-1}^I + d \left(\frac{f_I V_{k-1}^I}{\overline{m}d}\right) > \underline{f} V_{k-1}^I + d \left(\frac{\underline{f} V_{k-1}^I}{\overline{m}d}\right) = \left(\frac{\underline{f}\,(\overline{m}+1)}{\overline{m}}\right) V_{k-1}^I.$$

(4.13)

Therefore, buyer I's wealth at the end of time period k is

$$V_k^I > \left(\frac{\underline{f}}{\overline{N}+1}\right)^{a_k x_k^I} \left(\frac{\underline{f}\,(\overline{m}+1)}{\overline{m}}\right)^{l_k g_k^I} V_{k-1}^I. \tag{4.14}$$

Using (4.14), one can show inductively that

$$V_{T_s}^I > \left(\frac{\underline{f}}{\overline{N}+1}\right)^{\sum_{k=I}^{T_s}(a_k x_k^I)} \left(\frac{\underline{f}\,(\overline{m}+1)}{\overline{m}}\right)^{\sum_{k=I}^{T_s}(l_k g_k^I)} V_0. \tag{4.15}$$

Taking the logarithm of both sides of (4.15), it follows that

$$\ln V_{T_s}^I > \left\{\sum_{k=I}^{T_s}(a_k x_k^I) \ln\left(\frac{\underline{f}}{\overline{N}+1}\right) + \sum_{k=I}^{T_s}(l_k g_k^I) \ln\left(\frac{\underline{f}\,(\overline{m}+1)}{\overline{m}}\right) + \ln V_0\right\},$$

which further implies that

$$\frac{\ln V_{T_s}^I}{T_s - I + 1} >$$

$$\frac{1}{T_s - I + 1}\left\{\sum_{k=I}^{T_s}(a_k x_k^I) \ln\left(\frac{\underline{f}}{\overline{N}+1}\right) + \sum_{k=I}^{T_s}(l_k g_k^I) \ln\left(\frac{\underline{f}\,(\overline{m}+1)}{\overline{m}}\right) + \ln V_0\right\}.$$

Together with (4.11), this implies that

$$\lim_{s \to \infty} \Pr\left(\frac{\ln V_{T_s}^I}{T_s - I + 1} > \lambda\right) > 0.$$

Therefore,

$$\lim_{s \to \infty} \Pr\left(V_{T_s}^I > \exp\left((T_s - I + 1)\lambda\right)\right) > 0.$$

Since $\lim_{s\to\infty} \frac{\exp((T_s-I+1)\lambda)}{T_s} = \lim_{s\to\infty} \{\lambda \exp((T_s - I + 1)\lambda)\} = \infty$, it follows that for any $F > 0$,

$$\lim_{s\to\infty} \Pr\left(\frac{V^I_{T_s}}{T_s} > F\right) > 0.$$

□

Appendix B

Proposition 3. *If with a strictly positive probability, there exists an $\epsilon'_0 \in (0, \frac{1}{2}]$ and a subsequence $T_1, T_2, \ldots, T_s, \ldots$ such that for all s, $\frac{\sum_{k=1}^{T_s} a_k}{T_s} \geq 2\epsilon'_0$, then*

$$\lim_{s\to\infty} \Pr\left(\exists \text{ a seller } I', I' < s, s.t. \{z_{I'} = -1, (\theta_2^{I'}, \theta_3^{I'}) \in \Theta'(\epsilon'_0), f_{I'} \leq \overline{f}\} \big| G'\right) > 0,$$

where $0 < \overline{f} < 1$, $\Theta'(\epsilon'_0) = \{(\theta_2, \theta_3) : \theta_2 \geq 1 - \epsilon'_0, \theta_3 < \frac{\ln\left(\frac{f_{I'}}{m^2-1}+1\right)}{\ln\left(\frac{1}{1-\overline{f}}\right)}(\theta_2 - (1-\epsilon'_0))\}$ and G' represents the event, that there exists an $\epsilon'_0 \in (0, \frac{1}{2}]$ and a subsequence $T_1, T_2, \ldots, T_s, \ldots$ such that for all s, $\frac{\sum_{k=1}^{T_s} a_k}{T_s} \geq 2\epsilon'_0$.

Proof. This proposition uses exactly the same logic as Proposition 1. For the ease of notation and description of the proof, redefine R_t as follows. Define a random variable R'_t, where $t = 1, 2, \ldots$, as

$$R'_t = \begin{cases} 1 \text{ if } z_t = -1, (\theta_2^t, \theta_3^t) \in \Theta'(\epsilon'_0), f_t \leq \overline{f} \\ 0 \text{ otherwise,} \end{cases}$$

where $0 < \overline{f} < 1$ and $\Theta'(\epsilon'_0) = \{(\theta_2, \theta_3) : \theta_2 \geq 1 - \epsilon'_0, \theta_3 < \frac{\ln\left(\frac{f_{I'}}{m^2-1}+1\right)}{\ln\left(\frac{1}{1-\overline{f}}\right)}(\theta_2 - (1 - \epsilon'_0))\}$. The proof can be done by following through the proof of Proposition 1 after changing some notation. In the proof of Proposition 1, replace l_k with a_k and replace R_t with R'_t. As a result, replace $z_t = 1, (\theta_1^t, \theta_2^t) \in \Theta(\epsilon_0)$ and $f_t \geq \underline{f}$ with $z_t = -1, (\theta_2^t, \theta_3^t) \in \Theta'(\epsilon'_0)$ and $f_t \leq \overline{f}$, respectively. Replace "buyer I" with "seller I'." Replace I with I' and replace G with G'. Replace "z_t has support at 1" with "z_t has support at -1". □

Proposition 4. *If*

$$\lim_{s\to\infty} \Pr\left(\exists \text{ a seller } I' < s \text{ s.t. } \{z_{I'} = -1, (\theta_2^{I'}, \theta_3^{I'}) \in \Theta'(\epsilon'_0), f_{I'} \geq \overline{f}\} \big| G'\right) > 0, \tag{4.16}$$

Appendix B

where $0 < \overline{f} < 1$, $\Theta'(\epsilon_0') = \{(\theta_2, \theta_3) : \theta_2 \geq 1 - \epsilon_0', \theta_3 < \frac{\ln\left(\frac{f_{I'}}{\overline{m}^2-1}+1\right)}{\ln\left(\frac{1}{1-\overline{f}}\right)}(\theta_2 - (1 - \epsilon_0'))\}$ and G' represents the event that there exists an $\epsilon_0' \in (0, \frac{1}{2}]$ and there exists a subsequence $T_1, T_2, \ldots, T_s, \ldots$ such that for any s, $\frac{\sum_{k=1}^{T_s} a_k}{T_s} \geq 2\epsilon_0'$, then for any $F > 0$,

$$\lim_{s \to \infty} \Pr\left(\frac{V_{T_s}^{I'}}{T_s} \geq F\right) > 0.$$

Proof. The proof is identical to the proof of Proposition 2 of Appendix A with the following changes. Replace "buyer I" with "seller I'," replace I with I'. Inside the definition of x_k^I, replace $v_k^I > 0$ with $v_k^{I'} < 0$, and replace x_k^I with $x_k^{I'}$. Replace θ_2^I and θ_1^I with $\theta_2^{I'}$ and $\theta_3^{I'}$, respectively. Replace $\frac{\ln\left(\frac{f(\overline{m}+1)}{\overline{m}}\right)}{\ln\left(\frac{\overline{N}+1}{\underline{f}}\right)}$ with $\frac{\ln\left(\frac{f_{I'}}{\overline{m}^2-1}+1\right)}{\ln\left(\frac{1}{1-\overline{f}}\right)}$ and replace ϵ_0 with ϵ_0'. Replace $z_I = 1, (\theta_1^I, \theta_2^I) \in \Theta(\epsilon_0)$, $f_I \geq \underline{f}$ and G with $z_{I'} = -1, (\theta_2^{I'}, \theta_3^{I'}) \in \Theta'(\epsilon_0')$, $f_{I'} \leq \overline{f}$ and G', respectively. Replace the definition of $\underline{f}$, $\Theta(\epsilon_0)$ and G with the definition of $\overline{f}$, $\Theta'(\epsilon_0')$ and G' which are defined in Proposition 3 of Appendix B. Furthermore, $\frac{\underline{f}}{\overline{N}+1}$ is replaced with $1 - \overline{f}$ and $\frac{f(\overline{m}+1)}{\overline{m}}$ is replaced with $\frac{f_{I'}}{\overline{m}^2-1} + 1$. l_k are replaced with a_k and a_k is replaced with l_k.

The paragraph starts with the sentence "Consider buyer I's wealth at time period k" and ending with equation number (4.13) is replaced with the following:

Now, if $l_k = 1$ and $x_k^{I'} = 1$ then $p_k^f < p_k$ and $b_k^{I'} < p_k$, which further implies that $q_k^{I'} \geq -\frac{1}{(\overline{m}-1)} \frac{f_{I'} V_{k-1}^{I'}}{p_k^f}$. Hence, short seller I' potentially makes a loss (a negative profit) at time period k. At the end of time period k the wealth of short seller I' is

$$V_k^{I'} = V_{k-1}^{I'} + q_k^{I'}\left(p_k - p_k^f\right) \geq \left(1 + \left[\frac{f_{I'}}{\overline{m}-1} - \frac{p_k}{p_k^f}\frac{f_{I'}}{\overline{m}-1}\right]\right) V_{k-1}^{I'}$$

$$\geq \left(1 + \left[\frac{f_{I'}}{\overline{m}-1} - \left(\frac{\overline{m}d}{d}\right)\frac{f_{I'}}{\overline{m}-1}\right]\right) V_{k-1}^{I'}$$

$$= (1 - f_{I'}) V_{k-1}^{I'} \geq (1 - \overline{f}) V_{k-1}^{I'}.$$

If $a_k = 1$ and $g_k^{I'} = 1$ then $p_k^f > p_k$ and $b_k^{I'} = p_k$, which further implies that $q_k^{I'} = -\frac{1}{(\overline{m}-1)}\left[\frac{f_{I'} V_{k-1}^{I'}}{p_k^f}, \frac{f_{I'} V_{k-1}^{I'}}{p_k^f + d}\right]$. Hence, short seller I' makes a gain (a positive profit) at time period k. At the end of time period k, the wealth of short seller I' is

$$V_k^{I'} = V_{k-1}^{I'} + \left(p_k - p_k^f\right) q_k^{I'} \geq \left(1 + \left[\frac{f_{I'}}{\overline{m}-1} - \frac{p_k}{p_k^f} \frac{f_{I'}}{\overline{m}-1}\right]\right) V_{k-1}^{I'}$$

$$\geq \left(1 + \left[\frac{f_{I'}}{\overline{m}-1} - \left[\frac{\overline{m}}{\overline{m}+1}\right] \frac{f_{I'}}{\overline{m}-1}\right]\right) V_{k-1}^{I'} = \left(\frac{f_{I'}}{\overline{m}^2-1} + 1\right) V_{k-1}^{I'}. \quad \square$$

Appendix C

The Proof of Theorem 2: The proof is identical to the proof of Theorem 1 with the following changes: l_t and l_k are replaced with a_t and a_k, respectively. Replace ϵ_0 with ϵ_0'. Replace "Proposition 1 in Appendix A" with " by Proposition 3 in Appendix B" and as a result, replace "buyer I" with "seller I'," replace I with I' and replace $z_I = 1, (\theta_1^I, \theta_2^I) \in \Theta(\epsilon_0)$, $f_I \geq \underline{f}$ and G with $z_{I'} = -1, (\theta_2^{I'}, \theta_3^{I'}) \in \Theta'(\epsilon_0')$, $f_{I'} \leq \overline{f}$ and G' respectively. Replace the definition of $\underline{f}$, $\Theta(\epsilon_0)$, and G with the definition of $\overline{f}$, $\Theta'(\epsilon_0')$, and G' which are defined in Proposition 3 of Appendix B. Replace $\left(\theta_1^I, \theta_2^I, \theta_3^I, z_I, f_I\right)$ with $\left(\theta_1^{I'}, \theta_2^{I'}, \theta_3^{I'}, z_{I'}, f_{I'}\right)$.

Replace the paragraph beginning with "Notice that since ..." with "Notice that since the fraction of wealth of short seller I' spent on speculation is strictly less than 1, the wealth of short seller I' is always positive. (The importance of short seller I''s wealth remaining positive in any time period, is that if short seller I''s wealth is zero in one time period, then short seller I' will not be able to sell futures contracts in any subsequent time period and his or her wealth will be zero in all subsequent time periods.)" Replace the words "Proposition 2 in Appendix A" with "Proposition 4 in Appendix B." $\quad \square$

Appendix D

The Proof of Corollary 1: If for $t \geq 1$,

$$\Pr\left(\lim_{T \to \infty} \left(\frac{\ln V_T^t}{T}\right) = 0\right) = 1 \quad (4.17)$$

and if there exists a $u < +\infty$ such that

$$\Pr\left(\limsup_{T \to \infty} \left(\frac{\sum_{k=1}^T \ln V_T^k}{T}\right) < u\right) = 1, \quad (4.18)$$

then the result in Corollary 1 directly follows from the above equations. Now the following will show that (4.17) and (4.18) are true.

The Proof of Equation (4.17): Consider speculator t's wealth at the end of time period k. (i.e., V_k^t).

Appendix D

If $m_k = 1$, then $p_k^f = p_k$. Hence,

$$V_k^t = V_{k-1}^t. \tag{4.19}$$

If $a_k = 1$, then $p_k^f > p_k$. Since $V_k^t = V_{k-1}^t + q_k^t(p_k - p_k^f)$, using buyer t's or seller t's demand schedule, one can show that

$$\frac{p_k}{p_k^f} V_{k-1}^t < V_k^t < \left(1 + \frac{1}{\overline{m} - 1} f_t \left(1 - \frac{p_k}{p_k^f}\right)\right) V_{k-1}^t.$$

This further implies that

$$\frac{1}{\overline{N}+1} V_{k-1}^t < V_k^t < \left(1 + \frac{1}{\overline{m}-1}\right) V_{k-1}^t. \tag{4.20}$$

If $l_k = 1$, then $p_k^f < p_k$. Since $V_k^t = V_{k-1}^t + q_k^t(p_k - p_k^f)$, using buyer t's or seller t's demand schedule, one can show that

$$(1 - f_t) V_{k-1}^t < V_k^t < \left(1 + \frac{p_k}{p_k^f}\right) V_{k-1}^t.$$

This further implies that

$$(1 - f_t) V_{k-1}^t < V_k^t < (1 + \overline{m}) V_{k-1}^t. \tag{4.21}$$

Therefore, (4.19), (4.20), and (4.21) imply that at time k,

$$(1 - f_t)^{l_k} \left(\frac{1}{\overline{N}+1}\right)^{a_k} V_{k-1}^t < V_k^t < \left(1 + \frac{1}{\overline{m}-1}\right)^{a_k} (1 + \overline{m})^{l_k} V_{k-1}^t. \tag{4.22}$$

Using (4.22), one can show inductively that

$$(1 - f_t)^{\sum_{k=t}^{T} l_k} \left(\frac{1}{\overline{N}+1}\right)^{\sum_{k=t}^{T} a_k} V_0 < V_T^t < \left(1 + \frac{1}{\overline{m}-1}\right)^{\sum_{k=t}^{T} a_k} (1 + \overline{m})^{\sum_{k=t}^{T} l_k} V_0.$$

Since $f_t < 1$, $(1 - f_t) > 0$, the above equation further implies that

$$\frac{\sum_{k=t}^{T} l_k}{T} \ln(1 - f_t) + \frac{\sum_{k=t}^{T} a_k}{T} \ln\left(\frac{1}{\overline{N}+1}\right) + \frac{\ln V_0}{T} < \frac{\ln V_T^t}{T} < \frac{\sum_{k=t}^{T} a_k}{T} \ln\left(1 + \frac{1}{\overline{m}-1}\right)$$

$$+ \frac{\sum_{k=t}^{T} l_k}{T} \ln(1 + \overline{m}) + \frac{\ln V_0}{T}.$$

Since $\lim_{T \to \infty} \left(\frac{\ln V_0}{T} \right) = 0$, using Theorem 1 and Theorem 2, the above equation implies that

$$\Pr \left(\lim_{T \to \infty} \left(\frac{\ln V_T^t}{T} \right) = 0 \right) = 1.$$

The Proof of Equation (4.18): Consider the aggregate wealth of all speculators at the end of time period T, (i.e., $\sum_{k=1}^{T} V_T^k$). Since the aggregate wealth either comes from the initial wealth each speculator brings into the market or the gains or losses all speculators have made from the producers up to the end of time period T. That is,

$$\frac{\sum_{k=1}^{T} V_T^k}{T} = \frac{T V_0 + \sum_{k=1}^{T} \left(S_k^f (p_k - p_k^f) \right)}{T}.$$

Since $l_k + m_k + a_k = 1$, the above equation implies that

$$\frac{\sum_{k=1}^{T} V_T^k}{T} = V_0 + \frac{\sum_{k=1}^{T} \left(S_k^f (p_k - p_k^f) l_k \right)}{T} + \frac{\sum_{k=1}^{T} \left(S_k^f (p_k - p_k^f) m_k \right)}{T}$$

$$+ \frac{\sum_{k=1}^{T} \left(S_k^f (p_k - p_k^f) a_k \right)}{T}. \tag{4.23}$$

If $l_k = 1$, then $p_k^f < p_k$; which further implies that

$$0 \leq S_k^f (p_k - p_k^f) \leq \overline{S}(\overline{m}d - d). \tag{4.24}$$

If $m_k = 1$, then $p_k^f = p_k$; hence

$$S_k^f (p_k - p_k^f) = 0. \tag{4.25}$$

If $a_k = 1$, then $p_k^f > p_k$; hence

$$\overline{S}(d - \overline{m}d) \leq S_k^f (p_k - p_k^f) \leq 0. \tag{4.26}$$

Therefore, using (4.24), (4.25), and (4.26), (4.23) implies that

$$V_0 + \overline{S}(d - \overline{m}d) \frac{\sum_{k=1}^{T} a_k}{T} \leq \frac{\sum_{k=1}^{T} V_T^k}{T} \leq V_0 + \overline{S}(\overline{m}d - d) \frac{\sum_{k=1}^{T} l_k}{T}.$$

$$\Pr\left(\lim_{T\to\infty}\left(\frac{\sum_{k=1}^{T} V_T^k}{T}\right) = V_0\right) = 1. \qquad (4.27)$$

Since one can always redenominate wealth in units such that $V_0 < 1$, without loss of generality, assume that $V_0 < 1$. Since

$$\frac{\sum_{k=1}^{T} \ln V_T^k}{T} \leq \ln\left(\frac{\sum_{k=1}^{T} V_T^k}{T}\right),$$

using (4.27), (4.18) follows, where $u = \ln V_0$. □

References

Alchian, A. 1950. Uncertainty, evolution and economic theory. *Journal of Political Economy* 58:211–222.

Allen, B. 1981. Generic existence of equilibria for economies with uncertainty when prices convey information. *Econometrica* 49:1173–1199.

Biais, B. and Shadur, R. 2000. On the survival of irrational traders: a Darwinian approach, *European Economic Review* 44:469–490.

Billingsley, P. 1986. *Probability and measure*. New York: Wiley.

Blume, L. and Easley, D. 1992. Evolution and market behavior. *Journal of Economic Theory* 58: 9–40.

Bray, M. 1981. Futures trading, rational expectations, and the efficient markets hypothesis. *Econometrica* 49:575–596.

Castro, L.I. de, Marialaura, P., and Yannelis, N. 2011. "A new perspective to rational expectations:maximin rational expectations equilibrium". Working paper, Department of Economics, University of Illinois at Urbana Champaign.

Feiger, G.M. 1978. Divergent rational expectations equilibrium in a dynamic model of a futures market. *Journal of Economic Theory* 17:164–178.

Figlewski, S. 1978. Market 'efficiency' in a market with heterogeneous information. *Journal of Political Economy* 86:681–597.

Figlewski, S. 1982. Information diversity and market behavior, *Journal of Finance* 37:87–102.

Fischer, P.E. and R.E. Verrecchia. 1997. Steady state heuristic trade, mimeo, The Wharton School, University of Pennsylvania.

Friedman, M. 1953. *Essays in positive economics*. Chicago: University of Chicago Press.

Gnedenko, B.V. 1963. *The theory of probability*. New York: Chelsea Publishing Company.

Grossman, S.J. 1976. On the efficiency of competitive stock markets where traders have diverse information. *Journal of Finance* 31:573–585.

Grossman, S.J. 1978. Further results on the informational efficiency of competitive stock markets. *Journal of Economic Theory* 18:81–101.

Hellwig, M.F. 1980. On the aggregation of information in competitive markets. *Journal of Economic Theory* 22:477–498.

Kahneman, D., P. Slovic and A. Tversky, eds. 1982. *Judgment under uncertainty: heuristics and biases*. Cambridge: Cambridge University Press.

Kyle, A.S. and F.A. Wang. 1997. Speculation Duopoly with agreement to disagree: can overconfidence survive the market test? mimeo, Graduate School of Business, Columbia University.

Luo, G. 1995a. Evolution and market competition. *Journal of Economic Theory* 67:223–250.

Luo, G. 1995b. Evolutionary models of market behavior. Ph.D. Dissertation, University of Western Ontario.

Radner, R. 1979. Rational expectations equilibrium: generic existence and the information revealed by prices. *Econometrica* 47: 655–678.

Tversky, A. and D. Kahneman. 1974. Judgment under uncertainty: heuristics and biases. *Science* 185:1124–1131.

Chapter 5
Natural Selection, Random Shocks, and Market Efficiency in a Futures Market[1]

This chapter adds a random shock to the futures market to see if an informationally efficient equilibrium would still occur. In this chapter, the prices are modeled as continuous variables and traders can buy or sell with a single submission of their quotes. The conclusion is that, with probability one, if the volatility of the underlying spot market is sufficiently small, then the proportion of time that the futures price is sufficiently close to the fundamental value converges to one. However, the interval containing the fundamental value, where the futures price eventually lies, is influenced by the underlying volatility generated from the spot market. In other words, the accuracy of the information for which the market can eventually select, depends on the volatility generated from the random shock in the spot market. The more volatile the spot market, the more noisy is the information that gets selected for. As a result, the futures market moves further away from informational efficiency. Numerical examples are used to illustrate the cause of the convergence and how the wealth is redistributed among traders.

This chapter is organized into five sections. The next section describes the commodity futures market. Traders' predetermined behavior rules are defined in the third section. The results of the model are provided in the fourth section along with numerical illustrations. The last section concludes the chapter.

5.1 Introduction

A financial market is informationally efficient if the market price fully reflects all available information. In economics and finance traditional methodology usually explains the occurrence of informational efficiency in terms of actions of rational

---

[1] This chapter is based on my article published in the *Journal of Futures Markets* 21(6): 489–516, 2001.

agents. However, Patel et al. (1991) suggested that if the market has a sufficient degree of ability to transfer wealth among traders, this is sufficient to generate an informationally efficient market, regardless of whether traders are rational or not. Here, the biological term "natural selection" takes the form of transferring wealth from less fit traders to more fit ones in the market. This natural selection force in the market promotes an efficient outcome regardless of the rationality of traders.

The idea that markets work even when participants know very little about their environment or about other participants, was recognized by Hayek (1945) who marveled at the market price as an economizer of information despite "how little individual participants need to know" (p. 527).[2] Nevertheless, Hayek was never clear about how this evolved. It would seem that there must be an "invisible hand" process which leads the market to an efficient outcome. That is, there is an efficiency "pattern" that evolves not by conscious design but "instead through the (decentralized) interaction of agents having no such overall pattern in mind" (Nozick 1994, p. 314). For this efficiency pattern to occur in a market with diverse information, the market must serve as a natural selection device that screens out noisy information and only selects for accurate information.

How the market specifically works as a selection or filtering process in promoting an efficient outcome is illustrated in this chapter by through constructing a dynamic model of a commodity futures market. To illustrate the role of the market as a selection process, it is important that such a model allows for the transfer of wealth among traders and the accumulation of wealth across time. On the one hand, in the "oral tradition" of economics, it is sometimes argued that agents with inaccurate information may be driven, via bankruptcy, from the market by "natural forces" (Camerer 1987, p. 982) arising from the presence of more informed agents. On the other hand, there is the frequently provided counterargument that a constant inflow of new poorly informed traders is enough to disrupt any possible market filtering of information.[3] Therefore, to fully test the idea of natural selection in promoting market efficiency, it is also important that such a model allows for a continual inflow of traders with diverse noisy information signals.

There have been a few studies which examine the relationship between market efficiency and natural selection through wealth distribution. They include Feiger (1978), Figlewski (1978, 1982), and Luo (1998). Feiger's explanation of how an efficient equilibrium can evolve through wealth redistribution relies upon traders' rational expectations and uninformed traders learning from market prices to uncover information. Figlewski (1978, 1982) also explored the role of wealth redistribution in determining efficiency in the context of a speculative market with a finite number of traders endowed with differing quality of information. He assumed that traders maximize their utility and have the ability to make posterior updates of predictions from information gathered in the market. Figlewski (1982) showed

---

[2]This issue is also examined in an experimental context in Smith (1982).

[3]See Camerer (1987) for a list of arguments (and counterarguments) used to defend economic theories from the criticism that markets are not rational.

5.1 Introduction

that informational efficiency occurs in the long run only in the special situation where all traders have independent information. In a more recent paper, Luo (1998) examined the role of natural selection with respect to market efficiency, in the context of a futures market with discrete prices. Her paper makes a departure from the above papers in that for the attainment of informational efficiency through natural selection, no rationality is required on the part of traders.

This chapter is different from the aforementioned rationality approaches. Unlike Feiger (1978) and Figlewski (1978, 1982), in order to isolate the role of the market as a filtering process, in this chapter [like Luo (1998)], there is no requirement for rationality on the part of traders. Here traders are not maximizing particular objectives, nor are they receiving feedback from market prices or other traders' behavior. Traders merely act upon some predetermined or inherent behavior rules (described in detail in the next section). This chapter adopts an evolutionary approach of natural selection over these predetermined behavior rules. Unlike Figlewski (1982), informational efficiency can be obtained without the assumption that traders have independent information. One assumption of Figlewski (1978, 1982) that is critical in preventing informational efficiency is the idea that there is a fixed number of traders. In contrast, this chapter allows for an ongoing entry of new traders, with diverse prediction abilities. This chapter extends Luo (1998) to allow for continuous prices and traders who both buy and sell. Simulations are conducted to follow wealth redistribution among traders as the futures price converges to the fundamental value. Moreover, unlike Luo (1998), this chapter, by adding a random shock to the fundamental value in determining the spot price, is able to investigate the relationship between the degree of volatility in the spot market and the extent of convergence of the futures price to the fundamental value. While this relationship was explored through simulation by Figlewski (1978), this chapter is able to characterize this dependence analytically.

To illustrate the idea of natural selection in promoting market efficiency, this chapter presents a simple and straightforward model. The model is briefly described as follows. Consider a commodity futures market. The commodity is assumed to be nonstorable and must be sold in the spot market at the end of each time period. Correspondingly, the futures contracts are one-period in length. Traders enter the market sequentially over time at the beginning of each time period. Traders are engaged in buying or selling contracts to make speculative profits. The spot price consists of the fundamental value plus a random shock to the spot market. The fundamental value is determined in the beginning of each time period before the futures market opens, but is unknown to all market participants. The random shock is realized in the spot market at the end of each time period. In each time period, each trader's prediction about the fundamental value together with trader's wealth provides this trader's demand function for contracts. Each trader's wealth in each time period is defined to be the accumulated profits up to that time period. The futures market is a Walrasian market structure. Each time period, the futures price is the futures market clearing price which equates the aggregate net demand for contracts with the supply of contracts from producers in that time period.

To isolate the role of the market as a selection or filtering process, it is assumed that all traders are unsophisticated in the sense that traders do not adjust their behavior in response to other participants on the basis of their past market experiences. However, it is generally recognized that traders have access to a wide disparity of information. Thus, traders may have information signals with different degrees of reliability. This can be translated into differing abilities of traders in predicting the fundamental value of the spot price.[4] Specifically, upon the entry of each trader, each trader is endowed with an initial amount of wealth and a probability distribution of the prediction error with respect to the fundamental value. The endowment of the probability distribution is trader specific and it is fixed in all subsequent time periods. These probability distributions describe differing abilities of traders in predicting the fundamental value of the spot price and they reflect the diverse noisy information among traders. One trader is more informed (or possesses less noisy information and more accurate information) than another if this trader's probability distribution generates a higher probability of predicting arbitrarily close to the fundamental value than another trader's distribution does.

To easily convey the idea about how the market functions as a filtering process, an intuitive explanation begins with a model with no random shock to the spot market. In this model, traders with better predictions make gains at the expense of their trading counterparts. Therefore, traders with more accurate information tend to accumulate more wealth asymptotically than the traders with less accurate information. As a result, the predictions coming from traders with more accurate information get reflected into the futures price with a greater weight than the predictions from those traders with less accurate information. Over time, traders are constantly entering the market. Some of these traders are not well informed and some are very well informed. If, in each time period, there is a positive probability that the entering trader possesses more accurate information than any previously entering traders, the filtering process would constantly shift wealth from traders with less accurate information to traders with more accurate information. Thus, the filtering process eventually screens out less accurate information and selects for more accurate information. The futures price will be eventually driven to the fundamental value.

However, with the presence of the random shock to the spot market, the above story still works but with less precision. The more volatile the spot market is, the more noisy the information is for which the filtering process selects. As a result, the deviation of the futures market from informational efficiency gets larger. In other words, the width of the interval containing the fundamental value, where the futures price eventually lies, increases as the volatility of the underlying spot

---

[4]Furthermore, even if traders have access to the same information, they may disagree on its correct interpretation and may have differing abilities in processing the same information. Of course, this would further add to differing abilities of traders in predicting the fundamental value of the spot price. This would also be consistent with views of bounded rationality [e.g., Simon (1959, 1986) and Vriend (1996)].

market increases.[5] This latter result is distinctive and reinforces some earlier similar findings of Figlewski (1978). It is worth noting, however, that Figlewski (1978) in his seminal paper had to rely on simulations to illustrate this point; whereas, in this chapter, this result is achieved in a rigorous analytical way as part of a more general theorem.

One of the key ingredients for the functioning of natural selection in this futures market, is each trader's wealth constraint affecting the trader's demand and supply of futures contracts. The role of a wealth or budget constraint in producing an efficient outcomes is noted by Becker (1962) who argued that market rationality can result from agents' random choices being subject to budget constraints. Later on, Gode and Sunder (1993, 1997) built upon this idea and used experiments to demonstrate that allocative efficiency can be achieved even with zero-intelligence traders and the imposition of a budget constraint where no trader is allowed to sell below their costs or buy above their values. This chapter similarly finds that random or pervasive irrational behavior on the part of individual traders can coexist with a rational aggregate market. In the case of the aforementioned papers of Gode and Sunder, aggregate market rationality takes the form of allocative efficiency whereas here aggregate market rationality shows itself in long run informational efficiency. Nevertheless, there is one key difference between these two sets of models. In Gode and Sunder's allocative efficiency conclusions, the evolutionary idea of natural selection plays no role, whereas here there is a natural selection through time due to a constant reallocation of wealth away from traders with poor information and toward traders with the better information.

5.2 Commodity Futures Market

Consider a dynamic model of a commodity futures market. Time is discrete and indexed by t, where $t = 1, 2, \ldots$. The commodity is nonstorable and must be sold at the end of each time period. Hence, futures contracts are one-period in length. The futures market opens at the beginning of each time period. The futures market closes after all transactions in the futures market are completed. Traders participate in the futures market by buying or selling contracts. The aggregate supply of futures contracts from producers at time t, $t = 1, 2, \ldots$, denoted as S_t, is randomly determined each time period from an interval $[0, \overline{S}]$ according to a given probability distribution.[6] After the futures market closes, the spot market opens at the end of

---

[5]A similar descriptive story behind the above selection process can be found in Cootner (1967). Another market selection process for producers in an industry is formulated in Luo (1995) where efficient firms are selected for and a perfectly competitive market arises in the long run.

[6]To be consistent with the evolutionary framework, producers are also assumed to be irrational in the sense that producers have no understanding of the implication of the past futures prices and have no knowledge of the present futures price.

each time period. The spot price in each time period is determined in the spot market. The spot price consists of the fundamental value of the spot market and a random shock to the spot market (coming from either the consumers' demand or the producers' supply in the spot market). That is, the spot price at time period t, denoted by P_t, is modeled as

$$P_t = Z_t + \omega_t,$$

where Z_t represents the fundamental value of the spot market at time period t. Z_t is determined at the beginning of time period t before traders purchase or sell their contracts, but Z_t is unknown to all the market participants. It is assumed that $\{Z_t\}_{t \geq 1}$ is a random sequence taking values in an interval $[\underline{Z}, \overline{Z}]$, where $0 < \underline{Z} < \overline{Z} < \infty$. ω_t is a random shock to the spot market at time period t and ω_t is realized at the end of time period t. $\{\omega_t\}_{t \geq 1}$ is assumed to be an $i.i.d.$ random sequence taking values in an interval $[-\omega, \omega]$, where $\omega > 0$. ω_t has a symmetric density with $E(\omega_t) = 0$. To prevent the spot price being negative, it is assumed that $\omega \leq \underline{Z}$.[7]

It is assumed that the random shock at time t, ω_t, is independent of the fundamental value Z_s, for $s = 1, 2, \ldots$, and is independent of the aggregate supply of contracts from the producers S_t, for $t = 1, 2, \ldots$.

Traders are assumed to enter the market sequentially over time and participate with previously entered traders for the purpose of making speculative profits. At the beginning of time period t, where $t = 1, 2, \ldots$, a single trader (called trader t) is allowed to enter the market and this trader will continue to participate in all future time periods. The fundamental value at time t (Z_t) is determined before trader t enters the market, but unknown to all the market participants entering up to time period t. The timing of events for the model is illustrated in Fig. 5.1.

Each trader is assumed to be endowed with an initial wealth V_0 upon this trader's entry. Trader t's prediction or belief about the fundamental value at time s, where $s \geq t$, denoted by b_s^t, indicates that trader t is willing to buy the number of contracts at a price no higher than b_s^t up to whatever the trader's wealth permits and sell the number of contracts at a price no lower than b_s^t up to whatever the trader's wealth permits him or her to honor.

Specifically, denote trader t's wealth at the end of time period s, where $s \geq t$, as V_s^t and $V_{t-1}^t = V_0$. Denote the futures price at time s as P_s^f, where $s = 1, 2, \ldots$. Given trader t's prediction at time s, (where $s \geq t$), b_s^t, trader t's demand

---

[7]This decomposition of the spot price is consistent with many economic stories. One of such stories is as follows. The output level of each of a very large number of producers is determined (although unknown to other producers) at the beginning of the time period and the total output of all producers is delivered and sold in the spot market at the end of the time period. The intersection of a prespecified consumers' demand curve (determined at the beginning of the time period) with the producers' aggregate supply in the spot market determines the underlying spot price (or fundamental value, Z_t), although unknown to all participants, at the beginning of the time period. However, if a random shock is added to the consumers' demand or the producers' supply at the end of each time period, then this spot price (P_t) at the end of the time period becomes $P_t = Z_t + \omega_t$.

5.2 Commodity Futures Market

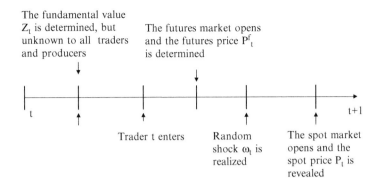

Fig. 5.1 The timing of events

for contracts at time period s is $\frac{V^t_{s-1}}{P^f_s}$ if $P^f_s < b^t_s$.[8] On the other hand, if $P^f_s > b^t_s$, trader t short sells contracts. Since the highest spot price is $\overline{Z} + \omega$, to ensure each trader honors his or her contracts when he or she is selling contracts, the supply of contracts from each trader is constrained such that this trader has enough money to cover his or her loss. Therefore, if $P^f_s > b^t_s$, the demand for contracts at time period s, where $s \geq t$, is $-\frac{V^t_{s-1}}{\overline{Z}+\omega-P^f_s}$. To summarize, trader t's demand for contracts at time period s, where $s \geq t$, is

$$q^t_s(P^f_s) = \begin{cases} \dfrac{V^t_{s-1}}{P^f_s} & \text{if } P^f_s < b^t_s \\[6pt] \left[-\dfrac{V^t_{s-1}}{\overline{Z}+\omega-P^f_s}, \dfrac{V^t_{s-1}}{P^f_s}\right] & \text{if } P^f_s = b^t_s \\[6pt] -\dfrac{V^t_{s-1}}{\overline{Z}+\omega-P^f_s} & \text{if } P^f_s > b^t_s. \end{cases} \quad (5.1)$$

An illustrative demand curve is in Fig. 5.2.

All payments among all participants in the futures market are settled at the end of each time period. Those who bought futures contracts must pay for the contracts at the futures price and in exchange receive payments for these contracts, valued at the spot price. Similarly, those who sold short futures contracts must pay for the contracts at the spot price and in exchange receive payments for these contracts, valued at the futures price. Hence, trader t's profit at the end of time period s is $(P_s - P^f_s)q^t_s$ and so trader t's wealth at the end of time period s is

---

[8] In the following it is assumed that traders actively use all of their wealth for speculation. However, even if traders withdraw for consumption a constant fraction of their wealth each time period, the results of the chapter remain the same.

Fig. 5.2 Trader ts demand for contracts at time s

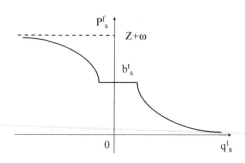

$$V_s^t = V_{s-1}^t + (P_s - P_s^f)q_s^t.$$

The futures price at time s, P_s^f, is the futures market clearing price, determined by the following equality of the aggregate net demand from traders with the aggregate supply of the producers,

$$\sum_{t=1}^{s} q_s^t(P_s^f) = S_s. \qquad (5.2)$$

The solution, P_s^f, to the above equation is unique because of the shape of the demand function and the vertical supply from producers. All transactions are executed at the futures market clearing price. If the maximum number of contracts demanded by traders at the futures market clearing price exceeds the number of contracts supplied by producers and if there are traders whose predictions coincide with the futures market clearing price, the remaining supply could be allocated among those traders proportionately to their wealth. Nevertheless, how the remaining supply is allocated does not affect the results of the chapter.

In fact, the above futures market mechanism is a Walrasian market. It is evident that the more wealth a trader has, the more contracts that this trader demands. Consequently, the more influence this trader's prediction has over the futures price.

5.3 Traders' Predetermined Behavior Rules

Given that the intention is to illustrate how the market functions as a filtering process that screens out traders with less accurate information and selects for traders with more accurate information, the role of the market needs to be isolated and highlighted. Therefore, with respect to modeling traders' predictions, the guiding principle is to model traders' behavior as unsophisticated. That is, traders will be modeled as unresponsive to other participants' behavior and the futures market

5.3 Traders' Predetermined Behavior Rules

environment.[9] To incorporate information about the fundamental value into the traders' predictions, one way of modeling traders' predictions is to assume that each trader's prediction errors with respect to the fundamental value obey his or her own inherent or preprogramed stationary distribution. This probability distribution function characterizes each trader's ability to predict the fundamental value and it reflects the accuracy level of the information this trader possesses. Different traders may have different abilities in predicting the fundamental value or different accuracy levels of information. As a result, different traders' prediction errors may have different probability distribution functions. This way of modeling a trader's ability is analogous to how the performance of a machine is measured by the probability distribution of its precision in meeting particular standards. Keeping each trader's distribution of prediction errors fixed through time is consistent with traders having systematical prediction biases.

Specifically, let b_s^t denote trader t's prediction about the fundamental value at time period s, where $s \geq t$, and let $b_s^t = Z_s + u_s^t$, where u_s^t is trader t's prediction error with respect to the fundamental value at time s.[10] The u_s^t may be correlated across traders. (This contrasts with Figlewski (1978, 1982) where to achieve informational efficiency in the long run, the u_s^t must be independent across traders.) It is assumed that trader t's prediction error at time $s, (s \geq t)$, u_s^t, is independent of Z_s and for all $s \geq t$, $u_s^t \in [-u, u]$. To ensure that the highest prediction does not exceed the highest spot price and the lowest prediction is positive, it is assumed that $u \leq \omega$. It is also assumed that for each t, u_s^t obeys the same probability distribution for all $s \geq t$. Hence, define a vector for trader t, where $t = 1, 2, ...$, as follows: for any given $\epsilon' > 0$,

$$\theta_1^t = \Pr\left(u_s^t \geq \epsilon'\right), \ \theta_2^t = \Pr\left(-\epsilon' \leq u_s^t \leq \epsilon'\right) \text{ and } \theta_3^t = \Pr\left(u_s^t \leq -\epsilon'\right).$$

The variables θ_1^t, θ_2^t, and θ_3^t define the probability of overpredicting, predicting correctly and underpredicting the fundamental value for trader t, respectively. This vector $(\theta_1^t, \theta_2^t, \theta_3^t)$ characterizes trader t's probability distribution of his or her prediction error with respect to the fundamental value, which reflects trader t's ability to predict the fundamental value.[11] Upon the beginning of trader t's entry period, trader t's vector (θ_1^t, θ_2^t) is randomly taken from a set $\{(\theta_1, \theta_2) \in (0, 1) \times (0, 1) : \theta_1 + \theta_2 < 1\}$ and $\theta_3^t = 1 - \theta_1^t - \theta_2^t$. Trader t's vector $(\theta_1^t, \theta_2^t, \theta_3^t)$ is determined in the beginning of time period t and it is fixed in any subsequent time period. This means that there is no adaptive learning or any strategic usage of any information from the markets or other markets' participants among all traders.

---

[9] Of course, traders with more sophisticated behavior could be added to the model, but this would make it more difficult in isolating the filtering role of the market.

[10] This modeling of predictions is the same as Grossman (1976, 1978), Figlewski (1978, 1982), and Hellwig (1980).

[11] No assumptions are made with respect to the type of distribution of the prediction error. This contrasts with most papers including Figlewski (1978, 1982), where normality is assumed.

Trader t acts upon his or her vector $(\theta_1^t, \theta_2^t, \theta_3^t)$ each time period. In other words, in each time period, trader t's prediction error is generated from his or her vector; hence, his or her prediction is determined. Given a trader's prediction at time s, this trader's demand for the number of contracts at time s is characterized by (5.1).

The sequence of traders' vectors $\{(\theta_1^t, \theta_2^t)\}_{t \geq 1}$ is independently and identically distributed according to the distribution function $F(\cdot)$ across traders $t = 1, 2, \ldots$.

Furthermore, it is assumed that in each time period there is a positive probability that an entering trader has an arbitrarily high probability of predicting arbitrarily close to the fundamental value. That is, for any given small positive ϵ,
$$\int_{1-\epsilon < \theta_2 < 1} dF(\theta_1, \theta_2) > 0.$$

In addition, it is also assumed that the random shock at time s, ($s \geq 1$), ω_s, is independent of all traders' prediction errors at all time periods, $u_{s'}^t$, where $s' \geq t \geq 1$.

The futures price at time s, P_s^f, is the futures market clearing price at time s, which is determined by (5.2). As can be seen the futures price P_s^f is a function of $S_1, S_2, \ldots, S_s; Z_1, Z_2, \ldots, Z_s; \omega_1, \omega_2, \ldots, \omega_{s-1}; u_1^t, u_2^t, \ldots, u_s^t$, for all $t \leq s$; and V_0.

5.4 Numerical Examples and Results

To see how the futures price moves over time in this market, a set of simulations is now conducted. For $t = 1, 2, \ldots$, define $\theta_1^t = \Pr(u_s^t > 0.10)$, $\theta_2^t = \Pr(-0.10 \leq u_s^t \leq 0.10)$, and $\theta_3^t = \Pr(u_s^t < -0.10)$. The vector $(\theta_1^t, \theta_2^t, \theta_3^t)$ characterizes trader t's probability distribution of his or her prediction error with respect to the fundamental value.

Consider a futures market with a random shock, ω_s, where $s \geq 1$, is a random draw from an interval $(-\omega, \omega) = (-3, 3)$ according to a symmetric doubly truncated normal distribution where the density function is $\sigma^{-1} Z\left(\frac{w_t}{\sigma}\right) \left[2\Phi\left(\frac{B}{\sigma}\right) - 1\right]^{-1}$, with parameter σ and $B = 2.999$. $Z(\cdot)$ is the unit normal probability density function and $\Phi(\cdot)$ is the corresponding cumulative distribution function.[12] As σ goes up (down), the variation in random shock also goes up (down). Other detailed characteristics of the market are described by (1), (2), (3), and (4) in Appendix A.

First, with $\sigma = 5.0$, 100 simulations are conducted and the market is followed from time period 1 to 3,000. The histogram in Fig. 5.3a shows that at time period 500, on average across 100 simulations, the percentages of time that $|P_s^f - Z_s| \geq 0.10$ and $|P_s^f - Z_s| < 0.025$ are 40% and 16%, respectively. By time period 3,000, on average across 100 simulations, the percentage of time that $|P_s^f - Z_s| \geq 0.10$ has decreased to 28% whereas the percentages of time that $|P_s^f - Z_s| < 0.025$ has increased to 19%. That is, as time goes by there is a lower proportion of time that

---

[12] The truncation keeps the upper bound of the spot price P_s from exceeding the highest bid 10.

5.4 Numerical Examples and Results

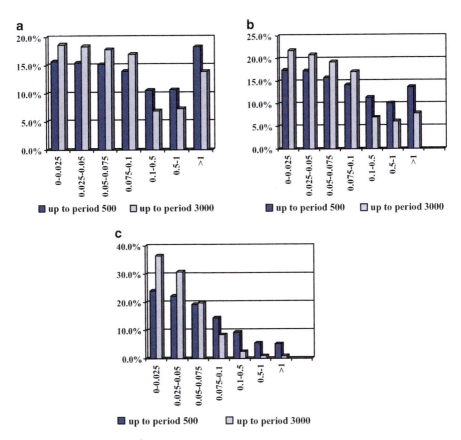

Fig. 5.3 Histogram of $|P_s^f - Z_s|$ as a percentage of times: (**a**) ω_t obeys a truncated normal distribution $\sigma = 5$, (**b**) ω_t obeys a truncated normal distribution $\sigma = 1.5$, and (**c**) No random shock to the economy

$|P_s^f - Z_s|$ is greater than 0.10 and there is a higher proportion of time that $|P_s^f - Z_s|$ is less than 0.025.

However, if the variation in the random shock gets smaller, does the futures price move closer to the fundamental value?

Now, a smaller variance in the random shock is chosen to conduct the second set of simulations. With all other aspects of the model remaining identical, $\sigma = 5.0$ is reduced to $\sigma = 1.5$. and 100 simulations are conducted and the market is followed from time 1 to 3,000. The histogram of the absolute deviation of the futures price from the fundamental value as a percentage of times is shown in Fig. 5.3b. Figure 5.3b shows the clustering of the futures price about the fundamental values, as time goes by. Furthermore, by time period 3,000, on average across 100 simulations, the percentages of time that $|P_s^f - Z_s| \geq 0.10$ and $|P_s^f - Z_s| < 0.025$ are 21% and 22%, respectively. This shows that, in comparison to the simulations with $\sigma = 5.0$, with $\sigma = 1.5$, there is a larger proportion of time that $|P_s^f - Z_s| <$ 0.025.

Now suppose that no random shock is assumed in the spot market (i.e., $\omega_t = 0$ for $t = 1, 2, \ldots$). A third set of simulations is conducted with the model described by the four assumptions in Appendix A along with no random shock assumption. Again, 100 simulations are conducted and the market is followed from time 1 to 3,000.

As expected, with no random shocks, convergence is much faster. The histogram of Fig. 5.3c shows that by time period $3,000$, on average across 100 simulations, the percentages of time that $|P_s^f - Z_s| \geq 0.10$ and $|P_s^f - Z_s| < 0.025$ are 4% and 37%, respectively. This shows that with no random shock, in comparison to the previous simulations with random shocks, there is an even larger proportion of time that $|P_s^f - Z_s| < 0.025$.

This provides good evidence that the smaller the volatility of the random shock to the spot market is, the higher the proportion of time that the futures price lies in a small interval containing the fundamental value, as time increases. This is precisely stated in the following theorem.

Theorem 1. *With probability 1 the following occurs: for any given positive ϵ, there exists a positive number $\overline{k}(\epsilon)$ such that, for the i.i.d. random shock sequence $\{\omega_t\}_{t \geq 1}$ with $\ln \underline{Z} - E(\ln(\underline{Z} + \omega_t)) \leq \overline{k}(\epsilon)$ and for any given positive $\epsilon' > 0$, there exists a time period $T'(\epsilon', \epsilon)$ such that for $T \geq T'(\epsilon', \epsilon)$,*

$$\frac{\#\left\{t \leq T : P_t^f \in [Z_t - \epsilon, Z_t + \epsilon]\right\}}{T} \geq 1 - \epsilon'.$$

Proof. See Appendix B for the proof. □

As shown in the appendix, the term $\ln \underline{Z} - E(\ln(\underline{Z} + \omega_t))$ is a function of all the moments of the random shock ω_t. This term reflects the volatility of the random shock ω_t. For example, if the random shock is normally distributed, the term $\ln \underline{Z} - E(\ln(\underline{Z} + \omega_t))$ is an increasing function of the variance of the random shock ω_t. Hence, Theorem 1 essentially says that, if the volatility of the random shock is sufficiently small, then the proportion of time, that the futures price is sufficiently close to the fundamental value of the spot price, converges to one with probability one. Theorem 1 also indicates that the smaller is the volatility of the random shock, the smaller is the width of the interval (containing the fundamental value), in which the futures price eventually lies with probability 1. This further suggests that if there is no random shock in any time period, then with probability 1, the width of the above interval is arbitrarily small. This is stated formally in the following corollary, which can be established directly from the above theorem.[13]

---

[13]This corollary is the same as Theorem 1 in Luo (1998) except the prices in this chapter are continuous.

5.4 Numerical Examples and Results

Table 5.1 Distribution of the proportion of wealth by trader-types

Trader-types (θ_2^t)	At time 1,000	At time 2,000	At time 3,000
0–0.50	0.378	0.331	0.203
0.50–0.75	0.314	0.291	0.229
0.75–0.90	0.228	0.228	0.229
0.90–0.95	0.045	0.083	0.156
0.95–1.00	0.035	0.067	0.182

Corollary 1. *If $\omega_t = 0$ for all t, then with probability 1 for any given $\epsilon, \epsilon' > 0$, there exists a time period $T^*(\epsilon', \epsilon)$ such that for $T \geq T^*(\epsilon', \epsilon)$,*

$$\frac{\#\left\{t \leq T : P_t^f \in [Z_t - \epsilon, Z_t + \epsilon]\right\}}{T} \geq 1 - \epsilon'.$$

While the convergence of the futures price is rigorously proven in Appendix B, the intuitive reason for convergence deserves further examination. In other words, what is the cause of the convergence of the futures price? For the purpose of dealing with this question, a trader is said to be more informed or possess more accurate information or less noisy information than others if this trader has a higher probability of predicting arbitrarily close to the fundamental value than others do. Since there is no learning or strategic behavior by participants in this model such that traders possessing less accurate information become the ones possessing more accurate information, the occurrence of convergence must be due to the constant redistribution of wealth among all traders. This constant redistribution process must be in favor of traders with a higher probability of predicting arbitrarily close to the fundamental value. That is, the proportion of wealth owned by traders with more accurate information increases relative to the proportion of the wealth owned by traders with less accurate information. Consequently, the more informed traders have more influence over the futures price than the less informed traders. It is the economic natural selection or the filtering process that screens out traders with less accurate information and selects for more accurate information.

To look at this issue, the distribution of wealth by trader-types, described by θ_2^t, is examined for the above simulation model with $\sigma = 1.5$ assumptions (1), (2), (3), and (4) in Appendix A. The distribution of the proportion of the wealth across all trader-types at time periods 1,000, 2,000, and 3,000 is shown in Table 5.1. The corresponding distribution of all trader-types, (here characterized by θ_2^t) at time periods 1,000, 2,000, and 3,000 is in Table 5.2.

As seen in Table 5.1, the proportion of the wealth owned by traders with θ_2^t lying in an interval [0.95,1.00) increases to 18.2% at time period 3,000 from 3.5% at time 1,000. In the meantime, the proportion of wealth owned by traders with θ_2^t lying in an interval (0,0.50) decreases to 20.3% at time 3,000 from 37.8% at time 1,000. From Table 5.2, it can be seen that the proportion of traders with θ_2^t lying in an interval [0.95,1.00) is relatively stable at about 0.05% over time. Both tables suggest that over time, more and more wealth is shifted to the traders with more accurate

Table 5.2 Distribution of trader-types

Trader-types (θ_2^t)	At time 1,000	At time 2,000	At time 3,000
0–0.50	0.8270	0.8363	0.8327
0.50–0.75	0.1552	0.1456	0.1487
0.75–0.90	0.0159	0.0161	0.0164
0.90–0.95	0.0015	0.0015	0.0016
0.95–1.00	0.0005	0.0005	0.0005

information from the traders with less accurate information as more traders with more accurate information enter the economy. This redistribution of wealth process goes on and on; eventually, the group of traders with θ_2^t arbitrarily close to 1 comes to dominate the markets and drives the futures price toward the fundamental value.

5.5 Conclusions

In the above, the idea that the market functions as a filtering process of information, promoting an efficient outcome, has been illustrated by using a dynamic model of a commodity futures market. To emphasize the concept of natural selection, the model allows for the continual inflow of traders with a wide spectrum of noisy information signals, the transfer of wealth among traders and accumulation of wealth across time.

To highlight the role of the market as a selection process of information, rather than the strategic moves of participants, traders are modeled as not being responsive to past market experiences. The model recognizes that traders' predictions reflect a wide disparity of information. Each trader is endowed with a probability distribution of the prediction error with respect to the fundamental value. Since in each time period there is a positive probability that a trader enters with a higher probability of predicting arbitrarily close to the fundamental value than any previously entered traders, over time as more traders enter the markets, if the volatility of the random shock is sufficiently small, then the proportion of time, the futures price is sufficiently close to the fundamental value of the spot price, converges to one. Nevertheless, the interval containing the fundamental value, where the futures price eventually lies, is influenced by the underlying volatility generated from the spot market. In other words, the accuracy of the information for which the market can eventually select, depends on the volatility generated from the random shock in the spot market. The more volatile the spot market, the more noisy is the information that gets selected for. As a result, the futures market moves further away from informational efficiency.

The explanation for the cause of the convergence of the futures price to the fundamental value, which is also supported by the simulations, is rather intuitive. That is, the market, as a filtering process, constantly shifts wealth from traders with less accurate information to traders with more accurate information. Over time as more traders enter the market with more accurate information, eventually, the traders with an arbitrarily high probability of predicting the fundamental value come to dominate the markets and drive the futures price toward the fundamental value of the spot market.

Appendix A

1. The fundamental value of the spot price at time s (z_s), where $s = 1, 2, ...$, is assumed to have a uniform distribution with its support $[\underline{Z}, \overline{Z}] = [3, 7]$.
2. The supply of contracts brought to the futures market by the producers at time i, S_i, is randomly drawn from the interval $(3, 7)$ according to a uniform distribution. This random draw of S_i is independent of the fundamental value Z_s, for all $s \geq 1$.
3. Each trader on entry is endowed with initial wealth $V_0 = 0.001$.

   Finally, all traders' predictions are modeled as being taken from a given distribution each time period. That is,
4. For $t = 1, 2, ...$, $(\theta_1^t, \theta_2^t, \theta_3^t)$ is drawn randomly and independently according to a uniform distribution from a cube defined by $\{(\theta_1, \theta_2, \theta_3) \in (0, 1) \times (0, 1) \times (0, 1) : \theta_1 + \theta_2 + \theta_3 = 1\}$. Trader t's prediction error in each time period is randomly and independently generated from the vector $(\theta_1^t, \theta_2^t, \theta_3^t)$ and trader t's prediction error at time s, ($s \geq t$), $u_s^t \in [-3, 3]$.

Appendix B

The purpose of this appendix is to provide a sketch of the proof of the result in Theorem 1. The result in Theorem 1 is proven by way of contradiction. Roughly speaking, if the result is not true, or in other words, if the futures price stays infinitely often away from the arbitrarily small interval containing the fundamental value, then there would exist a trader, say trader I, with a sufficiently large θ_2^I or sufficiently small θ_1^I and θ_3^I such that this trader's wealth grows exponentially over time and eventually this trader's average wealth over time explores to infinity. This contradicts the fact that the average total wealth in the market over time is bounded from above by a constant. Due to the complexity and the length of the proof, the proof is broken into two lemmas and one theorem. Lemma 1 shows the existence of such a trader with sufficiently large θ_2^I or sufficiently small θ_1^I and θ_3^I. Lemma 2 derives the lower bound for any trader's average logarithm wealth over time. This lower bound is made use of by the proof of Theorem 1 to show that under its contrapositive, the wealth for trader I presented in Lemma 1 would grow exponentially. What follows begins with a sketch of the proof of Lemma 1, followed by Proposition 1, which is required by Lemma 2. This is followed by a sketch of the proof of Lemma 2. The proof of Theorem 1 makes use of these two lemmas.

Lemma 1. *For any given $\delta > 0$ and for any given $\epsilon > 0$,*

$$\Pr\left(\exists \text{ trader } I \text{ such that } \left(\theta_2^I - 1 + \frac{1}{2}\delta\right) \ln\left(\frac{\overline{Z}}{Z - \epsilon}\right) + \theta_1^I \ln\left(\frac{Z}{Z + u}\right)\right.$$

$$\left. + \theta_3^I \ln\left(\frac{\omega}{Z + \omega}\right), \ + \theta_2^I \ln\left(\frac{\omega}{\omega + \epsilon'}\right) - \overline{k} > 0\right.$$

for some positive $\epsilon' < \epsilon$ and some positive $\overline{k}\bigg) = 1$.

Proof. This proof is done under the assumption that $(\theta_1^t, \theta_2^t, \theta_3^t)$ is independently and identically distributed across time $t = 1, 2, \ldots$, along with the second Borel Cantelli Lemma (see Billingsley (1995, p. 83)). The details of the proof are available from the author upon request. □

Proposition 1. *Let $\{X_t\}_{t \geq 1}$ be a random sequence with a finite expectation $E(X_t)$ and $|X_t| \leq M_1$, where M_1 is a finite positive number. Let Y_t, where $t = 1, 2, \ldots$, be a random variable with $|Y_t| \leq M_2$, where M_2 is a finite positive number. If X_t is independent of $Y_1, Y_2, \ldots, Y_t$, then for any given $\epsilon > 0$,*

$$\lim_{T \to \infty} \Pr\left(\left|\frac{\sum_{t=1}^{T}(X_t Y_t)}{T} - \frac{\sum_{t=1}^{T}(Y_t E(X_t))}{T}\right| < \epsilon\right) = 1.$$

Proof. The proof is available from the author upon request. □

To establish Lemma 2 below, the following definitions are needed.

Definition 1. For any given positive ϵ and ϵ' ($\epsilon' < \epsilon$), to describe the position of the futures price relative to the fundamental value plus ϵ, or minus ϵ, or plus ϵ', or minus ϵ', define $l_k, a_k, m_k, \overline{m}_k,$ and $\underline{m}_k$, where $k = 1, 2, \ldots$, as

$$l_k = \begin{cases} 1 \text{ if } P_k^f < Z_k - \epsilon \\ 0 \text{ otherwise,} \end{cases} \quad a_k = \begin{cases} 1 \text{ if } P_k^f > Z_k + \epsilon \\ 0 \text{ otherwise,} \end{cases}$$

$$m_k = \begin{cases} 1 \text{ if } Z_k - \epsilon' \leq P_k^f \leq Z_k + \epsilon' \\ 0 \text{ otherwise,} \end{cases} \quad \overline{m}_k = \begin{cases} 1 \text{ if } Z_k + \epsilon' < P_k^f \leq Z_k + \epsilon \\ 0 \text{ otherwise,} \end{cases}$$

and

$$\underline{m}_k = \begin{cases} 1 \text{ if } Z_k - \epsilon \leq P_k^f < Z_k - \epsilon' \\ 0 \text{ otherwise.} \end{cases}$$

Appendix B

Definition 2. For any given $\epsilon' > 0$, to describe the position of trader t's (where $t = 1, 2, ...,$) prediction error relative to $-\epsilon'$ and ϵ', define x_k^t, g_k^t and y_k^t, where $k \geq t$, as follows:

$$x_k^t = \begin{cases} 1 \text{ if } u_k^t > \epsilon' \\ 0 \text{ otherwise,} \end{cases} \quad g_k^t = \begin{cases} 1 \text{ if } -\epsilon' \leq u_k^t \leq \epsilon' \\ 0 \text{ otherwise,} \end{cases} \text{ and } y_k^t = \begin{cases} 1 \text{ if } u_k^t < -\epsilon' \\ 0 \text{ otherwise.} \end{cases}$$

Definition 3. Trader t (where $t = 1, 2, ...,$) is referred to as a buyer at time period k if trader t is purchasing contracts at time period k, (which occurs whenever $b_k^t > P_k^f$); trader t is referred to as a seller at time period k if trader t is selling contracts at time period k, (which occurs whenever $b_k^t < P_k^f$); trader t is referred to as a marginal buyer if trader t is actually purchasing contracts when $b_k^t = P_k^f$; trader t is referred to as a marginal seller if trader t is actually selling contracts when $b_k^t = P_k^f$. To describe whether trader t at one time period participates as a buyer, a seller, a marginal buyer or a marginal seller, define four random variables B_k^t, M_k^t, N_k^t, and S_k^t, where $k \geq t$, as

$$B_k^t = \begin{cases} 1 \text{ if } b_k^t > P_k^f \\ 0 \text{ otherwise,} \end{cases} \quad M_k^t = \begin{cases} 1 \text{ if } b_k^t = P_k^f, q_k^t > 0 \\ 0 \text{ otherwise,} \end{cases}$$

$$N_k^t = \begin{cases} 1 \text{ if } b_k^t = P_k^f, q_k^t < 0 \\ 0 \text{ otherwise,} \end{cases}$$

and define $S_k^t = 1 - B_k^t - M_k^t - N_k^t$.

Lemma 2. *Consider trader t's wealth at time T, where $t = 1, 2, ...,$ for any given $\epsilon > 0$ and for any $\epsilon' \in (0, \epsilon)$,*

$$\lim_{T \to \infty} \Pr \left(\frac{\ln V_T^t}{T - I + 1} > \frac{\sum_{k=1}^T (l_k + a_k) g_k^t}{T - I + 1} \ln \left(\frac{\overline{Z}}{\underline{Z} - \epsilon} \right) + \frac{\sum_{k=t}^T x_k^t}{T - t + 1} \ln \left(\frac{\underline{Z}}{\overline{Z} + u} \right) \right.$$

$$+ \frac{\sum_{k=t}^T y_k^t}{T - t + 1} \ln \left(\frac{\omega}{\overline{Z} + \omega} \right) + \frac{\sum_{k=t}^T g_k^t}{T - t + 1} \ln \left(\frac{\omega}{\omega + \epsilon'} \right)$$

$$\left. + (E(\ln(\underline{Z} + \omega_k)) - \ln \underline{Z}) \right) = 1.$$

Proof. There are five steps to the proof. Step 1 defines precisely the formula for trader t's wealth at time T (V_T^t).

$$V_T^t = \prod_{k=t}^{T} \left\{ \left(\frac{P_k}{P_k^f}\right)^{C_k} \left(\frac{\overline{Z}+\omega-P_k}{\overline{Z}+\omega-P_k^f}\right)^{D_k} \left(1 - r_k + r_k \frac{P_k}{P_k^f}\right)^{H_k} \right.$$

$$\left. \left(1 - r_k' + r_k'\left(\frac{\overline{Z}+\omega-P_k}{\overline{Z}+\omega-P_k^f}\right)\right)^{F_k} \right\} V_{t-1}^t, \qquad (5.3)$$

where $C_k = g_k^t(l_k + \underline{m}_k + m_k B_k^t) + x_k^t(l_k + \underline{m}_k + m_k + (a_k + \overline{m}_k)B_k^t) + y_k^t(l_k + \underline{m}_k)B_k^t$,

$D_k = g_k^t(a_k + \overline{m}_k + m_k S_k^t) + y_k^t(a_k + \overline{m}_k + m_k + (l_k + \underline{m}_k)S_k^t) + x_k^t(a_k + \overline{m}_k)S_k^t$,

$H_k = g_k^t m_k M_k^t + y_k^t(l_k + \underline{m}_k)M_k^t + x_k^t(a_k + \overline{m}_k)M_k^t$, and

$F_k = g_k^t m_k N_k^t + y_k^t(l_k + \underline{m}_k)N_k^t + x_k^t(a_k + \overline{m}_k)N_k^t$.

By taking logarithms of both sides of (5.3), setting $V_{t-1}^t = V_0$, and making use of the concavity of the function $\ln(\cdot)$, Step 2 establishes a lower bound for $\frac{\ln V_T^t}{T-t+1}$,

$$\frac{\ln V_T^t}{T-t+1} \geq \frac{1}{T-t+1} \left\{ \sum_{k=t}^{T} \left((C_k + H_k r_k) \ln\left(\frac{P_k}{P_k^f}\right)\right) \right.$$

$$\left. + \sum_{k=t}^{T} \left((D_k + F_k r_k') \ln\left(\frac{\overline{Z}+\omega-P_k}{\overline{Z}+\omega-P_k^f}\right)\right) + \ln V_0 \right\}.$$

As can be seen in the above, there are three components to this lower bound, two of which are random. Steps 3 and 4 determine probabilistic lower bound for the first two random components of this lower bound. This is done by using a Taylor expansion of $\ln(P_k) = \ln(Z_K + \omega_k)$ and $\ln(\overline{Z}+\omega-P_k) = \ln(\overline{Z}+\omega-(Z_K+\omega_k))$ and Proposition 1 to produce the following two equations.

$$\lim_{T \to \infty} \Pr \left(\frac{\sum_{k=t}^{T}\left((C_k + H_k r_k) \ln\left(\frac{P_k}{P_k^f}\right)\right)}{T-t+1} > \frac{\sum_{k=t}^{T}\left(g_k^t l_k \ln(\frac{\overline{Z}}{\overline{Z}-\epsilon})\right)}{T-t+1} \right.$$

$$+ \frac{\sum_{k=t}^{T}\left(x_k^t m_k \ln(\frac{\overline{Z}}{\overline{Z}+\epsilon'})\right)}{T-t+1} + \frac{\sum_{k=t}^{T}\left(g_k^t m_k (B_k^t + r_k M_k^t)(\ln(\frac{\overline{Z}}{\overline{Z}+\epsilon'}))\right)}{T-t+1}$$

$$+ \frac{\sum_{k=t}^{T}\left(x_k^t(a_k + \overline{m}_k)(B_k^t + r_k M_k^t) \ln(\frac{\overline{Z}}{\overline{Z}+u})\right)}{T-t+1}$$

$$\left. + \frac{\sum_{k=t}^{T}\left((C_k + H_k r_k)(E\ln(\overline{Z}+\omega_k) - \ln \overline{Z})\right)}{T-t+1} \right) = 1.$$

Appendix B

and

$$\lim_{T \to \infty} \Pr \left(\frac{\sum_{k=t}^{T} \left((D_k + F_k r'_k) \ln\left(\frac{\overline{Z}+\omega-P_k}{\overline{Z}+\omega-P_k^f}\right) \right)}{T-t+1} > \frac{\sum_{k=t}^{T} \left(g_k^t a_k \ln(\frac{\overline{Z}+\omega-Z}{\overline{Z}+\omega-(\underline{Z}+\epsilon)}) \right)}{T-t+1} \right.$$

$$+ \frac{\sum_{k=t}^{T} \left(y_k^t m_k \ln(\frac{\omega}{\omega+\epsilon'}) \right)}{T-t+1} + \frac{\sum_{k=t}^{T} \left(g_k^t m_k (S_k^t + r'_k N_k^t) \ln(\frac{\omega}{\omega+\epsilon'}) \right)}{T-t+1}$$

$$+ \frac{\sum_{k=t}^{T} \left(y_k^t (l_k + \underline{m}_k)(S_k^t + r'_k N_k^t) \ln(\frac{\omega}{\overline{Z}+\omega}) \right)}{T-t+1}$$

$$\left. + \frac{\sum_{k=t}^{T} \left((D_k + F_k r'_k) (E(\ln(\omega - \omega_k)) - \ln \omega) \right)}{T-t+1} \right) = 1.$$

Step 5 substitutes these two probabilistic lower bounds into the lower bound of $\frac{\ln V_T^t}{T-t+1}$ and simplifies it to give the results of Lemma 2. The details of the proof are available from the author upon request. □

The Proof of Theorem 1: This is shown by way of contradiction. Suppose that Theorem 1 is not true, then with a strictly positive probability the following occurs: there exists an ϵ_0 such that, for all $\overline{k}'$, it is possible to find an *i.i.d.* random sequence $\{\omega_k\}_{k \geq 1}$, with $\ln \underline{Z} - E(\ln(\underline{Z} + \omega_k)) \leq \overline{k}'$, for which there exists a $\delta_0 > 0$ and a subsequence $n_1, n_2, ..., n_T, ...$, such that for all $T \geq 1$, $\frac{\#\{k \leq n_T : P_k^f \notin [Z_k - \epsilon_0, Z_k + \epsilon_0]\}}{n_T} > \delta_0$. Since Lemma 1 implies that for this $\delta_0 > 0$ and for this $\epsilon_0 > 0$,

$$\Pr \left(\exists \text{ trader } I \text{ such that,} \left(\theta_2^I - 1 + \frac{1}{2}\delta_0 \right) \ln \left(\frac{\overline{Z}}{\underline{Z} - \epsilon_0} \right) \right.$$

$$+ \theta_1^I \ln \left(\frac{\overline{Z}}{\underline{Z} + u} \right) + \theta_3^I \ln \left(\frac{\omega}{\overline{Z}+\omega} \right) + \theta_2^I \ln \left(\frac{\omega}{\omega + \epsilon'_0} \right) - \overline{k} > 0,$$

$$\left. \text{for some positive } \epsilon'_0 < \epsilon_0 \text{ and some positive } \overline{k} \right) = 1. \quad (5.4)$$

and using the notation in definitions 1, 2, and 3 after replacing ϵ, ϵ' with ϵ_0 and ϵ'_0 respectively in the definitions 1, 2, and 3, the above statement can be restated as the following:

With a strictly positive probability the following occurs: there exists an ϵ_0 such that, for all $\overline{k}'$, it is possible to find an *i.i.d.* random sequence $\{\omega_k\}_{k \geq 1}$, with

$\ln \underline{Z} - E(\ln(\underline{Z} + \omega_k)) \leq \overline{k}'$, for which there exists a $\delta_0 > 0$ and a subsequence $n_1, n_2, \ldots, n_T, \ldots$, such that for all $T \geq 1$,

$$\frac{\sum_{k=1}^{n_T}(l_k + a_k)}{n_T} > \delta_0 > 0. \tag{5.5}$$

Consider trader I. The following shows that trader I's wealth grows exponentially whereas the aggregate wealth can only grow arithmetically. This is a contradiction.

Because trader I's prediction error u_k^I is independently and identically distributed across time k, the Strong Law of Large Number implies that with probability 1, as $T \to \infty$,

$$\frac{\sum_{k=I}^{n_T} g_k^I}{n_T - I + 1} \to \theta_2^I, \quad \frac{\sum_{k=I}^{n_T} x_k^I}{n_T - I + 1} \to \theta_1^I, \text{ and } \frac{\sum_{k=I}^{n_T} y_k^I}{n_T - I + 1} \to \theta_3^I. \tag{5.6}$$

Furthermore, noticing that,

$$\sum_{k=I}^{n_T}((l_k + a_k)g_k^I) = \sum_{k=I}^{n_T}((l_k + a_k)(1 - y_k^I - x_k^I))$$

$$\geq \sum_{k=I}^{n_T}((l_k + a_k) - (1 - g_k^I))$$

$$= (n_T - I + 1)\left[\left(\frac{\sum_{k=I}^{n_T}(l_k + a_k)}{n_T - I + 1} + \frac{\sum_{k=I}^{n_T} g_k^I}{n_T - I + 1}\right) - 1\right]. \tag{5.7}$$

Therefore, (5.4), (5.6), and (5.7) imply that

$$\Pr\left(\lim_{T\to\infty} \left(\frac{\sum_{k=I}^{n_T}((l_k + a_k)g_k^I)}{n_T - I + 1}\right) \ln\left(\frac{\overline{Z}}{\overline{Z} - \epsilon_0}\right) + \frac{\sum_{k=I}^{T} x_k^I}{n_T - I + 1} \ln\left(\frac{\underline{Z}}{\underline{Z} + u}\right)\right.$$

$$\left. + \frac{\sum_{k=I}^{T} y_k^I}{n_T - I + 1} \ln\left(\frac{\omega}{\overline{Z} + \omega}\right) + \frac{\sum_{k=I}^{T} g_k^I}{n_T - I + 1} \ln\left(\frac{\omega}{\omega + \epsilon_0'}\right)\right.$$

Appendix B

$$> \left(\theta_2^I - 1 + \frac{\sum_{k=I}^{n_T}(l_k + a_k)}{n_T - I + 1} \right) \ln\left(\frac{\overline{Z}}{\overline{Z} - \epsilon_0} \right)$$

$$+ \theta_1^I \ln\left(\frac{\overline{Z}}{\overline{Z} + u} \right) + \theta_3^I \ln\left(\frac{\omega}{\overline{Z} + \omega} \right) + \theta_2^I \ln\left(\frac{\omega}{\omega + \epsilon_0'} \right) \bigg| A \right) = 1, \quad (5.8)$$

where A denotes the event that there exists trader I, such that $(\theta_2^I - 1 + \frac{1}{2}\delta_0)\ln(\frac{\overline{Z}}{\overline{Z}-\epsilon_0}) + \theta_1^I \ln(\frac{\overline{Z}}{\overline{Z}+u}) + \theta_3^I \ln(\frac{\omega}{\overline{Z}+\omega}) + \theta_2^I \ln(\frac{\omega}{\omega+\epsilon_0'}) - \overline{k} > 0$, for some positive $\epsilon_0' < \epsilon_0$ and some positive $\overline{k}$.

Since if $\frac{\sum_{t=1}^{n_T}(l_k+a_k)}{n_T} > \delta_0$, then as $T \to \infty$,

$$\frac{\sum_{k=I}^{n_T}(l_k + a_k)}{n_T - I + 1} > \frac{1}{2}\delta_0. \quad (5.9)$$

Applying Bayes rule to (5.5) and (5.8), and using (5.9), it follows that

$$\Pr\left(\lim_{T \to \infty} \left(\frac{\sum_{k=I}^{n_T}((l_k + a_k)g_k^I)}{n_T - I + 1} \right) \ln\left(\frac{\overline{Z}}{\overline{Z} - \epsilon_0} \right) + \frac{\sum_{k=I}^{T} x_k^I}{n_T - I + 1} \ln\left(\frac{\overline{Z}}{\overline{Z} + u} \right) \right.$$

$$+ \frac{\sum_{k=I}^{T} y_k^I}{n_T - I + 1} \ln\left(\frac{\omega}{\overline{Z} + \omega} \right) + \frac{\sum_{k=I}^{T} g_k^I}{n_T - I + 1} \ln\left(\frac{\omega}{\omega + \epsilon_0'} \right)$$

$$> \left(\theta_2^I - 1 + \frac{1}{2}\delta_0 \right) \ln\left(\frac{\overline{Z}}{\overline{Z} - \epsilon_0} \right) + \theta_1^I \ln\left(\frac{\overline{Z}}{\overline{Z} + u} \right)$$

$$\left. + \theta_3^I \ln\left(\frac{\omega}{\overline{Z} + \omega} \right) + \theta_2^I \ln\left(\frac{\omega}{\omega + \epsilon_0'} \right) \bigg| (A, E) \right) = 1, \quad (5.10)$$

where E represents the following event: with a strictly positive probability the following occurs: there exists an ϵ_0 such that for all $\overline{k}'$, it is possible to find an $i.i.d.$ random sequence $\{\omega_k\}_{k \geq 1}$, with $\ln \overline{Z} - E(\ln(\overline{Z} + \omega_k)) \leq \overline{k}'$, for which there exists a $\delta_0 > 0$ and a subsequence $n_1, n_2, ..., n_T, ...$, such that for all T, $\frac{\sum_{k=1}^{n_T}(l_k+a_k)}{n_T} > \delta_0$.

Furthermore, noticing that for trader I, there exists some positive $\lambda > 0$, such that,

$$\left(\theta_2^I - 1 + \frac{1}{2}\delta_0\right) \ln\left(\frac{\overline{Z}}{\overline{Z} - \epsilon_0}\right) + \theta_1^I \ln\left(\frac{Z}{Z+u}\right) + \theta_3^I \ln\left(\frac{\omega}{\overline{Z}+\omega}\right)$$

$$+ \theta_2^I \ln\left(\frac{\omega}{\omega + \epsilon_0'}\right) - \overline{k} > \lambda. \tag{5.11}$$

Equations (5.10) and (5.11) imply that

$$\Pr\left(\lim_{T\to\infty}\left(\frac{\sum_{k=1}^{n_T}((l_k + a_k)g_k^I)}{n_T - I + 1}\ln\left(\frac{\overline{Z}}{\overline{Z} - \epsilon_0}\right) + \frac{\sum_{k=1}^{T} x_k^I}{n_T - I + 1}\ln\left(\frac{Z}{Z+u}\right)\right.\right.$$

$$\left.\left. + \frac{\sum_{k=1}^{T} y_k^I}{n_T - I + 1}\ln\left(\frac{\omega}{\overline{Z}+\omega}\right) + \frac{\sum_{k=1}^{T} g_k^I}{n_T - I + 1}\ln\left(\frac{\omega}{\omega + \epsilon_0'}\right) - \overline{k} > \lambda\right| (A, E)\right) = 1. \tag{5.12}$$

Equation (5.12) further implies that

$$\Pr\left(\lim_{T\to\infty}\left(\frac{\sum_{k=1}^{n_T}((l_k + a_k)g_k^I)}{n_T - I + 1}\ln\left(\frac{\overline{Z}}{\overline{Z} - \epsilon_0}\right) + \frac{\sum_{k=1}^{T} x_k^I}{n_T - I + 1}\ln\left(\frac{Z}{Z+u}\right)\right.\right.$$

$$\left.\left. + \frac{\sum_{k=1}^{T} y_k^I}{n_T - I + 1}\ln\left(\frac{\omega}{\overline{Z}+\omega}\right) + \frac{\sum_{k=1}^{T} g_k^I}{n_T - I + 1}\ln\left(\frac{\omega}{\omega + \epsilon_0'}\right) - \overline{k} > \lambda\right) > 0. \tag{5.13}$$

Lemma 2 implies that for trader I at time n_T, for this ϵ_0, and for $\epsilon_0' \in (0, \epsilon_0)$,

$$\lim_{T\to\infty}\Pr\left(\frac{\ln V_{n_T}^I}{n_T - I + 1} > \frac{\sum_{k=1}^{n_T}((l_k + a_k)g_k^I)}{n_T - I + 1}\ln\left(\frac{\overline{Z}}{\overline{Z} - \epsilon_0}\right)\right.$$

$$\left. + \frac{\sum_{k=1}^{n_T} x_k^I}{n_T - I + 1}\ln\left(\frac{Z}{Z+u}\right) + \frac{\sum_{k=1}^{n_T} y_k^I}{n_T - I + 1}\ln\left(\frac{\omega}{\overline{Z}+\omega}\right)\right.$$

$$+\frac{\sum_{k=I}^{n_T} g_k^I}{n_T - I + 1} \ln\left(\frac{\omega}{\omega + \epsilon_0'}\right) + (E(\ln(\underline{Z} + \omega_k)) - \ln \underline{Z})\Bigg) = 1. \quad (5.14)$$

Equations (5.13) and (5.14) imply that for any $i.i.d.$ random shock sequence $\{\omega_k\}_{k\geq 1}$ with $(\ln \underline{Z} - E(\ln(\underline{Z} + \omega_k))) \leq \overline{k}$, $\lim_{T\to\infty} \Pr\left(\frac{\ln V_{n_T}^I}{n_T - I + 1} > \lambda\right) > 0$. This further implies that for any given $F > 0$, for any $i.i.d.$ random shock sequence $\{\omega_k\}_{k\geq 1}$ with $(\ln \underline{Z} - E(\ln(\underline{Z} + \omega_k))) \leq \overline{k}$,

$$\lim_{T\to\infty} \Pr\left(\frac{V_{n_T}^I}{n_T - I + 1} > F\right) > 0, \quad (5.15)$$

However, since the maximum amount of wealth, which is injected into the market each time period, is bounded from above by a constant $(\overline{S}\,(\overline{Z} + \omega) + V_0)$; the average wealth (across time) of all the traders is bounded from above by this constant. This contradicts (5.15). □

References

Becker, G.S. 1962. Irrational behavior and economic theory. *Journal of Political Economy*. LXX:1–13.
Billingsley, P. 1995. *Probability and measure*. New York: John Wiley & Sons.
Camerer, C.F. 1987. Do biases in probability judgment matter in markets? *American Economic Review* 77:981–997.
Cootner, P.H. 1967. *The random character of stock market prices*. Rev. ed. Cambridge: M.I.T. Press.
Feiger, G.M. 1978. Divergent rational expectations equilibrium in a dynamic model of a futures market. *Journal of Economic Theory* 17:164–178.
Figlewski, S. 1978. Market 'efficiency' in a market with heterogeneous information. *Journal of Political Economy* 86(4):581–597.
Figlewski, S. 1982. Information diversity and market behavior. *Journal of Finance* 37:87–102.
Gode, D.K., and S. Sunder. 1993. Allocative efficiency of markets with zero-intelligence traders: market as a partial substitute for individual rationality *Journal of Political Economy* 101(1):119–137.
Gode, D.K., and S. Sunder. 1997. What makes markets allocationally efficient. *Quarterly Journal of Economics* 112(2):603–630.
Grossman, S.J. 1976. On the efficiency of competitive stock markets where traders have diverse information. *Journal of Finance* 31:573–585.
Grossman, S.J. 1978. Further results on the informational efficiency of competitive stock markets. *Journal of Economic Theory* 18:81–101.
Hayek, F.A. 1945. The uses of knowledge in society. *American Economic Review* 35:519–530.
Hellwig, M.F. 1980. On the aggregation of information in competitive markets. *Journal of Economic Theory* 22:477–498.
Luo, G.Y. 1995. Evolution and market competition. *Journal of Economic Theory* 67(1):223–250.

Luo, G.Y. 1998. Market efficiency and natural selection in a commodity futures market. *Review of Financial Studies* 11(3):647–674.
Nozick, R. 1994. Invisible-hand explanations. *American Economic Review* 84(2):314–318.
Patel, J., R. Zeckhauser, and D. Hendricks. 1991. The rationality struggle: illustrations from financial markets. *American Economic Review* 81(2):232–236.
Simon, H. 1959. Theories of decision-making in economic and behavioral science. *American Economic Review* 49:253–283.
Simon, H. 1986. Rationality in psychology and economics. *Journal of Business* 59:S209–S224.
Smith, V.L. 1982. Markets as economizers of information: experimental examination of the "Hayek hypothesis". *Economic Inquiry* 20(2):165–179.
Vriend, N.J. 1996. Rational behavior and economic theory. *Journal of Economic Behavior and Organization* 29:263–285.

Chapter 6
Evolution, Noise Traders, and Market Efficiency in a One-Sided Auction Market[1]

This chapter builds an evolutionary model of one-sided buyer auction market to examine if the informational efficiency would still occur as a long run outcome. Here, each trader's behavior is preprogramed with its own inherent and fixed probabilities of overpredicting, predicting correctly, and underpredicting the fundamental value of the asset. This chapter shows that, if each buyer's initial wealth is sufficiently small relative to the market supply and if the variation in the asset's random shock is sufficiently small, then as time gets sufficiently large, the proportion of time, that the asset price is arbitrarily close to the fundamental value, converges to one with probability one.

This chapter is organized into four sections. Section 6.2 outlines the model. The results can be found in Sect. 6.3. Section 6.4 summarizes and concludes the chapter.

6.1 Introduction

Traditionally, in the literature, the derivation of an informationally efficient market has tended to rely on the presence of traders' rational expectations, strategic usage of market information, or adaptive learning behavior where noise traders gradually become informed traders. However, due to individuals' limited ability to process and manage complex information, the assumption of rationality is challenged. This further calls into question the achievement of market efficiency. On the other hand, there is Friedman's 1953 well-known conjecture that, because noise traders will sooner or later lose money to the informed traders, the informed traders will come to dominate the market and drive the asset price toward the fundamental value. An intuitively appealing aspect of Friedman's conjecture is the idea of natural selection among traders.

---

[1]This chapter is based on my article published in the Journal of Financial Markets, 6, 163–197, 2003.

The idea of abandoning rationality on the part of traders is consistent with a growing literature in behavioral economics and finance. The behavioral approach focuses on the behavior patterns drawn from psychological theory (e.g., Kahneman et al. (1982)). Often judgmental decisions are based on cognitive rules of thumb used to simplify the decision-making process. Using such rules to assess uncertain events and make predictions, often leads to systematic errors or biases. In the context of a one-sided auction, such systematic errors take the form of consistent patterns of predicting biases, which are captured by the probabilities of overpredicting and underpredicting the asset value; these predicting probabilities become the key to modeling traders' behavior. In this chapter it is assumed that traders are rather unsophisticated and each trader consistently overpredicts or underpredicts with some fixed probabilities. In an evolutionary sense, each trader is genetically preprogrammed with its own inherent and fixed probabilities of overpredicting, underpredicting, and predicting correctly the asset value. Since a trader has a positive probability of overpredicting or underpredicting the asset value, the trader has a positive probability of acting upon noise as if it were information. Therefore, in this sense, traders are called noise traders in this chapter.

Within the context of a double-sided auction, Luo (1998, 2001) shows that with no requirement of traders' rationality such as rational expectations and adaptive learning, natural selection among traders through redistribution of wealth is sufficient to cause the convergence to an informationally efficient market. It is noteworthy, however, that in the context of a double-sided auction, the allowance for short sales implies that the supply of the asset is virtually elastic. While the majority of financial markets adopts a double-sided auction market, there is a significant number of markets which are essentially one-sided auction markets with a perfectly inelastic supply. A key distinction between a one-sided and a double-sided auction market is that traders in a double-sided auction market are allowed to short sell. In a one-sided auction market, short sales are not possible because of the lack of a secondary market. The absence of secondary markets often occurs in the sale of short-term commercial paper, municipal notes, non-negotiable certificates of deposit and private placements and sometimes occurs in markets for bonds (e.g., Japanese corporate bonds).[2] Other examples of one-sided auctions include the leasing of mineral rights, the leasing of oil drilling permits and the leasing of timber rights.[3] The recent emergence of internet online purchasing provides some other interesting examples.

There are three purposes of this chapter. The first purpose is to show that the market mechanism of a one-sided auction, itself, can promote an efficient outcome through natural selection. To this end, this chapter adopts the idea of natural

---

[2]Sometimes, secondary markets do exist for commercial paper and private placements. But usually the transaction costs of setting up these markets have proven to be prohibitive.

[3]Other examples of auctions, where there is a fixed supply of an asset and no short sales, can be found in both the theoretical and experimental economics literature (e.g., Wilson (1979) and Forsythe et al. (1982)).

6.1 Introduction

selection and formulates an evolutionary model of a one-sided buyer's auction market. It shows that even without a rationality assumption like rational expectations or adaptive learning and even when each trader merely acts upon its own inherent and fixed probabilities of overpredicting, predicting correctly, and underpredicting the asset value, an informationally efficient market can occur. This stands in contrast with the conventional literature which states that an efficient outcome is promoted through rational expectations or adaptive behavior on the part of market participants (e.g., Grossman (1976, 1978), Radner (1979), Hellwig (1980), Allen and Yannelis (2001),[4] and Castro et al. (2011)).

A second purpose of this chapter is to identify, in the context of this evolutionary approach, an alternative less restrictive condition for achievement of an efficient outcome in the one-sided auction market other than the one used in the double-sided auction market. For convergence to occur in the context of a double auction, Luo (1998, 2001) requires that in each time period there is a positive probability that the entering trader has an arbitrarily high probability of predicting the fundamental value correctly. Furthermore, within the context of a double auction the allowance for short sales implies that the supply of contracts is elastic. In contrast, in this chapter, the supply of the asset is perfectly inelastic and the market is a one-sided buyer auction. For convergence to occur, a less restrictive condition is that there is a positive probability in each time period that the entering trader has an arbitrarily low probability of overpredicting the fundamental value and has a probability, of predicting arbitrarily close to the fundamental value, being bounded away from zero by a positive number. This result is very intuitive. If traders who overpredict with a low probability (implying a small number of upward biases) are characterized as being relatively risk averse (in a behavioral finance sense (e.g., Sitkin and Pablo (1992)), for convergence to occur, it is sufficient that there are enough traders with a sufficient degree of risk aversion. The importance of the presence of these risk averse traders in the natural selection process leading to market efficiency, is consistent with Barrow (1992) and Olsen (1998) who see decision attributes that exhibit aversion to negative impacts (here caused by overpredicting) as having evolutionary value in selecting the long run outcome.

Nevertheless, to obtain convergence to efficiency, competition among traders is needed. That is, in a one-sided auction market where the market supply is perfectly inelastic, competition means that each trader's initial wealth must be sufficiently small relative to the fixed market supply. However, it is remarkable that even when there is a perfectly inelastic supply of the asset and even when the number of traders increases over time, with each entering trader coming in with a finite amount of wealth, the price can be eventually assured to remain in a small interval containing the fundamental value.

A third purpose of this chapter is to quantify the extent to which a variation in movement of the underlying asset's liquidation value around the fundamental value

---

[4] Allen and Yannelis (2001) present a comprehensive discussions on various rational equilibrium outcomes in various differential information economies.

influences the extent of convergence of the asset price to the fundamental value. This chapter, like Luo (2001), accounts for a random shock around the fundamental value. This chapter shows that, the bigger is the variation in the random shock about the fundamental value, the bigger is the variation of the asset price about the fundamental value.

The evolutionary approach in this chapter stands in contrast with recent literature which has analytically studied the impact of noise traders on the market price within the context of rational models. For example, De Long et al. (1990) study an overlapping generation model, where an informed trader and a noise trader both maximize their expected utilities. They find that the noise trader can cause the market price to deviate systematically away from its fundamental value.[5] For the convergence of the asset price to the fundamental value, rationality models (where utility or profit maximization occurs) sometimes rely on learning and imitation to make uninformed traders become more informed. For example, Grossman (1978) allows investors to acquire information about past distributions of prices which in turn produces more informed investors. This has also been explored in the experimental laboratory market. Plott and Sunder (1982) show that constant replication allows a learning by traders which resembles a rational expectations equilibrium.

Related literature in applying an evolutionary approach to examining market behavior are Blume and Easley (1992), Biais and Shadur (2000), and Luo (1995). Blume and Easley (1992) study a dynamic model of an asset market with a finite number of traders with different investment rules. They find that the market can select for an irrational rule and the market may not be efficient. Biais and Shadur (2000) apply Darwinian dynamics to the selection of the number of informed traders and noise traders based on their payoffs. They find that noise traders can persist in the long run. The results in the above two papers have illustrated that the natural selection in the market alone is not sufficient to generate an efficient market outcome. Luo (1995) further shows that natural selection, in conjunction with competition in the market, is sufficient to lead the market to select the most efficient firms (those producing at or near the minimum efficient scale) and as a result the market price converges to the perfectly competitive price.

This chapter shows analytically that the market can reach an efficient market outcome with the presence of irrational noise traders. The coexistence of market efficiency and participants' irrationality has also been illustrated in some recent experimental literature as well. For example, Gode and Sunder (1993) design a series of experiments to examine a double auction market where traders submit bids and offers randomly. They find that allocation efficiency in the double auction can be generated from individual participants' irrationality. Bosch and Sunder (2000) design a similar series of experiments to examine multimarket double auctions. They reach the same conclusion.

---

[5]Their results are partly due to the difference in the utility functions of both types of traders, the absence of wealth accumulation and the absence of wealth flows between the two types of traders.

6.2 The Model

Consider a conventional dynamic asset market where a market maker supplies one unit of a one-period risky asset each time period. Time is indexed by t, where $t = 1, 2, \ldots$. The asset market opens each time period. Traders can only buy shares of the asset from the market maker at the market clearing asset price. Denote the market clearing price at time s as p_s, where $s = 1, 2, \ldots$. No short selling is possible in this framework. Hence, all traders are buyers. In the following sections, the terms traders and buyers are used interchangeably. The risky asset is liquidated after the asset market closes at the end of each time period.[6] Denote v_t as the liquidation value of the risky asset at the end of time period t. It is assumed that $v_t = z_t \exp(w_t)$, where z_t represents the fundamental liquidation value of the asset at time t and determined in the beginning of time t and where w_t is a random shock to the economy and realized at the end of each time period t. It is assumed that the sequence $\{z_t\}_{t \geq 1}$ is a random sequence taking values from an interval $[\underline{z}, \overline{z}]$, where $0 \leq \underline{z} \leq \overline{z} < \infty$. The sequence $\{w_t\}_{t \geq 1}$ is assumed to be a i.i.d random sequence taking values from an interval $[-\underline{w}, \overline{w}]$, where $0 < \underline{w} < \infty$, $0 < \overline{w} < \infty$ and $E(w_t) = 0$ for all t. It is assumed that ω_t, where $t = 1, 2, \ldots$, is independent of z_s, where $s \geq 1$.

6.2.1 Traders' Prediction Errors

Traders enter the market sequentially over time. At the beginning of time period t, where $t = 1, 2, \ldots$, the fundamental value z_t is determined, but it is unknown to all market participants. At the beginning of time period t after the fundamental value z_t is determined, only one trader (called trader t) is allowed to enter the market and participate along with previously entered traders in the asset market. Trader t has a prediction (or belief) about the fundamental liquidation value each time period. Denote trader t's prediction (or belief) about the fundamental liquidation value at time s as b_s^t, where $s \geq t$. Define trader t's prediction error with respect to the fundamental liquidation value at time s ($s \geq t$) as $u_s^t = b_s^t - z_s$.[7] It is assumed that u_s^t is independent of $z_{s'}$, where $s' \geq 1$, and for all $s \geq t, u_s^t \in [-u, u]$,[8] and furthermore, for trader $t = 1, 2, \ldots$, u_s^t is independently and

---

[6] This one-sided buyer market with one unit of an asset being supplied each time period is also used in Blume and Easley (1992).

[7] This specification of beliefs or predictions is consistent with Grossman (1976, 1978), Figlewski (1978), and Hellwig (1980).

[8] For negative predictions not to occur, the lower bound for predictions is constrained to zero. That is $b_s^t = \max[z_s + u_s^t, 0]$.

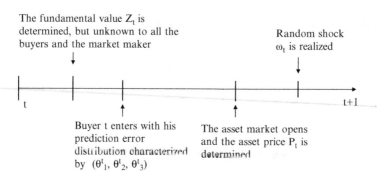

Fig. 6.1 The timing of events

identically distributed across times $s = t+1, t+2, \ldots$. Hence, for any given positive ϵ, denote

$$\theta_1^t = \Pr\left(u_s^t > -\frac{1}{3}\epsilon\right), \quad \theta_2^t = \Pr\left(-\frac{2}{3}\epsilon \le u_s^t \le -\frac{1}{3}\epsilon\right) \text{ and } \theta_3^t = \Pr\left(u_s^t < -\frac{2}{3}\epsilon\right),$$

where superscript t indicates buyer t. In other words, the variables θ_1^t, θ_2^t, and θ_3^t are trader t's probabilities of overpredicting, predicting correctly, and underpredicting the fundamental value. It is assumed that trader t's prediction error distribution characteristics (θ_1^t, θ_2^t) are randomly taken from the set $\Theta = \{(\theta_1, \theta_2) \in (0,1) \times (0,1) : \theta_1 + \theta_2 < 1\}$ according to a given distribution function $F(\cdot)$ in the beginning of this trader's entry period and $\theta_3^t = 1 - \theta_1^t - \theta_2^t$. Once trader t's vector $(\theta_1^t, \theta_2^t, \theta_3^t)$ is determined in the beginning of trader t's entry period, it is fixed thereafter in any subsequent time period. Figure 6.1 shows the timing of the above events.

The closer to zero a prediction error is, the more accurate the information is reflected in the prediction. This way of modeling the trader's beliefs reflects the fact that different traders may receive different signals about the fundamental value of the asset; or that, even though they receive the same signal, they may have different abilities to process the same information. From a behavioral finance perspective, the prediction error can be interpreted as a judgmental bias in the decision-making process. Based on the psychology literature, this judgmental bias tends to be displayed in a systematic pattern through time (see Tversky and Khaneman (1974) and Proposition 2 regarding inertia of Sitkin and Pablo (1992)). For this reason, a trader's probabilities of overpredicting, predicting correctly, and underpredicting is modeled as being fixed through time. In contrast to some of the literature (e.g., Grossman (1976, 1978), Figlewski (1978), and Hellwig (1980)), no precise assumptions are made about the shape of the distribution of the prediction error or the mean or variance of the prediction error.

6.2 The Model

Trader t's prediction or belief at time s, where $s \geq t$, is generated from trader t's prediction error probability distribution characterized by the vector $(\theta_1^t, \theta_2^t, \theta_3^t)$. Trader t's prediction or belief b_s^t at time s is this trader's reservation price or bid, indicating that trader t is willing to buy the number of shares of the asset that his or her wealth permits at a price no higher than b_s^t at time s. For this reason, the words prediction and bid are used interchangeably.

Here, there is no strategic interaction or learning among traders taking place. Traders merely act upon their predetermined probabilities of overpredicting, predicting correctly, and underpredicting the fundamental value. Using biological language, one may think of the vector $(\theta_1^t, \theta_2^t, \theta_3^t)$ as trader t's phenotype. This way of modeling traders' behavior isolates the impact of the market selection on traders' wealth dynamics and highlights the role that market selection plays in promoting long run market efficiency. Since each trader has a positive probability to underpredict or overpredict the fundamental liquidation value, each trader has a strictly positive probability of acting upon noise as if it were information.

For the simplicity, the following assumptions are used in this chapter.

It is assumed that $\{(\theta_1^t, \theta_2^t)\}_{t \geq 1}$ is independently and identically distributed according to the distribution function $F(\cdot)$ across traders $t = 1, 2, \ldots$.

It is also assumed that trader i's prediction error at time s, u_s^i, where $s \geq i \geq 1$, is independent of trader j's prediction error at time s', $u_{s'}^j$, where $s' \geq j \geq 1$ and $j \neq i$.

Furthermore, it is assumed that the random shock at times, ω_s, where $s \geq 1$, is independent of trader t's prediction error at time s', $u_{s'}^t$, where $s' \geq t \geq 1$.

Finally, define all the possible states of the world at time period t, where $t \geq 1$, as $\Omega_t = [-u, u]^t \times [\underline{z}, \overline{z}] \times [-\underline{\omega}, \overline{\omega}]$ with a typical element $\xi_t = (u_t^1, u_t^2, \ldots, u_t^t, z_t, \omega_t)$. ξ_t is the state of the world at time t. Denote $\Omega = \prod_{t=1}^{\infty} \Omega_t$. Let $\Im$ denote the product σ-field on Ω and let $\Pr(\cdot)$ denote the product probability. The probability space is $(\Omega, \Im, \Pr(\cdot))$. Let $\Omega^t = \prod_{i=1}^{t} \Omega_i$ for $t \geq 1$. Then the typical element in the set Ω^t is $(\xi_1, \xi_2, \ldots, \xi_t)$.

6.2.2 Traders' Wealth Dynamics in the Market Process

Each trader is assumed to have initial endowment of wealth V_0 in his or her entry time period. Each trader's wealth at the end of a time period is defined as accumulated profits up to the end of that time period. Denote trader t's wealth at the end of time period s (where $s \geq t \geq 1$) as V_s^t and $V_{t-1}^t = V_0$.[9] If trader t's

---

[9] Alternatively, one can assume different initial endowments of wealth for all traders. However, the same results with respect to convergence of the asset price will hold, provided that the initial endowment of wealth for all entering traders is bounded from above.

Fig. 6.2 Histogram of $|P_s - Z_s|$ as a percentage of times: (**a**) ω_t obeys a truncated normal with variance 0.01; (**b**) ω_t obeys a uniform distribution with variance 0.169

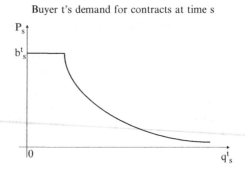

prediction or bid at time s, where $s \geq t$, is b_s^t, then trader t's demand for shares of the asset in time period s, where $s \geq t$, q_s^t, is[10]

$$q_s^t(p_s) = \begin{cases} \dfrac{V_{s-1}^t}{p_s} & p_s < b_s^t \\ \left[0, \dfrac{V_{s-1}^t}{p_s}\right] & p_s = b_s^t \\ 0 & p_s > b_s^t. \end{cases}$$

This demand function implies that if the asset price is below trader t's prediction, this trader is willing to purchase the number of shares that this trader's wealth permits; if the asset price is above trader t's prediction, this trader is not willing to purchase any share of the asset; if the asset price is equal to trader t's prediction, this trader is indifferent in purchasing any number of share lying between 0 and $\dfrac{V_{s-1}^t}{p_s}$. Figure 6.2 plots a trader's demand curve.

A trader is said to be active at one time period if the trader has actually purchased any shares at that time period. Therefore, if $q_s^t > 0$ then trader t is active in the time period s. If $q_s^t = 0$ then trader t is not active at time period s. A trader's profit at the end of time period s is $(v_s - p_s)q_s^t$. Hence, at the end of time period s, the wealth of trader t is[11] $V_s^t = V_{s-1}^t + (v_s - p_s)q_s^t$.[12]

---

[10] For simplicity it is assumed that each trader potentially invests all of his or her wealth in each period. The results of this chapter would still hold if each trader spends only a fraction of his or her total wealth on trading activity. A smaller fraction could reflect more risk aversion on the part of the trader.

[11] It is apparent that, given the demand function, any trader's wealth can never be negative. This is due to the fact that each trader begins with a positive level of initial wealth and short sales are not allowed.

[12] A related paper which examines the relationship between accuracy of agents' predictions, wealth accumulation and the convergence of prices to the true value, is Sandroni (2000).

6.2.3 The Asset Market Equilibrium

The asset market mechanism is organized as a one-sided auction market structure. The asset price is merely a Walrasian market clearing price. The asset market is assumed to have no traders at time 0. After time 0 traders enter sequentially. Since the traders' aggregate demand for the asset at time s is $\sum_{t=1}^{s} \left(q_s^t(p_s) \right)$ and since the market supply of the asset in each time period is 1 unit, the market clearing price at time s is the solution to the equation $\sum_{t=1}^{s} \left(q_s^t(p_s) \right) = 1$.

Clearly, the solution to the above equation is unique due to the shape of the traders' demand functions and the vertical supply function of the asset from the market maker.

All transactions are executed at the market clearing price. Traders with reservation bids or predictions above p_s will exhaust their wealth at time s. If the number of shares of the asset demanded at the market clearing price exceeds the total supply of the asset; and if there are traders whose reservation bids or predictions coincide with the market clearing price, the market maker allocates the supply of the asset among those traders proportionately to their wealth at the market clearing price.[13] Therefore, all traders with reservation bids equal to p_s at time s may not exhaust all of their wealth.

As can be seen, the asset price p_s is a function of the realizations of $z_1, z_2, \ldots, z_s$; and $\omega_1, \omega_2, \ldots, \omega_{s-1}$; and $u_1^t, u_2^t, \ldots, u_s^t$, for all $t \leq s$; and V_0. Hence, over time, the asset price follows a very complicated stochastic process.

In this one-sided auction market, the market serves as a selection process that evaluates all the traders with different prediction error distribution characteristics, rewarding traders who place good bids with gains (more wealth) and punishing traders who place bad bids with losses (less wealth). The more wealth a trader has, the more influence this trader has over the asset price. All traders impact the asset price through their predictions and the wealth they possess.

This chapter now uses the above evolutionary model of an asset market, to examine the relationship between the asset price and the fundamental value. In this exploration, one assumption is made about the distribution function $F(\cdot)$ from which $(\theta_1^t, \theta_2^t, \theta_3^t)$ for all t are drawn. This assumption says that in each time period there is a positive probability that an entering trader has an arbitrarily low probability of overpredicting the fundamental value and has a probability, of predicting arbitrarily close to the fundamental value, being bounded away from zero by a positive number. Since this assumption characterizes the distribution of traders' thetas $((\theta_1^t, \theta_2^t, \theta_3^t)$

---

[13]That is, for trader t where $b_s^t = p_s$, $q_s^t = \dfrac{V_{s-1}^t}{\sum_{t' \in M_s} V_{s-1}^{t'}} \left[1 - \sum_{t' \in A_s} q_s^{t'} \right]$ where $A_s = \{t' \mid b_s^{t'} > p_s\}$ and $M_s = \{t' \mid b_s^{t'} = p_s\}$. It would not alter the results if any alternative method of allocating shares of the asset is used in this situation.

for all t), this assumption is referred to as the θ−Assumption in the remainder of the chapter. More precisely, θ−**Assumption:** For any given small positive η and η',

$$\int_{\substack{0<\theta_1<\eta,\\ \theta_2>\eta'}} dF(\theta_1, \theta_2) > 0.$$

This is not a very demanding assumption. It merely says that with a positive probability (this probability could be extremely small), in each time period, the entering trader overpredicts less often (as a result, making losses less often) than any of previously entered traders. Note that the θ−Assumption does not mean that all entering traders must overpredict less often than any of previously entered traders. The key phrase in this assumption is "there is a positive probability" (this probability could be very small) that the entering trader in each time period overpredicts less often than any of previously entered traders.[14]

Since in this one-sided auction, losses are possibly realized when overbidding occurs, traders who overpredict with a sufficiently small probability can be viewed as avoiding risk of making losses due to placing a high weight on negative outcomes; hence, in the behavioral sense, such traders can be referred to as relatively risk averse (see Schneider and Lopes (1986) and Sitkin and Pablo (1992)). For this reason, one may interpret this assumption as an allowance for the entry of a sufficient number of buyers with a sufficient degree of risk aversion, who have a positive probability (however small) of bidding arbitrarily close to the fundamental value.

6.3 Convergence of the Asset Price to the Fundamental Value

This section shows analytically that with probability 1, if each trader's initial wealth is sufficiently small relative to the market asset supply and if the variation in the random shock is sufficiently small, then as time gets large, the proportion of time, that the asset price lying in an arbitrarily small interval, containing the fundamental value, converges to 1. This is shown in Theorem 3.

Before Theorem 3 is proven, two theorems are needed. Theorem 1 shows that the proportion of time, that the asset price is below the fundamental value by at least a small positive number ϵ, converges to zero with probability 1. Theorem 2 shows that if each trader's initial wealth is sufficiently small relative to the market asset supply and if the variation in the random shock to the economy is sufficiently small, then as time gets sufficiently large, the proportion of time, that the asset price is above the fundamental value by at least a small positive number ϵ, converges to zero with probability 1. Theorem 3 follows directly from Theorem 1 and Theorem 2. The result in Theorem 3 further suggests that in the limit, each individual trader's

---

[14] In fact, there can be a positive probability of traders with other types of predictive behavior. For example, such trader types could enter with prediction behavior that imitates past successful traders (e.g., Lettau (1997)). Nevertheless, as long as the θ−Assumption holds, the presence of these types of traders would not disrupt convergence.

6.3 Convergence of the Asset Price to the Fundamental Value

demand must be infinitesimally small relative to the market supply. This is formally established in Corollary 1.

For the establishment of the result in Theorem 1, the θ-Assumption plays a critical role. It allows enough "better buyers" to enter the market over time and eventually those "better buyers" prevent the asset price from staying below the fundamental value very often. The "better buyers" here refer to the buyers who enter the market with a sufficiently low probability of overpredicting the fundamental value and with some positive probability (which may be very small) of predicting arbitrarily close to the fundamental value.

Theorem 1.

$$\Pr\left(\text{for any given } \epsilon > 0, \text{ there exists a time period } T_1, \text{ such that for } T \geq T_1, \frac{\#\{t \leq T: p_t < z_t - \epsilon\}}{T} < \epsilon\right) = 1.$$

Proof. See Appendix A for the proof. □

After obtaining the result in Theorem 1, Theorem 2 shows that with probability 1 the following occurs: if each trader's initial wealth is sufficiently small relative to the market asset supply and if the variation in the random shock to the economy is sufficiently small, then as time gets sufficiently large, the proportion of time, that the asset price is above the fundamental value, converges to zero.

The intuition of the result in Theorem 2 is best explained as follows. Start by supposing that there is no random shock to the risky asset each time period. Then the liquidation value is the same as the fundamental value. In this case, buyers make a gain if the asset price is below the fundamental value and buyers make a loss if the asset price is above the fundamental price. Therefore, the average (across time) aggregate wealth of all buyers is bounded from above by term (1), the average maximum gains across the number of time periods when the asset price is below the fundamental value, minus term (2), the average minimum loss across the number of time periods when the asset price is above the fundamental value, plus term (3), the initial wealth V_0. Now suppose that there is a random shock each time period. Then the liquidation value differs from the fundamental value. If the random shock is positive (negative) at time t, ($t \geq 1$) then the liquidation value is above the fundamental value at time t and furthermore all buyers make an additional gain (loss) from the difference between the liquidation value and the fundamental value $v_t - z_t$ at time t as a result of the presence of the random shock. Therefore, the average (across time) aggregate wealth of all buyers is bounded from above by the average aggregate gains of all buyers coming from the positive random shock in addition to the above three terms describing the situation without the random shock.

Furthermore, the aggregate wealth of all buyers is always positive. Hence, we can rearrange the above to show that the proportion of time that the asset price is above the fundamental value is bounded from above by the summation of three terms: the first term, which is a positive constant multiplied by the proportion of time that the asset price is below the fundamental value; the second term, which is a product of the variation in the random shock (given that the shock is positive) and the proportion of time that the random shock is positive; and a third term, which is V_0. Theorem 1 says that, with probability one, the proportion of time, that the asset price is below the fundamental value, goes to zero as time gets large. As well, if the variation in the random shock is sufficiently small and the initial wealth is sufficiently small, then the proportion of time that the asset price is above the fundamental value can be made arbitrarily small, with probability one.[15] Hence, the result of Theorem 2 holds.

Theorem 2. *With probability 1, the following occurs: for any given $\epsilon > 0$, there exists a positive $\overline{k}$ and a positive $\overline{V}_0$ such that, if $E\left((\exp(\omega_t) - 1) | \omega_t > 0\right) \leq \overline{k}$ and if $V_0 \leq \overline{V}_0$, there exists a time period T_2, such that for all $T > T_2$,*

$$\frac{\#\{t \leq T : p_t > z_t + \epsilon\}}{T} < \epsilon.$$

Proof. See Appendix A for the proof. □

Theorem 3 brings together the results of the above two theorems and shows that for any ϵ-interval containing z_t, $[z_t - \epsilon, z_t + \epsilon]$, for a sufficiently small endowment of traders' initial wealth and for a sufficiently small amount of variation in the random shock, with probability one, the proportion of times that the asset price falls within this ϵ-interval containing the fundamental value z_t, $[z_t - \epsilon, z_t + \epsilon]$, converges to one as time gets large.

Theorem 3. *With probability 1, the following occurs: for any given $\epsilon > 0$, there exists a positive $\overline{k}$ and a positive $\overline{V}_0$ such that, if $E\left((\exp(\omega_t) - 1) | \omega_t > 0\right) \leq \overline{k}$ and if $V_0 \leq \overline{V}_0$, there exists a time period T^*, such that for all $T > T^*$,*

$$\frac{\#\{t \leq T : p_t \in [z_t - \epsilon, z_t + \epsilon]\}}{T} > 1 - 2\epsilon.$$

Proof. See Appendix A for the proof. □

Remark 1. The proof of Theorem 1 makes use of a set of buyers $\{t_1, t_2, \ldots, t_k, \ldots\}$ with their prediction errors distribution satisfying the following conditions $\epsilon_0 \theta_2^{t_k} \ln\left(\frac{z}{z - \frac{z}{3}\epsilon}\right) + \theta_1^{t_k} \ln\left(\frac{z}{z + u}\right) > 0$ and $\theta_2^{t_k} \geq c$ for some positive ϵ_0 and $c < 1$. These conditions are satisfied if $\theta_1^{t_k}$ is allowed to be arbitrarily close to zero provided that $\theta_2^{t_k} \geq c$ (the θ–Assumption). (Of course, the constant number c does not have to be very close to 1, instead, it can be a extremely small positive number.) This set of buyers play a determining role in driving the convergence result. The model deals with a one-sided, rather than a two-sided auction. With a relatively small variation in the random shock, buyers do not make any loss by underpredicting the fundamental value. This is due to buyers being inactive if the asset price is above the fundamental

---

[15] The variation in random shock here refers to $E\left((\exp(\omega_t) - 1) | \omega_t > 0\right)$.

6.3 Convergence of the Asset Price to the Fundamental Value

value. Buyers could make losses by overpredicting the fundamental value if the asset price is above the fundamental value. From a behavioral finance perspective, one can interpret traders with low probability of overpredicting the fundamental value (implying a small number of upward biases) as relatively risk averse. For this reason, the $\theta-$Assumption merely allows for the entry of a sufficient number of buyers with a sufficient degree of risk aversion and with a positive probability (however small) of bidding arbitrarily close to the fundamental value. The presence of this group of buyers provides the driving force for the long run convergence.

Remark 2. For the results to be achieved it is important that the competition among the buyers gets stronger as time increases. The model helps to achieve this by letting buyers with different characteristics of their prediction error distributions enter the market sequentially over time. As a result, the number of buyers increases to infinity as time goes to infinity.

Another ingredient of perfectly competitive markets is that each individual buyer is sufficiently small relative to the market or that each individual buyer's demand is initially sufficiently small relative to the market supply. In this model, where the initial wealth V_0 characterizes the size of the entering buyer relative to the market, a smaller V_0 represents less market power of entering traders and greater competition in the market. Technically, if the initial wealth V_0 is too large then in each time period the entering trader will cause the asset price to deviate away from its fundamental value with some positive probability.

Remark 3. Theorem 3 states that for a given ϵ-distance, for a sufficiently small V_0 and a sufficiently small variation in the random shock, with probability one, the proportion of time, that the deviation between the asset price and the fundamental value lies within this ϵ-distance, converges to one as time gets large. An empirical implication is, that for a given V_0, with a smaller variation in the random shock, there exists a corresponding smaller ϵ_1-distance, for which, with probability one, the proportion of time, that the deviation between the asset price and the fundamental value lies within this smaller ϵ_1-distance, converges to one as time gets large. This is consistent with the price of a more risky asset fluctuating in a wider range than the price of a less risky asset and the safe asset earning the certain return.

Nevertheless, it is remarkable that even though the number of traders increases over time, with each trader entering the market with a finite amount of wealth V_0 and with a perfectly inelastic supply of the asset, the price can eventually be assured never to explode outside a certain interval. Furthermore, for a given level of variation in random shock, the smaller is the initial V_0 of an entering trader, the smaller is the interval in which the asset price lies.

The result of Theorem 3 indicates that in the limit no individual buyer can influence the asset price. Otherwise, the long-run equilibrium would be destroyed. This further implies that the demand from each individual buyer must be infinitesimally small relative to the asset market supply in the limit. In other words, each individual buyer's wealth must be infinitesimally small relative to the aggregate wealth of all the buyers in the limit. The following corollary formally presents the results.

Corollary 1. *With probability 1, the following occurs: for any given $\epsilon' > 0$, there exists a positive $\overline{k}$ and a positive $\overline{V}_0$ such that, if $E\left((\exp(\omega_t) - 1)|\omega_t > 0\right) \leq \overline{k}$ and if $V_0 \leq \overline{V}_0$, there exists a time period T' such that for all $T > T'$, the ratio between buyer t's $(t = 1, 2, \ldots)$ wealth at the end of time period T (V_T^t) and the aggregate wealth of all the buyers at the end of time period T $\left(\sum_{t=1}^{T} V_T^t\right)$ is less than ϵ' (i.e., $\frac{V_T^t}{\sum_{t=1}^{T} V_T^t} \leq \epsilon'$).*

Proof. See Appendix A for the proof. □

6.4 Conclusions

This chapter uses an evolutionary idea of natural selection to examine the convergence of the asset price to its fundamental value in a one-sided auction market where traders are modeled as unsophisticated. Traders cannot learn or strategically use any information from the market or other participants and they merely act upon their preprogramed behavior rules, which reflect their inherent noisiness. Specifically, in this dynamic asset market, the market supplies one unit of a one period risky asset each time period. Traders enter the market sequentially over time. The liquidation value of the asset is the product of the fundamental value of the asset and the exponential of a random shock. The fundamental value of the asset is determined in the beginning of each time period, but unknown to any market participants. The random shock is realized at the end of each time period. Each trader's behavior is exogenously preprogrammed instead of endogenously derived from some optimization problem. In other words, each trader's behavior is characterized by his or her predetermined probabilities of overpredicting, predicting correctly, and underpredicting the fundamental liquidation value. Each trader's prediction in each time period is generated from a probability distribution described by his or her predetermined probabilities of overprediction, exact prediction and underprediction with respect to the fundamental liquidation value.

The asset market is a one-sided auction market. The market serves as a selection process which evaluates all the traders with different prediction error distributions, rewarding the traders who place good bids and taking money away from the traders who place bad bids. Over time this process gradually places more weight on the accurate information into the asset price and places less weight on noise into the asset price. Eventually the asset price only reflects the accurate information and eliminates noise. Informational efficiency occurs in the long run.

More precisely, as long as at any point in time there is a positive probability that the entering trader has an arbitrarily low probability of overpredicting the fundamental value and has a probability, of predicting arbitrarily close to the fundamental value, being bounded away from zero by a positive number, the following is true. With probability 1, if each trader's initial wealth is sufficiently small relative to the market supply and if the variation of the random shock is sufficiently small, then as time gets sufficiently large, the proportion of time, that the asset price is arbitrarily close to the fundamental value, converges to 1. In the limit, each individual's demand for the risky asset is infinitesimally small relative to the market supply. Consequently, no individual can influence the asset price.

In this one-sided auction market, losses are possibly incurred when overbidding occurs. From a behavioral finance perspective, one can interpret traders with low probability of overpredicting the fundamental value (implying a small number of upward biases) as relatively risk averse. For this reason, one may also interpret the θ-Assumption as an allowance for the entry of a sufficient number of buyers with a sufficient degree of risk aversion and with a positive probability (however small) of bidding arbitrarily close to the fundamental value. The presence of this group of buyers provides the driving force for the long run convergence.

Finally, the variation in the random shock about the fundamental value influences the extent to which efficiency occurs. The bigger is the variation in the random shock about the fundamental value, the bigger are the deviations of the asset price from the fundamental value.

Appendix C provides some numerical illustrations to help better understand the results.

Appendix A

This appendix consists of proofs for the results in Theorem 1, 2, 3, and Corollary 1. The proof in Theorem 1 makes use of the results in Lemma 1, Lemma 3, and Proposition 1 in Appendix B.

The Proof of Theorem 1: Define buyer t's pseudo-price at time s, denoted by p_s^t, where $s \geq t$, $t \geq 1$, as the solution to the equation $\sum_{i=1, i \neq t}^{s} q_s^i (p_s^t) = 1$. That is, buyer t's pseudo-price at time s, p_s^t, would be the market clearing price at time s if buyer t were not in the market. In other words, it would be the market clearing price which would occur without the demand from buyer t.

Also define an indicator variable at time s for buyer t, denoted as l_s^t, where $s \geq t$, $t \geq 1$, to describe the position of buyer t's pseudo price (p_s^t) relative to the fundamental value z_s at time s. Specifically, for any given $\epsilon > 0$,

$$l_s^t = \begin{cases} 1 & \text{if } p_s^t < z_s - \epsilon \\ 0 & \text{otherwise.} \end{cases}$$

Notice that if at any time s, the pseudo-price of any buyer is above $z_s - \epsilon$ then the asset price is above $z_s - \epsilon$. Use an indicator variable $\widetilde{l}_s = 0$ to describe whether the pseudo-price of any buyer is above $z_s - \epsilon$; otherwise $\widetilde{l}_s = 1$. Specifically, for $s \geq t$, $t \geq 1$,

$$\tilde{l}_s = \prod_{t=1}^{s} l_s^t.$$

The following shows that,

$$\Pr\left(\lim_{T\to\infty}\left(\frac{\sum_{s=1}^{T}\tilde{l}_s}{T}\right) = 0\right) = 1. \tag{6.1}$$

Define l_s^* to indicate whether the asset price is below $z_s - \epsilon$ at time s, where $s \geq 1$. That is,

$$l_s^* = \begin{cases} 1 & \text{if } p_s < z_s - \epsilon \\ 0 & \text{otherwise.} \end{cases}$$

If $l_s^* = 1$ then the asset price at time s is below $z_s - \epsilon$. Taking out any buyer's demand for the asset from the market demand function at time s means that the pseudo-price of that buyer is at least below $z_s - \epsilon$. That is, $l_s^* = 1$ implies that $l_s^t = 1$ for all $t = 1, 2, \ldots, s$ or $\tilde{l}_s = 1$. This further implies that,

$$\frac{\sum_{s=1}^{T} l_s^*}{T} \leq \frac{\sum_{s=1}^{T} \tilde{l}_s}{T}. \tag{6.2}$$

If (6.1) is true, then (6.1) and (6.2) imply that:

$$\Pr\left(\lim_{T\to\infty}\left(\frac{\sum_{s=1}^{T} l_s^*}{T}\right) = 0\right) = 1.$$

Therefore, Theorem 1 follows.

Now, the following proves that (6.1) is true. Before the proof of (6.1), some definitions of indicator variables are required. At time $s = 1, 2, \ldots$, l_s is defined to indicate whether the asset price is below $z_s - \frac{2}{3}\epsilon$.

$$l_s = \begin{cases} 1 & \text{if } p_s < z_s - \frac{2}{3}\epsilon \\ 0 & \text{otherwise.} \end{cases}$$

Define another random variable g_s^t to describe whether buyer t's prediction at time s is between $z_s - \frac{2}{3}\epsilon$ and $z_s - \frac{1}{3}\epsilon$. Specifically, define g_s^t, where $s \geq t$ and $t \geq 1$, as

$$g_s^t = \begin{cases} 1 & \text{if } -\frac{2}{3}\epsilon \leq u_s^t \leq -\frac{1}{3}\epsilon \\ 0 & \text{otherwise.} \end{cases}$$

Appendix A

Now, (6.1) is shown by way of contradiction. Suppose not, then

$$\Pr\left(\text{there exist a } \epsilon_0 > 0 \text{ and a subsequence } n_1, n_2, \ldots, n_T \ldots, \right. \\ \left. \text{such that for all } T = 1, 2, \ldots, \frac{\sum_{s=1}^{n_T} \widetilde{l_s}}{n_T} > \epsilon_0 \right) > 0. \quad (6.3)$$

Lemma 1 in Appendix B implies that for this ϵ_0 and ϵ; and for some positive $c < 1$,

$$\Pr(\text{there exists an infinite number of buyers in the set } \Theta(\epsilon_0, \epsilon, c)) = 1, \quad (6.4)$$

where $\Theta(\epsilon_0, \epsilon, c) = \{\text{buyer } t : \epsilon_0 \theta_2^t \ln(\frac{\bar{z}}{\bar{z}-\frac{2}{3}\epsilon}) + \theta_1^t \ln(\frac{\bar{z}}{\bar{z}+u}) > 0, \theta_2^t \geq c, \theta_1^t + \theta_2^t + \theta_3^t = 1\}$.

Now, consider buyer t in the set $\Theta(\epsilon_0, \epsilon, c)$. Since buyer t's pseudo-price at time i, p_i^t, is a function of $z_1, z_2, \ldots, z_i$; and $\omega_1, \omega_2, \ldots, \omega_{i-1}$; and $u_j^j, u_{j+1}^j, \ldots, u_i^j$, for $t \neq j \leq i$; and since buyer t's prediction error u_i^t is independent of $z_1, z_2, \ldots, z_i$; and $\omega_1, \omega_2, \ldots, \omega_{i-1}$; and $u_j^j, u_{j+1}^j, \ldots, u_i^j$, for $j \leq i$ and $j \neq t$; it follows that buyer t's prediction error is independent of his or her past and current pseudo-prices, that is, g_s^t is independent of l_i^t, for all $i \leq s$. Therefore, using Proposition 1 in Appendix B and using (6.4), it follows that,

$$\lim_{T \to \infty} \Pr\left(\frac{\sum_{s=t}^{n_T} (l_s^t g_s^t)}{n_T - t + 1} > \frac{E(g_s^t) \sum_{s=t}^{n_T} l_s^t}{n_T - t + 1} \bigg| t \in \Theta(\epsilon_0, \epsilon, c)\right) = 1. \quad (6.5)$$

Using Bayes rule, (6.4) and (6.5) imply that

$$\lim_{T \to \infty} \Pr\left(\frac{\sum_{s=t}^{n_T} (l_s^t g_s^t)}{n_T - t + 1} > \frac{E(g_s^t) \sum_{s=t}^{n_T} l_s^t}{n_T - t + 1} \text{ for all } t \in \Theta(\epsilon_0, \epsilon, c)\right) = 1. \quad (6.6)$$

Since $\frac{\sum_{s=1}^{n_T} \widetilde{l_s}}{n_T} > \epsilon_0$, for all T, implies that, for sufficiently large T and for $t \in \Theta(\epsilon_0, \epsilon, c)$, $\frac{\sum_{s=t}^{n_T} l_s^t}{n_T - t + 1} > \epsilon_0$ (due to $l_s^t \geq \widetilde{l_s}$); and since $E(g_s^t) = \theta_2^t$, applying Bayes rule to (6.3) and (6.6), it follows that,

$$\lim_{T \to \infty} \Pr \left(\frac{\sum_{s=t}^{n_T} \left(l_s^t g_s^t \right)}{n_T - t + 1} > \epsilon_0 \theta_2^t, \text{ for all } t \in \Theta(\epsilon_0, \epsilon, c) \middle| H(\epsilon_0) \right) = 1, \quad (6.7)$$

where $H(\epsilon_0)$ denotes the event that there exist a $\epsilon_0 > 0$ and a subsequence $n_1, n_2, \ldots, n_T, \ldots$ such that $\frac{\sum_{s=1}^{n_T} \tilde{l}_s}{n_T} > \epsilon_0$ for all $T = 1, 2, \ldots$

Since buyer $t \in \Theta(\epsilon_0, \epsilon, c)$, it follows that $\theta_2^t \geq c$. This together with (6.7) also implies that there exists a further subsequence $n_1', n_2', \ldots, n_T', \ldots$ of the sequence $n_1, n_2, \ldots, n_T, \ldots$, such that (see (Durrett, 1991, P. 40, (6.?) THEOREM))

$$\Pr \left(\liminf_{T \to \infty} \left(\frac{\sum_{s=t}^{n_T'} \left(l_s^t g_s^t \right)}{n_T' - t + 1} \right) > \epsilon_0 c, \text{ for all } t \in \Theta(\epsilon_0, \epsilon, c) \middle| H(\epsilon_0) \right) = 1. \quad (6.8)$$

In addition, using Lemma 3 in Appendix B, it follows that for this ϵ_0, ϵ; and for some positive number $c < 1$,

$$\Pr \left(\lim_{T \to \infty} \left(\frac{\sum_{s=t}^{n_T} \left(l_s^t g_s^t l_s \right)}{n_T - t + 1} \right) = 0, \text{ for all } t \in \Theta(\epsilon_0, \epsilon, c) \right) = 1. \quad (6.9)$$

Again, applying Bayes rule to (6.3) and (6.9), it follows that for this ϵ_0 and for some positive number $c < 1$,

$$\Pr \left(\lim_{T \to \infty} \left(\frac{\sum_{s=t}^{n_T} \left(l_s^t g_s^t l_s \right)}{n_T - t + 1} \right) = 0, \text{ for all } t \in \Theta(\epsilon_0, \epsilon, c) \middle| H(\epsilon_0) \right) = 1. \quad (6.10)$$

The intuition behind (6.10) is that if $l_s^t g_s^t l_s = 1$, then one can show that buyer t makes a positive expected profit at time s. If (6.10) is not true, then one can construct a contradiction by showing that with positive probability that the wealth of buyer t who is in the set $\Theta(\epsilon_0, \epsilon, c)$ would grow exponentially while the wealth, coming from the initial endowment of buyers and coming from the market maker, is injected into the market arithmetically.

Appendix A

Applying Bayes rule to (6.10) and (6.8), it follows that,

$$\Pr\left(\left\{\liminf_{T\to\infty} \frac{\sum_{s=t}^{n'_T}(l_s^t g_s^t)}{n'_T - t + 1} > \epsilon_0 c, \text{ for all } t \in \Theta(\epsilon_0,\epsilon,c)\right\},\right.$$

$$\left.\left\{\lim_{T\to\infty}\left(\frac{\sum_{s=t}^{n_T}(l_s^t g_s^t l_s)}{n_T - t + 1}\right) = 0, \text{ for all } t \in \Theta(\epsilon_0,\epsilon,c)\right\}\middle| H(\epsilon_0)\right) = 1. \quad (6.11)$$

Since for buyer $t \in \Theta(\epsilon_0,\epsilon,c), t \leq n'_T$,

$$\frac{\sum_{s=t}^{n'_T}(l_s^t g_s^t)}{n'_T - t + 1} = \frac{\sum_{s=t}^{n'_T}(l_s^t g_s^t l_s)}{n'_T - t + 1} + \frac{\sum_{s=t}^{n'_T}(l_s^t g_s^t (1 - l_s))}{n'_T - t + 1},$$

and using (6.11), it follows that,

$$\Pr\left(\liminf_{T\to\infty}\left(\frac{\sum_{s=t}^{n'_T}(l_s^t g_s^t (1 - l_s))}{(n'_T - t + 1)}\right) > \epsilon_0 c, \text{ for all } t \in \Theta(\epsilon_0,\epsilon,c)\middle| H(\epsilon_0)\right) = 1.$$

(6.12)

Now, the remaining part of the proof consists of two steps. Step 1 shows that (using (6.12)) with positive probability, $(1 - l_s) \sum_{\substack{t \in \Theta(\epsilon_0,\epsilon,c) \\ t \leq s}} (g_s^t l_s^t)$ is unbounded from above as $s \to \infty$. As a result, step 2 shows that with a positive probability the expected total profits of the number of buyers equal to $\sum_{\substack{t \in \Theta(\epsilon_0,\epsilon,c) \\ t \leq s}} (g_s^t l_s^t)$ tends to infinity as $s \to \infty$. This contradicts the fact that the total profits earned by all buyers in any one time period must be bounded from above. Therefore, (6.1) must be true.

Step 1: One observation that can be drawn from (6.12) is that $(1 - l_s) \sum_{\substack{t \in \Theta(\epsilon_0,\epsilon,c) \\ t \leq s}} (g_s^t l_s^t)$ must be unbounded as $s \to \infty$. That is,

$$\Pr\left(\text{for any given } M > 0, \text{ there exists a } s' \text{ such that, for some } s > s',\right.$$

$$\left.(1 - l_s) \sum_{\substack{t \in \Theta(\epsilon_0,\epsilon,c) \\ t \leq s}} (g_s^t l_s^t) \geq M \middle| (H(\epsilon_0), D_2)\right) = 1, \quad (6.13)$$

where D_2 denotes the event that $\lim\inf_{T\to\infty} \left(\frac{\sum_{s=t}^{n'_T} (l'_s g'_s (1-l_s))}{(n'_T - t + 1)} \right) > \epsilon_0 c$, for all $t \in \Theta(\epsilon_0, \epsilon, c)$. Otherwise, there would be a contradiction. The contradiction can be seen from the following analysis. Suppose that (6.13) is not true, then

$$\Pr\left(\text{there exists a positive number, say } B > 0, \text{ such that,} \right.$$

$$\left. (1-l_s) \sum_{\substack{t\in\Theta(\epsilon_0,\epsilon,c) \\ t\leq s}} (g'_s l'_s) \leq B, \text{ for all } s \middle| (H(\epsilon_0), D_2) \right) > 0. \quad (6.14)$$

Using (6.12) and (6.14), it follows that,

$$\Pr\left(\left\{ \exists B > 0, \text{ s.t. for all } s, \, (1-l_s) \sum_{\substack{t\in\Theta(\epsilon_0,\epsilon,c) \\ t\leq s}} (g'_s l'_s) \leq B \right\}, \text{ and} \right.$$

$$\left\{ \text{for all sufficiently large } T, \sum_{s=t}^{n'_T} (l'_s(1-l_s) g'_s) > \epsilon_0 c \left(n'_T - t + 1 \right), \right.$$

$$\left. \left. \text{for all } t \in \Theta(\epsilon_0, \epsilon, c) \text{ and } t \leq n'_T \right\} \middle| H(\epsilon_0) \right) > 0. \quad (6.15)$$

Since $\Theta(\epsilon_0, \epsilon, c)$ contains an infinite number of buyers, select the first $\overline{N}$ buyers, $t_1, t_2, \ldots, t_{\overline{N}}$, where $\overline{N} > \frac{2B}{\epsilon_0 c}$, from the set $\Theta(\epsilon_0, \epsilon, c)$. If $(1-l_s) \sum_{\substack{t\in\Theta(\epsilon_0,\epsilon,c) \\ t\leq s}} (g'_s l'_s) \leq B$, for all s then for $n'_T > t_{\overline{N}}$,

$$\sum_{s=1}^{n'_T} \left((1-l_s) \sum_{k=1,2,\ldots,\overline{N},} \left(\widetilde{l}_s^{t_k} \widetilde{g}_s^{t_k} \right) \right) \leq B n'_T, \quad (6.16)$$

where $\widetilde{l}_s^{t_k}$ and $\widetilde{g}_s^{t_k}$ for $k = 1, 2, \ldots,$ and for $s = 1, 2, \ldots,$ are defined as

$$\widetilde{l}_s^{t_k} = \begin{cases} l_s^{t_k} & \text{if } s \geq t_k \\ 0 & \text{if } s < t_k \end{cases} \text{ and } \widetilde{g}_s^{t_k} = \begin{cases} g_s^{t_k} & \text{if } s \geq t_k \\ 0 & \text{if } s < t_k. \end{cases}$$

If $\sum_{s=t_k}^{n'_T} (l_s^{t_k}(1-l_s) g_s^{t_k}) > \epsilon_0 c (n'_T - t_k + 1)$, for all sufficiently large T and for all $t_k \leq n'_T$, then

Appendix A

$$\sum_{k=1}^{\overline{N}} \sum_{s=t_k}^{n'_T} \left(l_s^{tk}(1-l_s) g_s^{tk} \right) > \epsilon_0 c \sum_{k=1}^{\overline{N}} \left(n'_T - t_k + 1 \right)$$

$$> \epsilon_0 c \overline{N} \left(n'_T - t_{\overline{N}} + 1 \right). \quad (6.17)$$

Since $\sum_{s=1}^{n'_T} \left((1-l_s) \sum_{k=1,2,\dots,\overline{N},} (\widetilde{g_s^{tk}} \widetilde{l_s^{tk}}) \right) = \sum_{k=1}^{\overline{N}} \sum_{s=t_k}^{n'_T} \left(l_s^{tk}(1-l_s) g_s^{tk} \right)$, and using (6.4), (6.15), (6.16), and (6.17), it follows that

$$\Pr\left(\overline{N} < \lim_{T \to \infty} \left(\frac{B n'_T}{\epsilon_0 c \left(n'_T - t_{\overline{N}} + 1 \right)} \right) = \frac{B}{\epsilon_0 c} \left| H(\epsilon_0) \right) > 0.$$

This further implies that

$$\Pr\left(\overline{N} < \frac{B}{\epsilon_0 c} \right) > 0.$$

This contradicts the fact that $\overline{N} > \frac{2B}{\epsilon_0 c}$. Therefore, (6.13) must be true. Now, (6.13) implies that

$$\Pr\left(\text{for any given } M > 0, \text{ there exists a } s' \text{ such that, for some } s > s', \right.$$

$$\left. (1 - l_s) \sum_{\substack{t \in \Theta(\epsilon_0, \epsilon, c) \\ t \leq s}} (g_s^t l_s^t) \geq M \right) > 0. \quad (6.18)$$

The intuition for Step 1 is as follows. Consider the infinite number of buyers in the set $\Theta(\epsilon_0, \epsilon, c)$. For each one of the buyers in the set, in order for the proportion of time that $l_s^t (1 - l_s) g_s^t = 1$ to be bounded from below, then the total number of times, that the joint event of $l_s^t = 1$ for every buyer t and $g_s^t = 1$ for every buyer t whenever $l_s = 0$, must go to infinity as $s \to \infty$, which in turn implies that $(1 - l_s) \sum_{\substack{t \in \Theta(\epsilon_0, \epsilon, c) \\ t \leq s}} (g_s^t l_s^t)$ is unbounded from above as $s \to \infty$.

Step 2: However, the following shows that if $(1 - l_s) \sum_{\substack{t \in \Theta(\epsilon_0, \epsilon, c) \\ t \leq s}} (g_s^t l_s^t)$ is unbounded from above as $s \to \infty$, then there exists a time period at which the expected total profits of a finite number of buyers in the set $\Theta(\epsilon_0, \epsilon, c)$ exceeds the total profits that could be possibly made by all the buyers in any one time period. This is illustrated in the following analysis. Since both the liquidation value and the asset price are bounded and since the supply of the asset each time period is 1 unit, the maximum profits that all the buyers could possibly make in any one time period is bounded from above by $\overline{z} \exp(\overline{\omega})$.

Equation (6.18) implies that for $M = \frac{3(\bar{z}\exp(\bar{w}))}{\underline{\epsilon q}}$,

$$\Pr\left(\exists s' \text{ s.t. for some } s > s', (1-l_s) \sum_{\substack{t\in\Theta(\epsilon_0,\epsilon,c) \\ t\leq s}} (g_s^t l_s^t) \geq \frac{3(\bar{z}\exp(\bar{w}))}{\underline{\epsilon q}}\right) > 0. \quad (6.19)$$

Since $\Theta(\epsilon_0, \epsilon, c)$ contains an infinite number of buyers, select $\overline{M}$ buyers, $t'_1, t'_2, \ldots,$ $t'_{\overline{M}}$, where $\overline{M} > \frac{2B}{\epsilon_0 c}$, from the set $\Theta(\epsilon_0, \epsilon, c)$. Hence, (6.4) and (6.19) imply that

$$\Pr\left(\exists s' \text{ such that, for some } s > s', \exists \{t'_1, t'_2, \ldots, t'_{\overline{M}}\}, \text{ where } \overline{M} > \frac{3(\bar{z}\exp(\bar{w}))}{\underline{\epsilon q}},\right.$$

$$\left. \text{s.t. } \left(g_s^{t'_1} l_s^{t'_1} = 1, g_s^{t'_2} l_s^{t'_2} = 1, \ldots, g_s^{t'_{\overline{M}}} l_s^{t'_{\overline{M}}} = 1\right) \text{ when } 1-l_s = 1\right) > 0. \quad (6.20)$$

Since at time period s, if $g_s^{t'_k} = 1$, $l_s^{t'_k} = 1$ and $(1-l_s) = 1$, then buyer t'_k bids in the interval $[z_s - \frac{2}{3}\epsilon, z_s - \frac{1}{3}\epsilon]$ while the pseudo price of buyer t'_k is below $z_s - \epsilon$ and the asset price is in the region $[z_s - \frac{2}{3}\epsilon, z_s - \frac{1}{3}\epsilon]$. This implies that buyer t'_k must be active and purchases at least a minimum quantity of shares of the asset $(\underline{q})$ which occurs in the extreme case where buyer t'_k's pseudo-price at time s, $p_s^{t'_k} = z_s - \epsilon$ and the asset price at time s is $p_s = z_s - \frac{2}{3}\epsilon$. (It can be shown that $\underline{q} = 1 - \frac{\bar{z}-\epsilon}{\bar{z}-\frac{2}{3}\epsilon}$.) Therefore, if for $k = 1, 2, \ldots, \overline{M}$, $g_s^{t'_k} = 1$, $l_s^{t'_k} = 1$ and $(1-l_s) = 1$, then

$$\sum_{k=1}^{\overline{M}} q_s^{t'_k} \geq \overline{M}\underline{q} \quad (6.21)$$

and

$$z_s - p_s \geq z_s - \left(z_s - \frac{1}{3}\epsilon\right) = \frac{1}{3}\epsilon. \quad (6.22)$$

Now consider the total expected profits of $\overline{M}$ buyers with $\left(g_s^{t'_1} l_s^{t'_1} = 1, g_s^{t'_2} l_s^{t'_2} = 1, \ldots, g_s^{t'_{\overline{M}}} l_s^{t'_{\overline{M}}} = 1\right)$ when $1-l_s = 1$. Denote D_3 as a set of buyers $\{t'_1, t'_2, \ldots, t'_{\overline{M}}\}$, where $\overline{M} > \frac{3(\bar{z}\exp(\bar{w}))}{\underline{\epsilon q}}$, such that $(g_s^{t'_1} l_s^{t'_1} = 1, g_s^{t'_2} l_s^{t'_2} = 1, \ldots, g_s^{t'_{\overline{M}}} l_s^{t'_{\overline{M}}} = 1)$ when $1-l_s = 1$. Using (6.21),

Appendix A

$$E\left((v_s - p_s) \sum_{k \in D_3}^{\overline{M}} q_s^{t_k'}\right) \geq \overline{M}\underline{q} E (v_s - p_s)$$

$$\geq \overline{M}\underline{q} E (z_s - p_s)$$

$$\geq \frac{1}{3} \epsilon \overline{M} \underline{q}. \tag{6.23}$$

The second to last inequality is due to $Ev_s \geq Ez_s$, (using $v_s = z_s \exp(\omega_s)$ and using Jensen's inequality). The last inequality is due to (6.22).

Using the definition of $\overline{M}$ and (6.23), it follows that

$$E\left((v_s - p_s) \sum_{k \in D_3}^{\overline{M}} q_s^{t_k'}\right) > \overline{z} \exp(\overline{\omega}). \tag{6.24}$$

However, the maximum amount of total profits that could be earned by all the buyers in the market in any one time period is bounded from above by $\overline{z}\exp(\overline{\omega})$. This contradicts (6.24). Therefore, (6.1) must be true. □

The Proof of Theorem 2: Consider the aggregate wealth of all the buyers at the end of time period T, which equals the aggregate gains that all the buyers have made up to time period T minus the aggregate losses that all the buyers have made up to time period T plus the aggregate initial wealth of all the buyers in the asset market at time T. That is,

$$\sum_{t=1}^{T} V_T^t = \sum_{k=1}^{T} \left((v_k - p_k) \left(\sum_{t=1}^{k} q_k^t\right)\right) + \sum_{k=1}^{T} V_0$$

$$= \sum_{k=1}^{T} (v_k - p_k) + \sum_{k=1}^{T} V_0 \quad \left(\text{since } \sum_{t=1}^{k} q_k^t = 1\right)$$

$$= \sum_{k=1}^{T} (v_k - z_k) + \sum_{k=1}^{T} (z_k - p_k) + \sum_{k=1}^{T} V_0. \tag{6.25}$$

To describe the position of p_t relative to z_t, define three indicator random variables $\widehat{m}_t, \widehat{l}_t$ and $\widehat{a}_t$, for $t = 1, 2, \ldots$, as follows: for any given $\epsilon > 0$,

$$\widehat{m}_t = \begin{cases} 1 & \text{if } z_t \leq p_t \leq z_t + \epsilon \\ 0 & \text{otherwise,} \end{cases} \quad \widehat{l}_t = \begin{cases} 1 & \text{if } p_t < z_t \\ 0 & \text{otherwise,} \end{cases} \text{ and }$$

$$\widehat{a}_t = \begin{cases} 1 & \text{if } p_t > z_t + \epsilon \\ 0 & \text{otherwise.} \end{cases}$$

Notice that $\widehat{l}_t + \widehat{a}_t + \widehat{m}_t = 1$ for any t. Equation (6.25) can be rewritten as the following:

$$\frac{\sum_{t=1}^{T} V_T^t}{T} = \frac{\sum_{k=1}^{T}(v_k - z_k)}{T} + \frac{\sum_{k=1}^{T}(\widehat{l}_k(z_k - p_k))}{T} + \frac{\sum_{k=1}^{T}(\widehat{a}_k(z_k - p_k))}{T}$$

$$+ \frac{\sum_{k=1}^{T}(\widehat{m}_k(z_k - p_k))}{T} + V_0. \qquad (6.26)$$

Since when $\widehat{m}_k = 1$, $z_k \leq p_k \leq z_k + \epsilon$, it follows that

$$\sum_{k=1}^{T}(\widehat{m}_k(z_k - p_k)) \leq 0. \qquad (6.27)$$

Since when $\widehat{l}_k = 1$, $p_k < z_k$ and furthermore, $z_k - p_k \leq \bar{z}$. Therefore,

$$\sum_{k=1}^{T}(\widehat{l}_k(z_k - p_k)) \leq \bar{z}\sum_{k=1}^{T}\widehat{l}_k. \qquad (6.28)$$

Since when $\widehat{a}_k = 1$, $p_k > z_k + \epsilon$ and furthermore, $z_k - p_k < -\epsilon$. Therefore,

$$\sum_{k=1}^{T}(\widehat{a}_k(z_k - p_k)) \leq -\epsilon\sum_{k=1}^{T}\widehat{a}_k. \qquad (6.29)$$

Using (6.27), (6.28), and (6.29), (6.26) becomes

$$\frac{\sum_{t=1}^{T} V_T^t}{T} \leq \bar{z}\frac{\sum_{k=1}^{T}\widehat{l}_k}{T} - \epsilon\frac{\sum_{k=1}^{T}\widehat{a}_k}{T} + \frac{\sum_{k=1}^{T}(v_k - z_k)}{T} + V_0. \qquad (6.30)$$

Since the asset price is strictly above zero and since all the buyers have initial endowments of wealth, it follows that for any T, $\sum_{t=1}^{T} V_T^t > 0$. This together with (6.30) implies that

$$\frac{\sum_{k=1}^{T}\widehat{a}_k}{T} \leq \frac{\bar{z}}{\epsilon}\frac{\sum_{k=1}^{T}\widehat{l}_k}{T} + \frac{\sum_{k=1}^{T}(v_k - z_k)}{\epsilon T} + \frac{V_0}{\epsilon}. \qquad (6.31)$$

Since $\frac{\sum_{k=1}^{T}(v_k-z_k)}{T} = \frac{\sum_{k=1}^{T}(z_k(\exp(\omega_k)-1))}{T}$, and denoting $I_{\omega_k>0} = \begin{cases} 1 \text{ if } \omega_k > 0 \\ 0 \text{ otherwise} \end{cases}$, it follows that

$$\frac{\sum_{k=1}^{T}(v_k - z_k)}{T} \leq \frac{\sum_{k=1}^{T}\left(\bar{z}(\exp(\omega_k)-1)I_{\omega_k>0}\right)}{\#\{k:\omega_k>0\}} \frac{\#\{k:\omega_k>0\}}{T}. \quad (6.32)$$

Since $\{\omega_k\}_{k\geq 1}$ is a *i.i.d* random sequence, using the Strong Law of Large Numbers, it follows that with probability 1, as $T \to \infty$,

$$\frac{\sum_{k=1}^{T}\left(\bar{z}(\exp(\omega_k)-1)I_{\omega_k>0}\right)}{\#\{k:\omega_k>0\}} \frac{\#\{k:\omega_k>0\}}{T} \to \bar{z}E\left((\exp(\omega_k)-1)|\,\omega_k>0\right)\Pr(\omega_k>0). \quad (6.33)$$

Since $0 < \Pr(\omega_k > 0) < 1$, (6.32) and (6.33) imply that with probability 1 the following occurs: for any given $\epsilon > 0$, there exists a positive $\bar{k}$ such that for any *i.i.d* random shock sequence $\{\omega_k\}_{k\geq 1}$ with $E\left((\exp(\omega_k)-1)|\,\omega_k>0\right) \leq \bar{k}$,

$$\lim_{T\to\infty}\left(\frac{\sum_{k=1}^{T}(v_k - z_k)}{T}\right) < \bar{z}\bar{k} \leq \frac{\epsilon^2}{3}. \quad (6.34)$$

The result in Theorem 1 implies that,

$$\Pr\left(\lim_{T\to\infty}\left(\frac{\sum_{k=1}^{T}\widehat{l}_k}{T}\right) < \frac{\epsilon^2}{3\bar{z}}\right) = 1. \quad (6.35)$$

Set $\overline{V}_0 \leq \frac{\epsilon^2}{3}$. This together with (6.31), (6.34) and (6.35) implies that with probability 1 the following occurs: for any given $\epsilon > 0$, there exist a positive $\bar{k}$ and a positive $\overline{V}_0$ such that, if $E\left((\exp(\omega_t)-1)|\,\omega_t>0\right) \leq \bar{k}$ and if $V_0 \leq \overline{V}_0$, there exists a time period T_2, such that for all $T > T_2$, $\frac{\sum_{k=1}^{T}\widehat{a}_k}{T} < \epsilon$. Therefore, the result in Theorem 2 follows. □

The Proof of Theorem 3: Notice that for any $T \geq 1$,

$$\frac{\#\{t \leq T : p_t < z_t - \epsilon\}}{T} + \frac{\#\{t \leq T : p_t > z_t + \epsilon\}}{T}$$
$$+ \frac{\#\{t \leq T : p_t \in [z_t - \epsilon, z_t + \epsilon]\}}{T} = 1.$$

Therefore, using the results in Theorem 1 and Theorem 2 and letting $T^* = \max\{T_1, T_2\}$, Theorem 3 follows from the above equation. □

The Proof of Corollary 1: Consider buyer t's average wealth across time at the end of time period T.

$$\frac{V_T^t}{T} = \frac{V_0 + \sum_{k=t}^{T}((v_k - p_k)q_k^t)}{T}. \tag{6.36}$$

Define two indicator random variables $\widetilde{l}_t$ and $\widetilde{a}_t$, for $t = 1, 2, \ldots$, as follows:

$$\widetilde{l}_t = \begin{cases} 1 & \text{if } p_t < z_t \\ 0 & \text{otherwise,} \end{cases} \quad \text{and} \quad \widetilde{a}_t = \begin{cases} 1 & \text{if } p_t \geq z_t \\ 0 & \text{otherwise.} \end{cases}$$

Notice that $\widetilde{l}_t + \widetilde{a}_t = 1$ for any t. Using the above definitions, (6.36) becomes

$$\frac{V_T^t}{T} = \frac{\sum_{k=t}^{T}\left(\widetilde{l}_k(v_k - p_k)q_k^t\right)}{T} + \frac{\sum_{k=t}^{T}\left(\widetilde{a}_k(v_k - p_k)q_k^t\right)}{T} + \frac{V_0}{T}. \tag{6.37}$$

Since, when $\widetilde{l}_k = 1$ at time k, $v_k - p_k = z_k \exp(\omega_k) - p_k < \overline{z}\exp(\overline{\omega})$, this together with $0 \leq q_k^t \leq 1$ implies that

$$\sum_{k=t}^{T}\left(\widetilde{l}_k(v_k - p_k)q_k^t\right) < \overline{z}\exp(\overline{\omega})\sum_{k=t}^{T}\widetilde{l}_k. \tag{6.38}$$

Since, when $\widetilde{a}_k = 1$, $v_k - p_k = z_k \exp(\omega_k) - p_k \leq z_k \exp(\omega_k) - z_k \leq \overline{z}(\exp(\overline{\omega}) - 1)$, this together with $0 \leq q_k^t \leq 1$ implies that

$$\sum_{k=t}^{T}(\widetilde{a}_k(v_k - p_k)q_k^t) \leq \overline{z}(\exp(\overline{\omega}) - 1)\sum_{k=t}^{T}\widetilde{a}_k. \tag{6.39}$$

Using (6.38) and (6.39), (6.37) becomes

$$\frac{V_T^t}{T} < \overline{z}\exp(\overline{\omega})\frac{\sum_{k=t}^{T}\widetilde{l}_k}{T} + \overline{z}(\exp(\overline{\omega}) - 1)\frac{\sum_{k=t}^{T}\widetilde{a}_k}{T} + \frac{V_0}{T}. \tag{6.40}$$

The result in Theorem 1 implies that, for any given $\epsilon > 0$,

$$\Pr\left(\lim_{T\to\infty}\left(\frac{\overline{z}\exp(\overline{\omega})\sum_{k=t}^{T}\widetilde{l}_k}{T}\right) \leq \frac{\epsilon}{3}V_0\right) = 1. \tag{6.41}$$

Appendix A

The result in Theorem 2 implies that

$$\Pr\left(\forall \epsilon > 0, \exists \overline{k} > 0 \text{ and } \overline{V}_0 > 0 \text{ such that, if } E((\exp(\omega_t) - 1) | \omega_t > 0) \leq \overline{k}\right.$$

$$\left. \text{and if } V_0 \leq \overline{V}_0, \exists T_2', \text{ s.t. for } T > T_2', \ \overline{z}(\exp(\overline{\omega}) - 1) \frac{\sum_{k=t}^{T} \widetilde{a}_k}{T} < \frac{\epsilon}{3} V_0 \right) = 1. \tag{6.42}$$

Notice that $\lim_{T \to \infty} \frac{V_0}{T} < \frac{\epsilon}{3} V_0$. This together with (6.40), (6.41), and (6.42) implies that

$$\Pr\left(\forall \epsilon > 0, \exists \overline{k} > 0 \text{ and } \exists \overline{V}_0 > 0 \text{ such that, if } E((\exp(\omega_t) - 1) | \omega_t > 0) \leq \overline{k} \right.$$
$$\left. \text{and if } V_0 \leq \overline{V}_0, \exists T_3, \text{ s.t. for } T > T_3, \ \frac{V_T^t}{T} < \epsilon V_0\right) = 1. \tag{6.43}$$

Now consider all the buyers' average wealth across times up to the end of time period T. Using (6.36) and since $\sum_{t=1}^{k} q_k^t = 1$, it follows that

$$\frac{\sum_{t=1}^{T} V_T^t}{T} = \frac{\sum_{k=1}^{T} V_0 + \sum_{k=1}^{T} (v_k - p_k)}{T}. \tag{6.44}$$

Since $\widetilde{l}_k + \widetilde{a}_k = 1$, (6.44) becomes

$$\frac{\sum_{t=1}^{T} V_T^t}{T} = \frac{\sum_{k=1}^{T} \left(\widetilde{l}_k (v_k - p_k)\right)}{T} + \frac{\sum_{k=1}^{T} (\widetilde{a}_k (v_k - p_k))}{T} + V_0. \tag{6.45}$$

Since $\widetilde{l}_k = 1$ implies that $z_k > p_k$ and $v_k - p_k > (\exp(\omega_k) - 1) z_k \geq (\exp(-\underline{\omega}) - 1)\underline{z}$, and since $\widetilde{a}_k = 1$ implies that $v_k - p_k \geq \overline{z} \exp(-\overline{\omega}) - (\overline{z} + u)$, using (6.45), it follows that

$$\frac{\sum_{t=1}^{T} V_T^t}{T} \geq ((\exp(-\underline{\omega}) - 1)\underline{z}) \frac{\sum_{k=1}^{T} \widetilde{l}_k}{T} + (\overline{z} \exp(-\overline{\omega}) - (\overline{z} + u)) \frac{\sum_{k=1}^{T} \widetilde{a}_k}{T} + V_0. \tag{6.46}$$

Given that $(\exp(-\underline{\omega}) - 1)\overline{z} < 0$, Theorem 1 implies that with probability 1 the following occurs: for any $\epsilon > 0$ and for any V_0,

$$\lim_{T \to \infty} \left(((\exp(-\underline{\omega}) - 1)\overline{z}) \frac{\sum_{k=1}^{T} \tilde{l}_k}{T} \right) \geq -\frac{\epsilon}{2} V_0. \qquad (6.47)$$

Given that $\overline{z} \exp(-\underline{\omega}) - (\overline{z} + u) < 0$, the result in Theorem 2 implies that with probability 1 the following occurs: for any $\epsilon > 0$, there exist a $\overline{k} > 0$ and a $\overline{V}_0 > 0$ such that, if $E((\exp(\omega_k) - 1)|\omega_t > 0) \leq \overline{k}$ and if $V_0 \leq \overline{V}_0$,

$$\lim_{T \to \infty} \left((\overline{z} \exp(-\underline{\omega}) - (\overline{z} + u)) \frac{\sum_{k=1}^{T} \tilde{a}_k}{T} \right) \geq -\frac{\epsilon}{2} V_0. \qquad (6.48)$$

Therefore (6.46), (6.47), and (6.48) imply that with probability 1 the following occurs: for any $\epsilon > 0$, there exist a $\overline{k} > 0$ and a $\overline{V}_0 > 0$ such that, if $E((\exp(\omega_k) - 1)|\omega_t > 0) \leq \overline{k}$ and if $V_0 \leq \overline{V}_0$,

$$\lim_{T \to \infty} \left(\frac{\sum_{t=1}^{T} V_T^t}{T} \right) \geq -\epsilon V_0 + V_0. \qquad (6.49)$$

Using (6.43) and (6.49), it follows that with probability 1 the following occurs: for any $\epsilon > 0$, there exist a $\overline{k} > 0$ and a $\overline{V}_0 > 0$ such that, if $E((\exp(\omega_k) - 1)|\omega_t > 0) \leq \overline{k}$ and if $V_0 \leq \overline{V}_0$,

$$\lim_{T \to \infty} \left(\frac{V_T^t}{\frac{\sum_{t=1}^{T} V_T^t}{T}} \right) < \frac{\epsilon V_0}{(1 - \epsilon) V_0}. \qquad (6.50)$$

Let $\epsilon' = \frac{\epsilon}{(1-\epsilon)}$, Corollary 1 follows from (6.50). $\square$

Appendix B

This appendix consists of three lemmas and one proposition. Lemmas 1 and 2 are used to established Lemma 3. Proposition 1, Lemmas 1 and 3 are used to prove Theorem 1. Proposition 1 is also used to prove Lemma 2.

Proposition 1. *Let $\{X_t\}_{t \geq 1}$ be a random sequence with a finite expectation $E(X_t)$ and $|X_t| \leq M_1$, where M_1 is a finite positive number. Let Y_t, where $t = 1, 2, \ldots$, be a random variable with $|Y_t| \leq M_2$, where M_2 is a finite positive number. If X_t is independent of $Y_1, Y_2, \ldots, Y_t$, then for any given $\epsilon > 0$,*

$$\lim_{T \to \infty} \Pr \left(\left| \frac{\sum_{t=1}^{T} (X_t Y_t)}{T} - \frac{\sum_{t=1}^{T} (Y_t E(X_t))}{T} \right| < \epsilon \right) = 1.$$

Proof. Let $X_t = E(X_t) + \epsilon_t$. Since $\{X_t\}_{t \geq 1}$ is a random sequence with $E(X_t) < \infty$ and $|X_t| \leq M_1$, it follows that $\{\epsilon_t\}_{t \geq 1}$ is a random sequence with $E\epsilon_t = 0$ and $|\epsilon_t| \leq M_1 < \infty$. Therefore, for all $t = 1, 2, \ldots$,

$$\frac{\sum_{t=1}^{T} (X_t Y_t)}{T} = \frac{\sum_{t=1}^{T} (Y_t E(X_t))}{T} + \frac{\sum_{t=1}^{T} (\epsilon_t Y_t)}{T}. \tag{6.51}$$

Consider the last term in the above equation $\frac{\sum_{t=1}^{T} (\epsilon_t Y_t)}{T}$. Since X_t is independent of Y_t, ϵ_t is independent of Y_t, and it follows that

$$E \left(\frac{\sum_{t=1}^{T} (\epsilon_t Y_t)}{T} \right) = \frac{\sum_{t=1}^{T} (E(\epsilon_t) E(Y_t))}{T} = 0. \tag{6.52}$$

Notice that

$$\mathrm{Var} \left(\frac{\sum_{t=1}^{T} (\epsilon_t Y_t)}{T} \right) = \frac{\sum_{t=1}^{T} (\mathrm{Var}(\epsilon_t Y_t))}{T^2} + \frac{2}{T^2} \sum_{t=1}^{T} \sum_{s>t}^{T} (E(\epsilon_t Y_t \epsilon_s Y_s) - E(\epsilon_t Y_t) E(\epsilon_s Y_s)). \tag{6.53}$$

Since X_s is independent of $Y_1, \ldots, Y_s$, ϵ_s is also independent of $Y_1, \ldots, Y_s$. Given $E\epsilon_t = 0$ for any t, it follows that the last term in the above equation is equal to zero. That is,

$$\frac{2}{T^2} \sum_{t=1}^{T} \sum_{s>t}^{T} (E(\epsilon_t Y_t \epsilon_s Y_s) - E(\epsilon_t Y_t) E(\epsilon_s Y_s)) = 0. \tag{6.54}$$

Since $|\epsilon_t| \leq M_1 < \infty$ and since $|Y_t| \leq M_2 < \infty$, it follows that $\text{Var}(\epsilon_t Y_t) \leq M_3$, where M_3 is a finite positive number. Therefore,

$$0 \leq \frac{1}{T^2} \sum_{t=1}^{T} (\text{Var}(\epsilon_t Y_t)) \leq \frac{1}{T} M_3. \tag{6.55}$$

Equations (6.53), (6.54) and (6.55) imply that

$$\text{Var}\left(\frac{\sum_{t=1}^{T} (\epsilon_t Y_t)}{T}\right) \to 0 \text{ as } T \to \infty. \tag{6.56}$$

Given (6.52) and (6.56), using Markov's Theorem, see (Gnedenko, 1962, pp. 232), it follows that for any given $\epsilon > 0$,

$$\lim_{T \to \infty} \Pr\left(\left|\frac{\sum_{t=1}^{T} (\epsilon_t Y_t)}{T}\right| < \epsilon\right) = 1. \tag{6.57}$$

Using (6.51) and (6.57), Proposition 1 follows. □

Lemma 1. *For any given $\delta, \epsilon > 0$ and for some positive $c < 1$,*

$$\Pr\left(\textit{There exists an infinite number of buyers in the set } \Theta(\delta, \epsilon, c)\right) = 1,$$

where $\Theta(\delta, \epsilon, c) = \{\textit{buyer } t : \delta \theta_2^t \ln\left(\frac{z}{z - \frac{z}{3}\epsilon}\right) + \theta_1^t \ln\left(\frac{z}{z+u}\right) > 0, \theta_2^t \geq c, \theta_1^t + \theta_2^t + \theta_3^t = 1\}$.

Proof. As noted in the text, $\{(\theta_1^t, \theta_2^t)\}_{t \geq 1}$ is independently and identically distributed. Hence, define a random variable R_t, where $t = 1, 2, \ldots$, as the following: for any given arbitrarily small $\delta, \epsilon > 0$ and some positive $c < 1$,

$$R_t = \begin{cases} 1 & \text{if buyer } t \in \Theta(\delta, \epsilon, c) \\ 0 & \text{otherwise,} \end{cases}$$

Appendix B

where $\Theta(\delta, \epsilon, c) = \left\{ \text{buyer } t : \delta\theta_2^t \ln\left(\frac{\bar{z}}{\bar{z}-\frac{2}{3}\epsilon}\right) + \theta_1^t \ln\left(\frac{\bar{z}}{\bar{z}+u}\right) > 0, \theta_2^t \geq c, \theta_1^t + \theta_2^t + \theta_3^t = 1 \right\} \neq \emptyset$. It follows that $\{R_t = 1\}_{t \geq 1}$ is also a $i.i.d.$ random sequence. If the distribution function $F(\cdot)$ satisfies the θ–Assumption, then $\Pr(R_t = 1) = \Pr(\text{buyer } t \in \Theta(\delta, \epsilon, c)) = \int_{\substack{\delta\theta_2 + \theta_1 D > 0, \\ \theta_2 \geq c}} dF(\theta_1, \theta_2) > 0$, for any t, where $D = \frac{\ln\left(\frac{\bar{z}}{\bar{z}+u}\right)}{\ln\left(\frac{\bar{z}}{\bar{z}-\frac{2}{3}\epsilon}\right)}$. Therefore,

$$\sum_{t=1}^{\infty} \Pr(R_t = 1) = \infty. \tag{6.58}$$

Using (6.58) and the Second Borel Cantelli Lemma, see (Billingsley, 1995, pp. 83),

$$\Pr\left(\sum_{t=1}^{\infty} R_t = \infty\right) = 1. \tag{6.59}$$

Equation (6.59) further implies that for any given arbitrarily small $\delta, \epsilon > 0$ and some positive $c < 1$,

Pr (There exists an infinite number of buyers in the set $\Theta(\delta, \epsilon, c)) = 1$.

Lemma 1 follows. □

Lemma 2. *Consider buyer t's wealth at time period T, V_T^t, and show that for any given $\epsilon > 0$,*

$$\lim_{T \to \infty} \Pr\left(\frac{\ln V_T^t}{T-t+1} \geq \frac{\sum_{k=t}^{T}\left(l_k g_k^t l_k^t\right)}{T-t+1} \ln\left(\frac{\bar{z}}{\bar{z}-\frac{2}{3}\epsilon}\right) + \frac{\sum_{k=t}^{T} x_k^t}{T-t+1} \ln\left(\frac{\bar{z}}{\bar{z}+u}\right) + \frac{\ln V_0}{T-t+1} \right) = 1.$$

Proof. Consider buyer t's wealth at time period k, where $k \geq t$, $t = 1, 2, \ldots$,

$$V_k^t = V_{k-1}^t + (v_k - p_k)q_k^t. \tag{6.60}$$

If buyer t's prediction at time k coincides with the asset price, then buyer t is referred to as a marginal trader. In this case, buyer t's wealth may not be fully used up. Hence $q_k^t \in \left(0, \frac{V_{k-1}^t}{p_k}\right]$. Denote $q_k^t = r_k \left(\frac{V_{k-1}^t}{p_k}\right)$, where $r_k \in (0, 1]$. Clearly, r_k

is independent of the random shock ω_i for all $i \geq k$. For the sake of the following discussion, define an indicator random variable M_k^t for $k \geq t$ to describe whether buyer t at time k is a marginal trader. That is,

$$M_k^t = \begin{cases} 1 & \text{if } b_k^t = p_k \\ 0 & \text{otherwise.} \end{cases}$$

Define another random variable H_k^t, where $k \geq t$, to describe whether buyer t is active at time k, that is,

$$H_k^t = \begin{cases} 1 & \text{if } q_k^t > 0 \\ 0 & \text{otherwise.} \end{cases}$$

Define random variables x_k^t and y_k^t, where $k \geq t$, to describe the position of buyer t's prediction error relative to $-\frac{2}{3}\epsilon$ or $-\frac{1}{3}\epsilon$ at time k. That is, for any given $\epsilon > 0$,

$$y_k^t = \begin{cases} 1 & \text{if } u_k^t < -\frac{2}{3}\epsilon \\ 0 & \text{otherwise,} \end{cases} \quad \text{and} \quad x_k^t = \begin{cases} 1 & \text{if } u_k^t > -\frac{1}{3}\epsilon \\ 0 & \text{otherwise.} \end{cases}$$

Finally, define two random variables m_k and a_k, where $k \geq 1$, as the following:

$$m_k = \begin{cases} 1 & \text{if } z_k - \frac{2}{3}\epsilon \leq p_k \leq z_k \\ 0 & \text{otherwise,} \end{cases} \quad \text{and} \quad a_k = \begin{cases} 1 & \text{if } p_k > z_k \\ 0 & \text{otherwise.} \end{cases}$$

In addition to the above notation, the notation (i.e., l_k, g_k^t and l_k^t) defined in the proof of Theorem 1 is also used here.

Consider the following mutually exclusive cases where buyer t is a nonmarginal trader at time k, i.e., $b_k^t > p_k$:

1. $l_k = 1$ and $g_k^t = 1$ meaning that $p_k < z_k - \frac{2}{3}\epsilon$ and $-\frac{2}{3}\epsilon \leq u_k^t \leq -\frac{1}{3}\epsilon$;
2. $l_k = 1$ and $x_k^t = 1$ meaning that $p_k < z_k - \frac{2}{3}\epsilon$ and $u_k^t > -\frac{1}{3}\epsilon$;
3. $l_k = 1$, $y_k^t = 1$, $(1 - M_k^t) = 1$ and $H_k^t = 1$ meaning that $p_k < z_k - \frac{2}{3}\epsilon$; $u_k^t < -\frac{2}{3}\epsilon$; and buyer t is active at time k;
4. $a_k = 1$, $x_k^t = 1$, $(1 - M_k^t) = 1$ and $H_k^t = 1$ meaning that $p_k > z_k$; $u_k^t > -\frac{1}{3}\epsilon$; and buyer t is active at time k;
5. $m_k = 1$, $x_k^t = 1$, $(1 - M_k^t) = 1$ and $H_k^t = 1$ meaning that $z_k - \frac{2}{3}\epsilon \leq p_k \leq z_k$; $u_k^t > -\frac{1}{3}\epsilon$; and buyer t is active at time k;
6. $m_k = 1$, $g_k^t = 1$, $(1 - M_k^t) = 1$ and $H_k^t = 1$ meaning that $z_k - \frac{2}{3}\epsilon \leq p_k \leq z_k$; $-\frac{2}{3}\epsilon \leq u_k^t \leq -\frac{1}{3}\epsilon$; and buyer t is active at time k.

In conclusion, for $b_k^t > p_k$, buyer t uses all of his or her wealth at time period k, i.e., $q_k^t = \frac{V_{k-1}^t}{p_k}$. Using (6.60), it follows that, if $b_k^t > p_k$,

$$V_k^t = \left(\frac{v_k}{p_k}\right)^{g_k^t l_k + x_k^t l_k + H_k^t(1-M_k^t)y_k^t l_k + H_k^t(1-M_k^t)x_k^t a_k + H_k^t(1-M_k^t)x_k^t m_k + H_k^t(1-M_k^t)g_k^t m_k} V_{k-1}^t.$$

(6.61)

Appendix B

Consider the following mutually exclusive cases where buyer t is a marginal trader at time k, i.e., $b_k^t = p_k$:

7. $l_k = 1$, $y_k^t = 1$, $M_k^t = 1$ meaning that $p_k < z_k - \frac{2}{3}\epsilon$; $u_k^t < -\frac{2}{3}\epsilon$; and buyer t is a marginal trader at time k;
8. $a_k = 1$, $x_k^t = 1$, $M_k^t = 1$ meaning that $p_k > z_k$; $u_k^t > -\frac{1}{3}\epsilon$; and buyer t is a marginal trader at time k;
9. $m_k = 1$, $x_k^t = 1$, $M_k^t = 1$ meaning that $z_k - \frac{2}{3}\epsilon \leq p_k \leq z_k$; $u_k^t > -\frac{1}{3}\epsilon$; and buyer t is a marginal trader at time k;
10. $m_k = 1$, $g_k^t = 1$, $M_k^t = 1$ meaning that $z_k - \frac{2}{3}\epsilon \leq p_k \leq z_k$; $-\frac{2}{3}\epsilon \leq u_k^t \leq -\frac{1}{3}\epsilon$; and buyer t is a marginal trader at time k.

In conclusion, for $b_k^t = p_k$, buyer t may not use up all of his or her wealth, hence, $q_k^t = r_k \frac{V_{k-1}^t}{p_k}$ where $r_k \in (0, 1]$. Using (6.60), it follows that, if $b_k^t = p_k$,

$$V_k^t = \left(1 - r_k + r_k \left(\frac{v_k}{p_k}\right)\right)^{M_k^t y_k^t l_k + M_k^t x_k^t a_k + M_k^t x_k^t m_k + M_k^t g_k^t m_k} V_{k-1}^t. \quad (6.62)$$

Therefore, at the end of time period k, bringing together (6.61) and (6.62) produces

$$V_k^t = \left(\frac{v_k}{p_k}\right)^{g_k^t l_k + x_k^t l_k + H_k^t(1-M_k^t)y_k^t l_k + H_k^t(1-M_k^t)x_k^t a_k + H_k^t(1-M_k^t)x_k^t m_k + H_k^t(1-M_k^t)g_k^t m_k}$$

$$\cdot \left(1 - r_k + r_k \left(\frac{v_k}{p_k}\right)\right)^{M_k^t y_k^t l_k + M_k^t x_k^t a_k + M_k^t x_k^t m_k + M_k^t g_k^t m_k} V_{k-1}^t.$$

One can show inductively that

$$V_T^t = \prod_{k=t}^{T} \left\{ \left(\frac{v_k}{p_k}\right)^{g_k^t l_k + x_k^t l_k + H_k^t(1-M_k^t)y_k^t l_k + H_k^t(1-M_k^t)x_k^t a_k + H_k^t(1-M_k^t)x_k^t m_k + H_k^t(1-M_k^t)g_k^t m_k} \right.$$

$$\left. \cdot \left(1 - r_k + r_k \left(\frac{v_k}{p_k}\right)\right)^{M_k^t y_k^t l_k + M_k^t x_k^t a_k + M_k^t x_k^t m_k + M_k^t g_k^t m_k} \right\} V_{t-1}^t.$$

Let $V_{t-1}^t = V_0$, take the logarithm of both sides, and divide by $T - t + 1$

$$\frac{\ln V_T^t}{T - t + 1} = \frac{1}{T - t + 1} \left\{ \sum_{k=t}^{T} ([g_k^t l_k + x_k^t l_k + H_k^t(1 - M_k^t)y_k^t l_k \right.$$

$$\left. + H_k^t(1 - M_k^t)x_k^t a_k + H_k^t(1 - M_k^t)x_k^t m_k + H_k^t(1 - M_k^t)g_k^t m_k] \ln\left(\frac{v_k}{p_k}\right)\right)$$

$$+ \sum_{k=t}^{T} \left[\left(M_k^t y_k^t l_k + M_k^t x_k^t a_k + M_k^t x_k^t m_k + M_k^t g_k^t m_k \right) \right.$$

$$\left. \times \ln \left(1 - r_k + r_k \left(\frac{v_k}{p_k} \right) \right) \right] + \ln V_0 \Bigg\}$$

Furthermore, since $\ln(\cdot)$ is concave, $\ln \left(1 - r_k + r_k \left(\frac{v_k}{p_k} \right) \right) \geq (1 - r_k) \ln (1) + r_k \ln \left(\frac{v_k}{p_k} \right) = r_k \ln \left(\frac{v_k}{p_k} \right)$, it follows that

$$\frac{1}{T-t+1} \ln V_T^t \geq \frac{1}{T-t+1} \left(A_{1T} + A_{2T} + A_{3T} + \ln V_0 \right),$$

where
$$\begin{cases}
A_{1T} = \sum_{k=t}^{T} \left(g_k^t l_k \ln \left(\frac{v_k}{p_k} \right) \right), \\
A_{2T} = \sum_{k=t}^{T} \left(\left[x_k^t l_k + H_k^t (1 - M_k^t) y_k^t l_k + H_k^t (1 - M_k^t) x_k^t m_k \right. \right. \\
\qquad \left. + H_k^t (1 - M_k^t) g_k^t m_k \right] \ln \left(\frac{v_k}{p_k} \right) \Big) \\
\qquad + \sum_{k=t}^{T} \left[\left(M_k^t y_k^t l_k + M_k^t x_k^t m_k + M_k^t g_k^t m_k \right) r_k \ln \left(\frac{v_k}{p_k} \right) \right], \\
A_{3T} = \sum_{k=t}^{T} \left[H_k^t (1 - M_k^t) x_k^t a_k \ln \left(\frac{v_k}{p_k} \right) \right] + \sum_{k=t}^{T} \left[M_k^t x_k^t a_k r_k \ln \left(\frac{v_k}{p_k} \right) \right].
\end{cases}$$
(6.63)

Now, the convergence of A_{1T}, A_{2T} and A_{3T} are shown respectively in Steps 1, 2 and 3.

Step 1: Since the asset price at time k, p_k, is a function of $z_1, z_2, \ldots, z_k$; and $\omega_1, \omega_2, \ldots, \omega_{k-1}$; and $u_t^t, u_{t+1}^t, \ldots, u_k^t$, for all $t \leq k$; and since ω_k is independent of $z_1, z_2, \ldots, z_k$; and $\omega_1, \omega_2, \ldots, \omega_{k-1}$; and $u_t^t, u_{t+1}^t, \ldots, u_k^t$, for all $t \leq k$; it follows that ω_k is independent of p_k. This further implies that ω_k is independent of g_i^t and l_i, for all $t \leq i \leq k$. This together with $\ln v_k = \ln z_k + \omega_k$, and Proposition 1 in Appendix B implies that

$$\frac{A_{1T}}{T-t+1} = \frac{\sum_{k=t}^{T} \left(g_k^t l_k \left((\ln z_k - \ln p_k) + \omega_k \right) \right)}{T-t+1}$$

$$\rightarrow \frac{\sum_{k=t}^{T} \left(g_k^t l_k (\ln z_k - \ln p_k) \right)}{T-t+1} + \frac{\sum_{k=t}^{T} \left(g_k^t l_k E(\omega_k) \right)}{T-t+1} \text{ in probability.} \quad (6.64)$$

Appendix B

Since $l_k = 1$ implies that $p_k < z_k - \frac{2}{3}\epsilon$, $\ln z_k - \ln p_k \geq \ln(\frac{z_k}{z_k - \frac{2}{3}\epsilon}) \geq \ln(\frac{\bar{z}}{\bar{z} - \frac{2}{3}\epsilon}) > 0$. Therefore, this together with $E(\omega_k) = 0$, implies that (6.64) becomes

$$\lim_{T \to \infty} \Pr\left(\frac{A_{1T}}{T-t+1} \geq \frac{\sum_{k=t}^{T} \left(g_k^t l_k \ln\left(\frac{\bar{z}}{\bar{z} - \frac{2}{3}\epsilon}\right) \right)}{T-t+1} \right) = 1. \quad (6.65)$$

Step 2: For the same reasons as outlined at the beginning of Step 1, the random shock at time k, ω_k, is independent of $M_i^t, y_i^t, x_i^t, g_i^t, l_i, m_i, r_i, H_i^t$ for all $t \leq i \leq k$. This together with $\ln v_k = \ln z_k + \omega_k$ and Proposition 1 in Appendix B implies that,

$$\frac{A_{2T}}{T-t+1} = \frac{1}{T-t+1} \sum_{k=t}^{T} \left([x_k^t l_k + H_k^t(1-M_k^t)y_k^t l_k + H_k^t(1-M_k^t)x_k^t m_k \right.$$

$$\left. + H_k^t(1-M_k^t)g_k^t m_k + M_k^t y_k^t l_k r_k + M_k^t x_k^t m_k r_k + M_k^t g_k^t m_k r_k \right]$$

$$\times (\ln z_k - \ln p_k + \omega_k))$$

$$\to \frac{1}{T-t+1} \sum_{k=t}^{T} \left([x_k^t l_k + H_k^t(1-M_k^t)y_k^t l_k + H_k^t(1-M_k^t)x_k^t m_k \right.$$

$$\left. + H_k^t(1-M_k^t)g_k^t m_k + M_k^t y_k^t l_k r_k + M_k^t x_k^t m_k r_k + M_k^t g_k^t m_k r_k \right]$$

$$\times (\ln z_k - \ln p_k + E(\omega_k))) \text{ in probability.} \quad (6.66)$$

Now, since $E(\omega_k) = 0$, and since the equation $l_k = 1$ or $m_k = 1$ implies that $p_k \leq z_k$, it follows that if $l_k = 1$ or $m_k = 1$, then $\ln z_k - \ln p_k \geq 0$. Therefore, (6.66) becomes

$$\lim_{T \to \infty} \Pr\left(\frac{A_{2T}}{T-t+1} \geq 0 \right) = 1. \quad (6.67)$$

Step 3: Similarly, since $\ln v_k = \ln z_k + \omega_k$ and since ω_k is independent of H_i^t, M_i^t, x_i^t, a_i, and r_i for all $t \leq i \leq k$, using Proposition 1 in Appendix B,

$$\frac{A_{3T}}{T-t+1} \to \frac{\sum_{k=t}^{T} \{(H_k^t(1-M_k^t)x_k^t a_k + M_k^t x_k^t a_k r_k)((\ln z_k - \ln p_k) + E(\omega_k))\}}{T-t+1}$$

$$\times \text{ in probability.} \quad (6.68)$$

148   6 Evolution, Noise Traders, and Market Efficiency in a One-Sided Auction Market

Since $a_k = 1$ implies $p_k > z_k$, it follows that if $a_k = 1$, then $0 > \ln(\frac{z_k}{p_k}) > \ln(\frac{z}{\bar{z}+u})$; and furthermore, $H_k^t(1 - M_k^t)x_k^t a_k + M_k^t x_k^t a_k r_k \leq x_k^t$ and $E(\omega_k) = 0$. Therefore, this together with (6.68) implies that

$$\lim_{T \to \infty} \Pr\left(\frac{A_{3T}}{T-t+1} \geq \frac{\sum_{k=t}^{T} \{x_k^t \ln(\frac{z}{\bar{z}+u})\}}{T-t+1} \right) = 1. \tag{6.69}$$

Using (6.63), (6.65), (6.67), and (6.69), it follows that

$$\lim_{T \to \infty} \Pr\left(\frac{\ln V_T^t}{T-t+1} \geq \frac{\sum_{k=t}^{T}\{g_k^t l_k \ln(\frac{\bar{z}}{\bar{z}-\frac{2}{3}\epsilon}) + x_k^t \ln(\frac{z}{\bar{z}+u})\} + \ln V_0}{T-t+1} \right) = 1. \tag{6.70}$$

Since $g_k^t l_k \geq g_k^t l_k l_k^t$, using (6.70), Lemma 2 follows. □

Lemma 3. *For any given $\delta, \epsilon > 0$, for some positive number $c < 1$ and for any subsequence $n_1, n_2, \ldots, n_T, \ldots$,*

$$\Pr\left(\lim_{T \to \infty} \frac{\sum_{s=t}^{n_T}(l_s^t g_s^t l_s)}{n_T - t + 1} = 0, \text{ for all } t \in \Theta(\delta, \epsilon, c) \right) = 1,$$

where $\Theta(\delta, \epsilon, c)$ is defined in Lemma 1. That is,

$$\Theta(\delta, \epsilon, c) = \left\{ \text{buyer } t : \delta \theta_2^t \ln\left(\frac{z}{\bar{z} - \frac{2}{3}\epsilon}\right) + \theta_1^t \ln\left(\frac{z}{\bar{z}+u}\right) \right. \\ \left. > 0, \; \theta_2^t \geq c, \; \theta_1^t + \theta_2^t + \theta_3^t = 1 \right\}.$$

Proof. Lemma 1 implies that for any given $\delta, \epsilon > 0$ and for some positive $c < 1$,

Pr (there exists an infinite number of buyers in the set $\Theta(\delta, \epsilon, c)) = 1$, (6.71)

where $\Theta(\delta, \epsilon, c) = \{\text{buyer } t : \delta \theta_2^t \ln(\frac{z}{\bar{z}-\frac{2}{3}\epsilon}) + \theta_1^t \ln(\frac{z}{\bar{z}+u}) > 0, \; \theta_2^t \geq c, \; \theta_1^t + \theta_2^t + \theta_3^t = 1\}$.

Now, consider buyer t in the set $\Theta(\delta, \epsilon, c)$. If the following equation is true,

Appendix B

$$\Pr\left(\lim_{T\to\infty}\left(\frac{\sum_{s=t}^{n_T}(l_s^t g_s^t l_s)}{n_T - t + 1}\right) = 0 \bigg| t \in \Theta(\delta,\epsilon,c)\right) = 1, \quad (6.72)$$

then using Bayes rule, (6.71) and (6.72) implies that

$$\Pr\left(\lim_{T\to\infty}\left(\frac{\sum_{s=t}^{n_T}(l_s^t g_s^t l_s)}{n_T - t + 1}\right) = 0, \text{ for all } t \in \Theta(\delta,\epsilon,c)\right) = 1.$$

Therefore, Lemma 3 follows. Now, the following proves (6.72). The proof is shown by way of contradiction. Suppose not, then

$$\Pr\bigg(\text{there exist a } \delta_0 > 0 \text{ and a further subsequence } n_1^0, n_2^0, \ldots, n_T^0, \ldots$$

of the subsequence $n_1, n_2, \ldots, n_T, \ldots$, such that,

$$\frac{\sum_{s=t}^{n_T^0}(l_s^t g_s^t l_s)}{n_T^0 - t + 1} > \delta_0 \theta_2^t, \text{ for all } T \geq 1 \bigg| t \in \Theta(\delta,\epsilon,c)\bigg) > \delta_0. \quad (6.73)$$

Lemma 2 implies that for buyer $t \in \Theta(\delta,\epsilon,c)$ and at time period n_T^0,

$$\lim_{T\to\infty}\Pr\left(\frac{\ln V_{n_T^0}^t}{n_T^0 - t + 1} \geq \frac{\sum_{s=t}^{n_T^0}(l_s^t g_s^t l_s)}{n_T^0 - t + 1}\ln\left(\frac{\bar{z}}{\bar{z}-\frac{2}{3}\epsilon}\right) + \frac{\sum_{s=t}^{n_T^0} x_s^t}{n_T^0 - t + 1}\ln\left(\frac{\bar{z}}{\bar{z}+u}\right)\right.$$

$$\left. + \frac{\ln V_0}{n_T^0 - t + 1} \bigg| t \in \Theta(\delta,\epsilon,c)\right) = 1. \quad (6.74)$$

Consider buyer $t \in \Theta(\delta,\epsilon,c)$. Since $\{u_s^t\}_{s\geq t}$ is a i.i.d. random sequence, $\{x_s^t\}_{s\geq t}$ is a i.i.d. random sequence. The Strong Law of Large numbers implies that given $t \in \Theta(\delta,\epsilon,c)$,

$$\frac{\sum_{s=t}^{n_T^0} x_s^t}{n_T^0 - t + 1} \to \theta_1^t \text{ as } T \to \infty \text{ with probability 1.} \quad (6.75)$$

Equations (6.73), (6.74), and (6.75) imply that

$$\lim_{T \to \infty} \Pr\left(\frac{\ln V_{n_T^0}^t}{n_T^0 - t + 1} \geq \left. 8\theta_2^t \ln\left(\frac{z}{z - \frac{2}{3}\epsilon}\right) + \theta_1^t \ln\left(\frac{z}{z + u}\right) \right| t \in \Theta(\delta, \epsilon, c) \right) > 0. \tag{6.76}$$

Since $t \in \Theta(\delta, \epsilon, c)$ implies that for some positive λ, $8\theta_2^t \ln\left(\frac{z}{z - \frac{2}{3}\epsilon}\right) + \theta_1^t \ln\left(\frac{z}{z+u}\right) > \lambda$, this together with (6.76) implies that

$$\lim_{T \to \infty} \Pr\left(\left. \frac{\ln V_{n_T^0}^t}{n_T^0 - t + 1} \geq \lambda \right| t \in \Theta(\delta, \epsilon, c) \right) > 0.$$

This together with (6.71) further implies that for any given $F > 0$,

$$\lim_{T \to \infty} \Pr\left(\frac{V_{n_T^0}^t}{n_T^0} > F \right) > 0. \tag{6.77}$$

However, since the aggregate profits of all the buyers in any one time period is bounded from above, the average total wealth of all the buyers across time is also bounded from above. It follows that the average total wealth of any one buyer across time is bounded from above. This contradicts (6.77).

Therefore, (6.72) must be true. □

Appendix C

The purpose of Appendix C is to add some numerical evidence to highlight the importance of the θ−Assumption in the convergence of the asset price to its fundamental value. Four sets of simulations are conducted. They illustrate: (a) If all traders are too noisy in the sense that all traders have too high of a probability of overpredicting and underpredicting the asset's fundamental value, convergence does not seem to occur. (b) A sufficient condition for convergence is that in each time period there is a positive probability that an entering trader has an arbitrarily high probability of predicting arbitrarily close to the fundamental value. In other words, if for any given arbitrarily small $\eta > 0$, $\Pr(\theta_2^t \in (1 - \eta, 1)) > 0$ for all $t \geq 1$, then convergence does occurs. It is also shown that if the variation in the random shock is smaller, the convergence band is smaller. (c) Another sufficient condition (but weaker than that described in (b)) for convergence is that there is a positive probability in each time period that the entering trader has an arbitrarily low probability of overpredicting the fundamental value and has a probability, of predicting arbitrarily close to the fundamental value, being bounded away from zero by a positive number. That is, for any given arbitrarily small positive η and η', $\Pr(\theta_1^t \in (0, \eta), \theta_2^t > \eta') > 0$ for all $t \geq 1$. Note that both conditions described in (b) and (c) satisfy the θ−Assumption described in the text.

Appendix C   151

All of the following numerical illustrations share the following characteristics:
1. The fundamental value of the asset at time s (z_s), where $s = 1, 2, \ldots$, is assumed to have a uniform distribution with its support $[\underline{z}, \overline{z}] = [3, 7]$.
2. For $t \geq 1$, trader t's prediction errors u_s^t are randomly drawn from an interval $[-3, 3]$ according to $(\theta_1^t, \theta_2^t, \theta_3^t)$, where $\theta_1^t = \Pr(u_s^t > 0)$, $\theta_2^t = \Pr(-0.10 \leq u_s^t \leq 0)$, and $\theta_3^t = \Pr(u_s^t < -0.10)$.
3. All traders on entry are endowed with their initial wealth $V_0 = 0.001$.

C.1 Failure of Convergence with Too Noisy Traders

The proportion of time, that the asset price is arbitrarily close to the fundamental value, does not converge to one if all traders are too noisy, in the sense that all traders have a sufficiently higher probability of overpredicting the fundamental value. To illustrate this, in the first set of simulations, together with characteristics (1), (2), and (3), all traders' prediction errors are assumed to have a uniform distribution with its support $[-3, 3]$ and $\theta_1^t = \theta_2^t = \theta_3^t = \frac{1}{3}$ for all $t \geq 1$. The random shock w_t has a symmetric doubly truncated normal distribution where the density function of w_t is $\sigma^{-1} Z\left(\frac{w_t}{\sigma}\right) \left[2\Phi\left(\frac{B}{\sigma}\right) - 1\right]^{-1}$ where $\sigma = 0.1000$, $B = 0.356$, $Z(\cdot)$ is the unit normal probability density function and $\Phi(\cdot)$ is the corresponding cumulative distribution function. The truncation keeps the upper bound of v_s from exceeding the highest bid 10. 100 simulations are conducted and the market is followed from time period 1 to 3000. Figure 6.3 shows the proportion of time that the absolute deviation between the asset price and the fundamental value lies in the intervals $I_i = [(i-1) \times 0.025, i \times 0.025)$ for $i = 1, 2, 3, 4$; $I_5 = [0.10, 0.50)$; $I_6 = [0.50, 1.00)$ and $I_7 = [1.0, \infty)$ up to time periods 500, 1500, and 3000. Figure 6.3 shows no sign of convergence. The proportion of time that $|p_s - z_s|$ lies in the various intervals is relatively stable across time periods 500, 1500, and 3000; in particular, by time period 3000, 88% of the time $|p_s - z_s| \geq 0.10$.

It is clear that convergence does not occur if traders are too noisy. The entry of a large number of traders together with the law of large numbers is not sufficient to guarantee convergence.

C.2 Convergence when the Probability of Predicting the Fundamental Value is Allowed to be Arbitrarily Close to 1

The second set of simulations is conducted under the assumption that, with a positive probability, the entering trader has an arbitrarily high probability of predicting arbitrarily close to the fundamental value. That is, for any given small $\eta > 0$, $\Pr(\theta_2^t \in (1 - \eta, 1)) > 0$ for all $t \geq 1$.

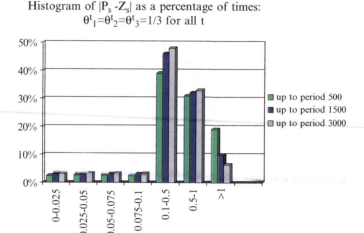

Fig. 6.3 Histogram of $|P_s - Z_s|$ as a percentage of times: $\theta_1^t = \theta_2^t = \theta_3^t = 1/3$ for all t

The vector $(\theta_1^t, \theta_2^t, \theta_3^t)$, which characterizes trader t's probability distribution of his or her prediction error, is drawn randomly according to a uniform distribution from a plane defined by $\{(\theta_1, \theta_2, \theta_3) \in (0, 1) \times (0, 1) \times (0, 1) : \theta_1 + \theta_2 + \theta_3 = 1\}$.

1. The random shock w_t obeys a symmetric doubly truncated normal distribution where its density function is $\sigma^{-1} Z\left(\frac{w_t}{\sigma}\right) \left[2\Phi\left(\frac{B}{\sigma}\right) - 1\right]^{-1}$ where $\sigma = 0.1000$ and $B = 0.356$.

   One hundred simulations are conducted and the market is followed from time period 1 to 3000. Figure 6.4a indicates that the proportion of time, that the asset price is closer to the fundamental value of the asset, gets larger as time gets larger. At time period 500, on average across 100 simulations, $\frac{\#\{s \le 500 : |p_s - z_s| \ge 0.10\}}{500} = 0.30$ and $\frac{\#\{s \le 500 : |p_s - z_s| < 0.025\}}{500} = 0.22$. By time period 3000, on average across 100 simulations, $\frac{\#\{s \le 3000 : |p_s - z_s| \ge 0.10\}}{3000} = 0.13$ and $\frac{\#\{s \le 3000 : |p_s - z_s| < 0.025\}}{3000} = 0.45$.

2. However, if $E((\exp(w_t)) - 1 | w_t > 0)$ gets larger, the convergence band gets wider. To illustrate this, a uniform density of w_t is chosen, where $w_t \in [-.356, .356]$. Given this density, $E(w_t) = 0$ and $\text{Var}(w_t) = 0.1689813$. This compares with a variance of 0.0099497 for the density of w_t described in (i) when $\sigma = 0.1000$. The corresponding histogram for this larger variance is in Fig. 6.4b. Here the convergence is not as tight. By time period 3000, on average across 100 simulations, $\frac{\#\{s \le 3000 : |p_s - z_s| < 0.10\}}{3000} = 0.79$. This compares with 87% observed in Fig. 6.4a.

Appendix C

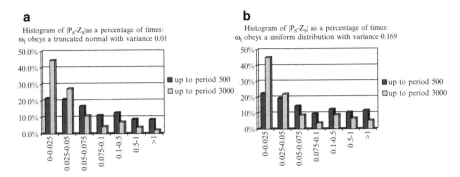

Fig. 6.4 Histogram of $|P_s - Z_s|$ as a percentage of times: (**a**) ω_t obeys a truncated normal with variance 0.01; (**b**) ω_t obeys a uniform distribution with variance 0.169

C.3 Convergence when the Probability of Predicting the Fundamental Value is Constrained to be Less than a Number Below 1

The fourth set of simulations is conducted under the assumption that for any given small positive η and η', $\Pr(\theta_1^t \in (0, \eta), \theta_2^t > \eta') > 0$, for all $t \geq 1$. That is, if for all traders the probability of predicting correctly the fundamental value is constrained to be positive but less than a number below 1; and if with a positive probability in each time period a trader, with an arbitrarily low probability of overpredicting the fundamental value, is allowed to enter the market, then convergence can still occur. To illustrate this, a set of 100 simulations is conducted, where the random shock ω_t has a truncated symmetric normal distribution with $\sigma = 0.10$ and $B = 0.356$ (like that specified in C.2(i)), and there is the constraint $\theta_2^t \leq 0.2$, for all buyers $t \geq 1$. θ_2^t is drawn according to a uniform distribution from $(0, 0.2]$. (θ_1^t, θ_3^t) are then drawn according to a uniform distribution from a set $\{(\theta_1, \theta_3) \in (0, 1 - \theta_2^t) \times (0, 1 - \theta_2^t), \theta_1^t + \theta_3^t = 1 - \theta_2^t\}$. This does allow for the entry of a trader with the probability of overpredicting (θ_1^t) the fundamental value (z_t) being arbitrarily close to zero. Here, as shown in Fig. 6.5, there is a sign of convergence. By time period 3000, on average across 100 simulations, $\frac{\#\{s \leq 3000: |p_s - z_s| < 0.10\}}{3000} = 0.57$, which compares with a value of 0.33 at time 500. Nevertheless, convergence is not as fast as in the simulations where no upper bound is placed on θ_2^t, for all $t \geq 1$.[16]

---

[16]For the simulations, as T grows, the computer (c.p.u.) time to complete the simulations grows in proportion to T^2. To conduct 100 simulations in a reasonable length of c.p.u. time, T was constrained to be 3000. However, for five simulations the time was extended to 5000. By time period 5000, on average across five simulations, $\frac{\#\{s \leq 5000: |p_s - z_s| < 0.10\}}{5000} = 0.64$. This shows further convergence.

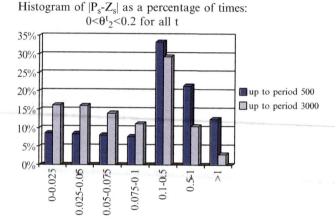

Fig. 6.5 Histogram of $|P_s - Z_s|$ as a percentage of times: $0 < \theta_2^t < 0.2$ for all t

References

Allen, B., and N.C. Yannelis. 2001. Differential information economies: An introduction. *Economic Theory* 18:263–273.
Barrow, J.H. 1992. *The Adapted Mind*. New York: Oxford Press.
Biais, B., and R. Shadur. 2000. "On the Survival of Irrational Traders: A Darwinian Approach", *European Economic Review* 44:469–490.
Billingsley, P. 1995. *Probability and Measure*. New York: John Wiley & Sons.
Blume, L., and D. Easley. 1992. "Evolution and Market Behavior", *Journal of Economic Theory* 58:9–40.
Bosch, A and S. Sunder. 2000. "Tracking the Invisible Hand: Convergence of Double Auctions to Competitive Equilibrium", *Computational Economics* 16(3):257–284.
Castro, L.I. de, Marialaura, P., and Yannelis, N. 2011. "A new perspective to rational expectations:maximin rational expectations equilibrium". Working paper, Department of Economics, University of Illinois at Urbana Champaign.
De Long, J.B., A. Shleifer, L. H. Summers and R. J. Waldmann. 1990. "Noise Trader Risk in Financial Markets". *Journal of Political Economy* 98:703–738.
Durrett, R. 1991. *Probability: Theory and Examples* Belmont, CA: Wadsworth & Brooks/Cole.
Figlewski, S. 1978. "Market 'Efficiency' in a Market with Heterogeneous Information". *Journal of Political Economy* 86(4):581–597.
Forsythe, R., Palfrey, T.R., and C. R. Plott. 1982. "Asset Valuation in an Experimental Market". *Econometrica* 50:537–567.
Friedman, M. 1953. *Essays in Positive Economics*. Chicago: University of Chicago Press.
Gnedenko, B.V. 1962. *The Theory of Probability*. New York, NY: Chelsea Publishing Company.
Gode, D.K., and S. Sunder. 1993. "Allocative Efficiency of Markets with Zero-Intelligence Traders: Market as a Partial Substitute for Individual Rationality". *Journal of Political Economy* 101(1):119–137.
Grossman, S. J. 1976. "On the Efficiency of Competitive Stock Markets where Traders Have Diverse Information". *Journal of Finance* 31:573–585.
Grossman, S.J. 1978. "Further Results on the Informational Efficiency of Competitive Stock Markets". *Journal of Economic Theory* 18:81–101.

References

Hellwig, M.F. 1980. "On the Aggregation of Information in Competitive Markets". *Journal of Economic Theory* 22:477–498.

Kahneman, D., Slovic, P., and A. Tversky (eds.). 1982. *Judgment under Uncertainty: Heuristics and Biases.* Cambridge: Cambridge University Press.

Lettau, M. 1997. "Explaining the Facts with Adaptive Agents: The Case of Mutual Fund Flows". *Journal of Economic Dynamics and Control* 21:1117–1147.

Luo, G. 1995. "Evolution and Market Competition". *Journal of Economic Theory* 67:223–250.

Luo, G. 1998. "Market Efficiency and Natural Selection in a Commodity Futures Market". *Review of Financial Studies* 11(3):647–674.

Luo, G. 2001. "Natural Selection and Market Efficiency in a Futures Market with Random Shocks. *Journal of Futures Markets* 21(6):489–516.

Olsen, R.A. 1998. "Behavioral finance and its Implications for Stock-price Volatility". *Financial Analysts Journal* 54(2):10–18.

Plott, C.R., and S. Sunder. 1982. "Efficiency of Experimental Security Markets with Insider Information: An Application of Rational-Expectations Models". *Journal of Political Economy* 90(4):663–698.

Radner, R. 1979. "Rational Expectations Equilibrium: Generic Existence and the Information Revealed by Prices". *Econometrica* 47:655–678.

Sandroni, A. 2000. "Do Markets Favor Agents Able to Make Accurate Predictions?" *Econometrica* 68:1303–1341.

Schneider, S.L., and L.L. Lopes. 1986. "Reflection in Preferences under Risk: Who and When may Sugget Why?" *Journal of Experimental Psychology: Human Perception and Performance* 12:535–548.

Sitkin, S.B., and A.L. Pablo. 1992. "Reconceptualizing the Determinants of Risk Behavior". *Academy of Management Review* 17(1):9–38.

Tversky, A., and D. Khaneman. 1974. "Judgment under Uncertainty: Heuristics and Biases". *Science* 185:1124–1131.

Wilson, R. 1979. "Auctions of Shares". *Quarterly Journal of Economics* 93(4):675–690.

Chapter 7
The Evolution of Money as a Medium of Exchange in a Primitive Economy[1]

This chapter uses an evolutionary approach to explain the origin of money as media of exchange in a primitive economy, where agents specialize in production for the purpose of trading for their own consumption goods. A general class of dynamics (consistent with Darwinian dynamics) is applied to the selection of strategies. The model produces many of the well-known results regarding the importance of intrinsic value and the proportion of agents specializing in different goods. In addition, the model also shows the importance of initial trading strategies and of the mutations of agents' strategies in selecting equilibria.

The chapter begins by discussing the framework of the model in Sect. 7.2. Section 7.3 describes how the strategies evolve over time and the selection of equilibria. Section 7.4 examines the role of the mutation hypothesis in selecting equilibria and Sect. 7.5 concludes the chapter.

> we can only come fully to understand the origin of money by learning to view the establishment of the social procedure, with which we are dealing, as the spontaneous outcome, the unpremeditated resultant, of particular, individual efforts of the members of a society, who have little by little worked their way to a discrimination of the different degrees of saleableness in commodities.   ......Karl Menger (1892)

7.1 Introduction

Although a lot of recent literature has addressed the existence of money, few papers [with the exception of Jones (1976), Oh (1989), Marimon et al. (1990), Wright (1995), and Renero (1998)] analytically address the dynamic selection process that leads to an equilibrium. In this chapter a model is constructed which uses an evolutionary process for explaining the emergence of media of exchange.

---

[1]This chapter is based on my article published in the *Journal of Economic Dynamics & Control* 23: 415–458, 1999.

Unlike agents in the papers of Jones (1976) and Oh (1989), this model does not have a selection mechanism where agents explicitly gather information or take account of the probabilities that a randomly encountered individual would wish to buy or sell a particular good. Strategies do not arise from rational agents maximizing expected utility (as in Kiyotaki and Wright (1989) and Renero (1998)) nor from the agents being artificially intelligent (using some global search algorithm to search in a space of possible decision rules, as in Marimon et al. (1990)). In addition, this model is distinct from that of Wright (1995) which places the rational agents of the Kiyotaki and Wright (1989) model in an evolutionary framework which endogenizes agent types. As Wright (1995, p. 205) suggests in his conclusions, "it may be more natural or interesting to apply the evolutionary approach to trading strategies rather than (or in addition to) the choice of (agent) types". This is the direction pursued in this chapter. Here an evolutionary model of trading strategies is proposed where agents behave with bounded rationality and follow very primitive rules of adaptation.[2] At the population level, these rules produce strategy dynamics, which are consistent with Darwinian dynamics.

Even though agents in this model are not very rational, with respect to the selection of media of exchange, the model produces many of the well-known results of Kiyotaki and Wright (1989) and Wright (1995) regarding the importance of intrinsic value and the proportion of agents specializing in different goods. In addition, the model also shows the importance of initial trading strategies and of the mutations of agents' strategies in selecting equilibria. Different initial points can lead the economy to different equilibria.[3] While varying the proportion of agents specializing in different goods tends to increase the number of stable equilibria, increasing the size of some of the mutation rates tends to narrow down the number of stable equilibria. Furthermore, for sufficiently large mutation rates, the fundamental equilibrium is the only equilibrium that can be selected, regardless of the initial trading strategies and the proportion of agents specializing in different goods.

In the late eighteenth century, Adam Smith (1776) advanced the idea that production specialization is the driving force for a medium of exchange to occur. Because of production specialization, each individual producer may not consume whatever he or she produces and will want to consume other producers' goods. To do this, trade would have to occur. Without a central market auctioneer, some producers may engage in direct trade for their consumption goods, while others would engage in indirect trade and hold the traded commodities for further trades at a later time for their consumption goods.

---

[2]The editor has drawn my attention to another related paper written recently by Sethi (1999) which analyzes the Kiyotaki–Wright model using an evolutionary game theoretic framework.

[3]Within the context of a dynamic programing model where the expected discounted utility is maximized by traders, Renero (1998) also finds that initial conditions matter; however, his conclusions, unlike those of this chapter, are that many of the conventional equilibria found in the literature (e.g., Kiyotaki and Wright (1989), Aiyagari and Wallace (1991)) are not stable.

7.1 Introduction

Menger (1892) provided an additional theory of "saleableness" to explain the origin of money. People's willingness to accept a certain commodity depends on beliefs about the same willingness on the part of other traders. Among the factors that limit commodities' saleableness, Menger included such intrinsic values of commodities as "the degree to which goods lend themselves to transport," and "the cost of storing them" (pp. 246–247). A critical element in Menger's discussion is seeing the evolution of money as a learning process that takes place over generations of individuals. As part of this process, he sees "practice and habit" (p. 249) and the imitation of successful traders contributing to the evolution of money. This view is later reinforced by Einzig (1966, p. 15): "primitive man is not a rationally calculating being...His progress toward the adoption of money...is very often unconscious." But "at a comparatively advanced stage...primitive communities (are) able...to imitate each other's currencies and to learn by the achievements and mistakes of their ancestors or neighbours."

To summarize the above, what matter in the evolution of money are the desire to acquire a consumption good produced by someone else, the commodities' intrinsic values (such as storability), extrinsic beliefs about the willingness on the part of other traders to accept certain commodities, and the evolutionary process of imitating successful traders. The following model reflects these views by extending the model of Kiyotaki and Wright (1989) to include dynamic processes of learning from an evolutionary perspective. All agents begin with given initial strategies. These initial trading strategies may be based on the agents' extrinsic beliefs and may have their origins in social customs, and most probably do not arise from any optimal planning. In a sense, agents are born with these strategies. Through time agents tend to imitate strategies which are more successful at the margin than other strategies. In other words, "there is no better method of enlightening anyone about his economic interests than that he perceive the economic success of those who use the right means to secure their own" (Menger 1892, p. 249). As a result of this natural imitation of successful strategies, uniform strategies may gradually evolve on a population basis. In turn, this produces a particular set of media of exchange. Nevertheless, a key contribution of the evolutionary perspective is that it recognizes the limited ability of agents to optimally respond to their environment. Agents through simple imitation are myopic: they may not react by immediately imitating successful strategies and sometimes they may even play an arbitrary strategy regardless of its suitability.

Similar to the conclusions of Kiyotaki and Wright (1989), this chapter shows that the intrinsic value of a commodity (here characterized by storability) is a critical determinant of the media of exchange. However, when the discussion moves away from Kiyotaki and Wright (1989) stationary environment of equal proportions of rational agents, and instead applies a class of dynamics consistent with Darwinian dynamics to the selection of strategies, this chapter provides some additional insights. In addition to intrinsic values, the other principle ideas that matter in determining media of exchange are the proportion of agents specializing in different products (which determines the probability of meeting and ultimately affects the saleableness of commodities)(also noted by Wright (1995)), agents' initial trading strategies, and the probability of agents playing arbitrary strategies. As a result, in addition to the equilibria found in Kiyotaki and Wright (1989), and Wright (1995), more equilibria are found. Moreover, within the context of the evolutionary approach of this chapter, a method is provided for computing the basins of attraction for various equilibria (see Theorem 1 and Lemmas 1 and 2 of Appendix A). It is worth noting that these basins of attraction can be computed for a very general class of dynamics without knowledge of the specific functional form of the dynamic process.

The evolutionary model can produce many equilibria which correspond to one medium of exchange, two media of exchange, or three media of exchange.[4] While very small mutation rates do not disrupt any of the asymptotically stable equilibria, with sufficiently large mutation rates, the number of the asymptotically stable equilibria can be reduced to one unique equilibrium – the fundamental equilibrium, where the most storable good serves as the medium of exchange. In other words, if mutation rates are sufficiently large that each agent, regardless of his or her relative success in consuming, is more likely to switch to trading for the more storable good with someone who does not have the agent's consumption good, then the economy converges to the fundamental equilibrium, This is true regardless of where the economy starts (i.e., where the initial trading strategies are) and regardless of the proportion of agents specializing in different goods.

7.2 Framework

7.2.1 Physical Environment

There are three types of infinitely-lived agents in the economy. Agents of type i consume good i and produce good $i + 1$ (modulo 3).[5] (Fiat money can also serve as a medium of exchange in this model; but, for simplicity of analysis, this chapter focuses on commodity money.) There is a continuum of agents of type i ($i = 1, 2, 3$). The proportion of agents of type i in the economy is denoted by P_i, where $P_1 + P_2 + P_3 = 1$. It is assumed that P_i is fixed over time. Time is indexed by day t, $t = 0, 1, 2, \ldots$. At the beginning of each day, each agent produces one unit of his or her production good for the purpose of trade. All goods perish at the end of each day. If, by the end of the day, an agent has acquired his or her consumption good, consumption occurs at the end of the day. Within each day there are two

---

[4]The coexistence of more than one commodity serving as a medium of exchange is well documented (e.g., cattle, goats, and cloth of the Wabena of Tanganyika Territory in Africa in the early twentieth century; tobacco and sugar in seventeenth century North America; and wadmal (spun from the fleece of the sheep) and fish in fifteenth century Iceland (Quiggin 1949).

[5]Just as Aiyagari and Wallace (1991) generalize the Kiyotaki–Wright model to N goods, the following model can be generalized to N commodities and N agents. Further discussion of this generalization is provided later.

7.2 Framework

trading sessions: the morning trading session and the afternoon trading session. In each trading session, all agents are randomly matched in pairs and trade bilaterally. At the end of each day, each agent decides on his or her trading strategy for the following day. These decisions are based on information regarding prior success of other agents of the same type and this information can be obtained from random pairwise matching of agents of the same type at the end of each day.[6]

7.2.2 The Trading Sessions

Trade only occurs if both agents are willing to trade. Trade takes the form of a one-to-one swap. Clearly, since in this framework no two agents produce goods which are mutually acceptable consumption goods for each other, in the morning session there is a lack of double coincidence of wants in this bilateral trading process. In this framework, it is assumed that each agent only trades if he or she can potentially benefit from trade. Therefore, in the afternoon of each day an agent trades only for his or her own consumption good.[7] It is assumed that all agents, including agents successful in the morning, participate in the afternoon. However, in the afternoon, if any agent happens to meet an agent who was successful in acquiring his or her consumption good in the morning, no trade occurs.[8]

Since all agents trade for only their own consumption goods in the afternoon trading session, based on their trading strategies used in the morning trading session, each type of agent is further classified. Agents of type i, where $i = 1, 2, 3$, consist of $i(1)$ and $i(2)$ subtype agents where $i(1)$ is the agent subtype who trades only for his or her own consumption in the morning and $i(2)$ is the agent subtype who trades for any good in the morning trading session. There is a continuum of agents of subtype $i(1)$ and of agents of subtype $i(2)$. For example, if agent $3(1)$ meets agent

---

[6]The model is basically that of Kiyotaki and Wright (1989) with two differences: all goods are perishable and trade occurs over the two trading sessions (the morning and afternoon). The above assumptions considerably reduce the complexity of calculating the distribution of agents' holdings over time and thus the computation of equilibria.

[7]This assumption prevents trade from occurring in the afternoon session when only one party wants to trade. This assumption can be justified if any trade incurs an arbitrarily small transaction cost, this paper's results would remain basically unchanged. Nevertheless, it is interesting to consider an alternative model where the framework remains the same, but traders make trades in the afternoon as long as one party wants to trade. In this case, it is easy to show that, in terms of the notation of the latter part of this section, $\frac{P^t_{i(2)}(s)}{\bar{P}^t_{i(2)}} = \frac{P^t_{i(1)}(s)}{\bar{P}^t_{i(1)}}$ for all t, and the economy converges to the fundamental equilibrium where the most storable good is the unique medium of exchange.

[8]This assumption is reflected in the following probability calculations. The framework could be altered by not allowing successful morning traders to participate in the afternoon. While the essence of the results would remain the same, the following probability calculations would have to be slightly altered.

Table 7.1 Proportions of agent-pairs in the morning session

Paired agents	Proportion of paired agents	Trade	Notes
$i(1), i(1)$	$\left(P_i P^t_{i(1)}\right)^2$	No	
$i(1), i(2)$	$2(P_i)^2 P^t_{i(1)} P^t_{i(2)}$	No	
$i(1), (i+1)(1)$	$2 P_i P_{i+1} P^t_{i(1)} P^t_{(i+1)(1)}$	No	
$i(1), (i+1)(2)$	$2 P_i P_{i+1} P^t_{i(1)} P^t_{(i+1)(2)}$	No	
$i(1), (i-1)(1)$	$2 P_i P_{i-1} P^t_{i(1)} P^t_{(i-1)(1)}$	No	
$i(1), (i-1)(2)$	$2 P_i P_{i-1} P^t_{i(1)} P^t_{(i-1)(2)}$	Yes	$(i-1)(2)[i+1]^*$
$i(2), i(2)$	$(P_i)^2 P^t_{i(2)} P^t_{i(2)}$	No	
$i(2), (i+1)(1)$	$2 P_i P_{i+1} P^t_{i(2)} P^t_{(i+1)(1)}$	Yes	$i(2)[i-1]$
$i(2), (i+1)(2)$	$2 P_i P_{i+1} P^t_{i(2)} P^t_{(i+1)(2)}$	Yes	$i(2)[i-1]$
$i(2), (i-1)(1)$	$2 P_i P_{i-1} P^t_{i(2)} P^t_{(i-1)(1)}$	No	
$i(2), (i-1)(2)$	$2 P_i P_{i-1} P^t_{i(2)} P^t_{(i-1)(2)}$	Yes	$(i-1)(2)[i+1]$
$(i+1)(1), (i+1)(1)$	$(P_{i+1})^2 P^t_{(i+1)(1)} P^t_{(i+1)(1)}$	No	
$(i+1)(1), (i+1)(2)$	$2(P_{i+1})^2 P^t_{(i+1)(1)} P^t_{(i+1)(2)}$	No	
$(i+1)(1), (i-1)(1)$	$2 P_{i+1} P_{i-1} P^t_{(i+1)(1)} P^t_{(i-1)(1)}$	No	
$(i+1)(1), (i-1)(2)$	$2 P_{i+1} P_{i-1} P^t_{(i+1)(1)} P^t_{(i-1)(2)}$	No	
$(i+1)(2), (i+1)(2)$	$(P_{i+1})^2 P^t_{(i+1)(2)} P^t_{(i+1)(2)}$	No	
$(i+1)(2), (i-1)(1)$	$2 P_{i+1} P_{i-1} P^t_{(i+1)(2)} P^t_{(i-1)(1)}$	Yes	$(i+1)(2)[i]$
$(i+1)(2), (i-1)(2)$	$2 P_{i+1} P_{i-1} P^t_{(i+1)(2)} P^t_{(i-1)(2)}$	Yes	$(i+1)(2)[i]$
$(i-1)(1), (i-1)(1)$	$(P_{i-1})^2 P^t_{(i-1)(1)} P^t_{(i-1)(1)}$	No	
$(i-1)(1), (i-1)(2)$	$2(P_{i-1})^2 P^t_{(i-1)(1)} P^t_{(i-1)(2)}$	No	
$(i-1)(2), (i-1)(2)$	$(P_{i-1})^2 P^t_{(i-1)(2)} P^t_{(i-1)(2)}$	No	
	Sum = 1		

*$(i-1)(2)[i+1]$ indicates that agent $(i-1)(2)$ is holding good $i+1$ as a result of the morning session

2(2) in the morning, trade will take place since agent 3(1) wishes to exchange good 1 for good 3 with agent 2(2), who wishes to give agent 3(1) good 3 for good 1; and then agent 2(2) carries good 1 to the afternoon hoping to meet an agent 1 who was unable to trade in the morning trading session. The proportions of agents of type i at time t who are $i(1)$ and $i(2)$ are denoted as $P^t_{i(1)}$ and $P^t_{i(2)}$, respectively. Therefore, $P^t_{i(1)} + P^t_{i(2)} = 1$. This further implies that the proportions of agents at time t who are $i(1)$ and $i(2)$ are equal to $P_i P^t_{i(1)}$ and $P_i P^t_{i(2)}$, respectively.

In the morning trading session, all agents are matched randomly in pairs. In day t, for $i = 1, 2, 3$ and $k = 1, 2$, the proportion of agent pairs corresponding to agent $i(k)$ matching with another agent $i(k)$ is $(P_i)^2 (P^t_{i(k)})^2 = (\overline{P}^t_{i(k)})^2$, where $\overline{P}^t_{i(k)} = P_i P^t_{i(k)}$. The proportion of agent pairs in day t corresponding to agent $i(k)$ matching with agent $i'(k')$, where $i \neq i'$ and $k \neq k'$, is $2\overline{P}^t_{i(k)} \overline{P}^t_{i'(k')}$ for $i, i' = 1, 2, 3$ and $k, k' = 1, 2$. All the proportions of agent pairs sum to 1. See Table 7.1 for more detail.

7.2 Framework

Therefore, the proportion of the total population which consists of $i(2)$ subtype agents who are successful in acquiring their own consumption goods in the morning of day t is

$$\overline{P}^t_{i(2)} \overline{P}^t_{(i-1)(2)}. \tag{7.1}$$

The proportion of the population, which contains $i(2)$ subtype agents who are successful in acquiring their own consumption goods in the afternoon of day t, consists of the following two cases:

Case 1: The proportion of the total population which consists of untraded $i(2)$ agents from the morning session who meet, in the afternoon session, traded $(i+1)(2)$ agents from the morning session holding good i, is

$$\left(\overline{P}^t_{i(2)} \overline{P}^t_{i(1)} + \overline{P}^t_{i(2)} \overline{P}^t_{i(2)} + \overline{P}^t_{i(2)} \overline{P}^t_{(i-1)(1)}\right)\left(\overline{P}^t_{(i-1)(1)} \overline{P}^t_{(i+1)(2)} + \overline{P}^t_{(i-1)(2)} \overline{P}^t_{(i+1)(2)}\right)$$

$$= \left(P_i \overline{P}^t_{i(2)} + \overline{P}^t_{i(2)} \overline{P}^t_{(i-1)(1)}\right) P_{i-1} \overline{P}^t_{(i+1)(2)}.$$

Case 2: The proportion of the total population which consists of traded $i(2)$ agents from the morning session who meet, in the afternoon trading session, untraded $i-1$ agents from the morning session, is

$$\left(\overline{P}^t_{i(2)} \overline{P}^t_{(i+1)(1)} + \overline{P}^t_{i(2)} \overline{P}^t_{(i+1)(2)}\right)\left(\overline{P}^t_{i(1)} \overline{P}^t_{(i-1)(1)} + \overline{P}^t_{i(2)} \overline{P}^t_{(i-1)(1)} + \left(\overline{P}^t_{(i-1)(1)}\right)^2\right.$$

$$\left. + 2\overline{P}^t_{(i-1)(1)} \overline{P}^t_{(i-1)(2)} + \left(\overline{P}^t_{(i-1)(2)}\right)^2 + \overline{P}^t_{(i-1)(2)} \overline{P}^t_{(i+1)(1)} + \overline{P}^t_{(i-1)(1)} \overline{P}^t_{(i+1)(1)}\right)$$

$$= P_{i+1} \overline{P}^t_{i(2)} \left(P_i \overline{P}^t_{(i-1)(1)} + P_{i-1} \overline{P}^t_{(i+1)(1)} + (P_{i-1})^2\right).$$

Therefore, the proportion of the total population which consists of $i(2)$ subtype agents who are successful in acquiring their own consumption goods in the afternoon session of day t is

$$\left(P_i \overline{P}^t_{i(2)} + \overline{P}^t_{i(2)} \overline{P}^t_{(i-1)(1)}\right) P_{i-1} \overline{P}^t_{(i+1)(2)} + P_{i+1} \overline{P}^t_{i(2)}$$

$$\times \left(P_i \overline{P}^t_{(i-1)(1)} + P_{i-1} \overline{P}^t_{(i+1)(1)} + (P_{i-1})^2\right). \tag{7.2}$$

Thus, adding expressions (7.1) and (7.2) indicates that the proportion of the total population which is made up of $i(2)$ subtype agents who are successful in acquiring their own consumption goods by the end of day t, denoted by $P^t_{i(2)}(s)$, is

$$P^t_{i(2)}(s) = \overline{P}^t_{i(2)} \overline{P}^t_{(i-1)(2)} + \left(P_i \overline{P}^t_{i(2)} + \overline{P}^t_{i(2)} \overline{P}^t_{(i-1)(1)}\right) P_{i-1} \overline{P}^t_{(i+1)(2)}$$

$$+ P_{i+1} \overline{P}^t_{i(2)} \left(P_i \overline{P}^t_{(i-1)(1)} + P_{i-1} \overline{P}^t_{(i+1)(1)} + (P_{i-1})^2\right). \tag{7.3}$$

Similarly, the proportion of the total population which is made up of $i(1)$ subtype agents who are successful in acquiring their own consumption goods in the morning session of day t is

$$\overline{P}^t_{i(1)} \overline{P}^t_{(i-1)(2)}. \tag{7.4}$$

The proportion of the total population which contains $i(1)$ subtype agents who are successful in acquiring their own consumption goods in the afternoon session of day t is the proportion of the total population which contains untraded $i(1)$ agents from the morning session who meet, in the afternoon session, traded $(i+1)(2)$ agents from the morning session holding good i. That is,

$$\left(\left(\overline{P}^t_{i(1)}\right)^2 + \overline{P}^t_{i(1)} \overline{P}^t_{i(2)} + \overline{P}^t_{i(1)} \overline{P}^t_{(i-1)(1)} + \overline{P}^t_{i(1)} \overline{P}^t_{(i+1)(1)} + \overline{P}^t_{i(1)} \overline{P}^t_{(i+1)(2)} \right)$$
$$\times \left(P_{i-1} \overline{P}^t_{(i+1)(2)} \right) = \left(\left(\overline{P}^t_{i(1)}\right)^2 + \overline{P}^t_{i(1)} \overline{P}^t_{i(2)} + \overline{P}^t_{i(1)} \overline{P}^t_{(i-1)(1)} + \overline{P}^t_{i(1)} P_{i+1} \right)$$
$$\times P_{i-1} \overline{P}^t_{(i+1)(2)}. \tag{7.5}$$

Therefore, the proportion of the total population which consists of $i(1)$ subtype agents who are successful in acquiring their own consumption goods by the end of day t, denoted by $P^t_{i(1)}(s)$, is the summation of (7.4) and (7.5). That is,

$$P^t_{i(1)}(s) = \overline{P}^t_{i(1)} \overline{P}^t_{(i-1)(2)} + \left(P_i \overline{P}^t_{i(1)} + \overline{P}^t_{i(1)} \overline{P}^t_{(i-1)(1)} + \overline{P}^t_{i(1)} P_{i+1} \right) P_{i-1} \overline{P}^t_{(i+1)(2)}. \tag{7.6}$$

Therefore, the probability that agent $i(k)$ is successful in acquiring his or her own consumption good in day t is $\frac{P^t_{i(k)}(s)}{\overline{P}^t_{i(k)}}$, for $i = 1, 2, 3$ and $k = 1, 2$.

Each agent, whether successful or unsuccessful in acquiring his or her consumption good at the end of day t, is allowed to continue to produce one unit of his or her production good for trade in day $t + 1$.

The above has described the setting for the trading which takes place within a day and summarized the success of agents at the end of each day. The purpose of the next two sections is to describe how trading strategies may evolve from day to day.

7.3 Evolution of Strategies

There are many possible learning or imitation micro stories regarding agents' adaptive behavior from day to day. In this chapter, the intention is to concentrate on fairly primitive rules of adaptation. Very little sophistication is presumed on the part of agents. Section 7.3.1 provides an example based on micro behavior of imitation by agents. Here, through random sampling from the same population, imitation of successful agents occurs. There are other variants of imitation, some of which are driven by dissatisfaction (e.g., Bjornerstedt and Weibull (1996)) and some of which take the form of imitating only successful agents (Weibull 1995). This motivates a more general class of dynamics described in Sect. 7.3.2. Under this general class of dynamics, the equilibria selection results are described in Sect. 7.3.3.

7.3.1 Example 1: Random Sampling Among the Same Population

This example describes a very basic type of imitation on the part of agents. Suppose, at the end of time period t ($t \geq 0$), each agent of each population is allowed to randomly meet another agent in the same population. If this agent meets a successful agent of another subtype in the same population he or she will use this successful agent's strategy in day $t + 1$ with some probability; otherwise, this agent will play the same strategy in day $t + 1$ as in day t. Specifically, consider agent $i(k)$, where $i = 1, 2, 3$ and $k = 1, 2$. At the end of day t agent $i(k)$ randomly meets an i-type agent in the population i. If this i-type agent is a successful agent of another subtype $i(k')$, where $k' \neq k$, then agent $i(k)$ imitates and plays the strategy of agent $i(k')$ with probability $\lambda_{i(k)}$, where $\lambda_{i(k)} \in [0, 1]$, in day $t + 1$; otherwise agent $i(k)$ will play the same strategy in day $t + 1$. The size of $\lambda_{i(k)}$ is positively correlated with the willingness of agent $i(k)$ to switch from strategy $i(k)$ to $i(k')$. This willingness could be based on many factors such as agents' abilities to change, or their perceptions about the characteristics of the commodities. In this chapter, the characteristic of interest is the storability of commodities carried from the morning session to the afternoon session.[9]

---

[9]Notice that $\lambda_{i(k)}$ is a model parameter and reflects relative storability among commodities. More precisely, the $\lambda_{i(k)}$ is a function of relative storability and does not depend on time. The justification for this is as follows. Since the behavior of agents $i(1)$ and $i(2)$ differs only with respect to meeting agent type $i + 1$ in the morning and since in the afternoon both subtypes of agents behave the same in that they only trade for their own consumption goods, it follows that an alternative way of viewing agents' subtypes in the morning of each day is to see agent i as deciding on whether, in the event of meeting agent $i + 1$ in the morning (which occurs with a constant probability of P_{i+1}), he or she will trade with agent $i + 1$ (i.e., choose strategy i(2)) or will not trade with agent $i + 1$ (i.e., choose strategy i(1)). Suppose such factors as inertia and portability, that may influence $\lambda_{i(k)}$, are set aside and $\lambda_{i(k)}$ is hypothesized to be only a function of storability. Since the expected storage costs, conditional on not meeting agent $i + 1$, incurred by agents i(1) and i(2) are identical, what only matters in determining the $\lambda_{i(k)}$ (the probability of switching strategies) is the relative storage costs incurred as a result of meeting $i + 1$. Suppose good i costs c_i to store from morning to afternoon. In the event of meeting agent $i + 1$, agent $i(1)$ would not trade and would only incur a storage cost of c_{i+1} in storing good $i + 1$ until the afternoon. Agent $i(2)$ would trade with $i + 1$ and would incur a storage cost of c_{i-1} until the afternoon. Therefore, $\lambda_{i(k)}$, the probability of agent

Therefore, the dynamic equations of motion describing the above process are as follows:

$$P_{i(2)}^{t+1} = P_{i(2)}^{t} + P_{i(1)}^{t}\lambda_{i(1)}\frac{P_{i(2)}^{t}(s)}{P_i} - P_{i(2)}^{t}\lambda_{i(2)}\frac{P_{i(1)}^{t}(s)}{P_i}, \quad \text{for } i = 1, 2, 3, \quad (7.7)$$

where $P_{i(1)}^{t}\lambda_{i(1)}\frac{P_{i(2)}^{t}(s)}{P_i}$ is the proportion of i agents flowing from the $i(1)$ subpopulation to the $i(2)$ subpopulation, and $P_{i(2)}^{t}\lambda_{i(2)}\frac{P_{i(1)}^{t}(s)}{P_i}$ is the proportion of i agents flowing from the $i(2)$ subpopulation to the $i(1)$ subpopulation. $P_{i(2)}^{t}(s)$ and $P_{i(1)}^{t}(s)$ are defined in (7.3) and (7.6), respectively.

Notice that agent $I(2)$ possibly engages in indirect trade for good $i-1$ (where $i-1$ is not the consumption good of agent $i(2)$) in the morning and carries commodity $i-1$ to the afternoon. If commodity $i-1$ is perceived by agent i to be less (more) storable relative to good $i+1$, $\lambda_{i(2)}$ will be relatively big (small) in comparison to $\lambda_{i(1)}$. For example, if commodity 1 is the most storable good then the probability of agent $2(1)$ imitating the strategy of the successful agent $2(2)$ is higher than the probability of agent $2(2)$ imitating the strategy of the successful agent $2(1)$. That is, $\lambda_{2(1)} > \lambda_{2(2)}$.

The above example illustrates an evolution of strategies which moves in the direction of strategies where agents have the highest probability of being successful in acquiring their own consumption goods. This motivates the following general class of dynamics.

7.3.2 The General Class of Dynamics

Definition 7.1. Define a class of dynamics F for this economy which can be described by the system of equations of motion

$$P_{i(2)}^{t+1} - P_{i(2)}^{t} = f_i\left(P_{1(2)}^{t}, P_{2(2)}^{t}, P_{3(2)}^{t}; \lambda\right) \quad \text{for } i = 1, 2, 3,$$

where $\lambda = (\lambda_{1(2)}, \lambda_{1(1)}, \lambda_{2(2)}, \lambda_{2(1)}, \lambda_{3(2)}, \lambda_{3(1)})$, $f_i(\cdot) : [0,1]^3 \to [-1,1]$, and $f_i(\cdot)$ has the following properties:

(1) $f_i\left(P_{1(2)}^{t}, P_{2(2)}^{t}, P_{3(2)}^{t}; \lambda\right)$ is continuous in the first three arguments,
(2) $f_i\left(P_{1(2)}^{t}, P_{2(2)}^{t}, P_{3(2)}^{t}; \lambda\right) = 0$ for $P_{i(2)}^{t} \in \{0, 1\}$, $i = 1, 2, 3$, and
(3) $f_i\left(P_{1(2)}^{t}, P_{2(2)}^{t}, P_{3(2)}^{t}; \lambda\right) > 0$ if and only if $\frac{P_{i(2)}^{t}(s)}{\lambda_{i(2)}\overline{P}_{i(2)}^{t}} > \frac{P_{i(1)}^{t}(s)}{\lambda_{i(1)}\overline{P}_{i(1)}^{t}}$ for $P_{i(2)}^{t} \in (0, 1)$.

---

i switching from strategy k to k' ($k \neq k'$), is a parameter which is an increasing function of $(-1)^k(c_{i-1} - c_{i+1})$.

7.3 Evolution of Strategies

In fact, in Example 1, $f_i\left(P^t_{1(2)}, P^t_{2(2)}, P^t_{3(2)}; \lambda\right) = P^t_{i(1)}\lambda_{i(1)}\frac{P^t_{i(2)}(s)}{P_i} - P^t_{i(2)}\lambda_{i(2)}\frac{P^t_{i(1)}(s)}{P_i}$. It is easy to show that each f_i in the example satisfies the three properties outlined in Definition 1. Moreover, the above general class of dynamics encompasses replicator dynamics (Taylor and Jonker 1978) in addition to many types of selection dynamics coming from adaptation by myopic imitation (see Weibull (1995) for a survey of such models). For more detail on how some of these other dynamics relate to this money framework and to this general class of dynamics, see Luo (1995).[10]

In the above dynamics F, property (2) simply says that the above difference equations have fixed points (or steady states), which correspond to all combinations of pure strategies. (With a slight alteration to the above dynamics F, there may be mixed strategies that are also equilibria, but for the purpose of illustrating the relevance of the evolutionary approach in determining media of exchange the focus will be on the pure strategy steady states.[11]) Property (3) describes the fact that the fitter strategies should increase relative to the less fit strategies. In a given time period, the fitter strategy in a population is the strategy which yields the higher discounted percentage (discounted by the storability parameter) of agents successful in acquiring their own consumption goods. For example, within population i, if the discounted percentage of those $i(2)$ agents who play successfully (in acquiring their own consumption goods by the end of the day) is higher than the discounted percentage of those $i(1)$ agents who play successfully, strategy $i(2)$ is considered to be the fittest of the two strategies; and, in the next time period, the fraction of i agents who play strategy $i(2)$ should increase. In other words, "strategies that are 'good' replies to the distribution of actions chosen by the current population" are "played by a larger fraction of the population in the next period." (Mailath 1992, p. 259). This essentially is the underlying idea of Darwinian dynamics.

---

[10]If, instead, an alternative dynamic, the best reply dynamic (see Kandori et al. (1993)) is applied to the selection of strategies, then not all combinations of pure strategies would be steady states. However, all of the asymptotically stable equilibria in this paper are the same asymptotically stable equilibria under the best reply dynamic. Furthermore, the open balls characterized in all propositions of this paper would also support the respective asymptotically stable equilibria under the best reply dynamic. Property (i), as outlined in the definition of the basin of attraction in Theorem 1 of Appendix A, indicates that for all points in the basin of attraction, the strategy corresponding to the respective asymptotically stable equilibrium is the strategy with the higher relative payoff. But this precisely describes a basin of attraction for the corresponding asymptotically stable equilibrium of the best reply dynamic model (since in the best reply dynamic model players play the strategy with the higher relative payoff).

[11]I have also explored an extension of the model which allows for mixed strategy equilibria. Definition 1 would have to be altered slightly. In addition to properties (1), (2), and (3), an additional property is added: $f_i\left(P^t_{1(2)}, P^t_{2(2)}, P^t_{3(2)}; \lambda\right) = 0$ if $\frac{P^t_{i(2)}(s)}{\lambda_{i(2)}\overline{P}^t_{i(2)}} = \frac{P^t_{i(1)}(s)}{\lambda_{i(1)}\overline{P}^t_{i(1)}}$ for $P^t_{i(2)} \in (0,1)$, and for $i = 1, 2, 3$. Mixed strategy equilibria only exist under specific restrictions on the parameters. For example, the equilibrium $(x, 1, 0)$ for $0 < x < 1$ identified by Kehoe et al. (1993) exists only if $2(P_1 + P_3) = \frac{\lambda_{1(2)}}{\lambda_{1(1)}}$. For this reason, this paper focuses only on pure strategy equilibria.

The parameter vector (P_1, P_2, P_3) characterizes the distribution of agent types specializing in different production-consumption activities and is also the probability distribution of each agent meeting each population; and the parameter vector $(\lambda_{1(2)}, \lambda_{1(1)}, \lambda_{2(2)}, \lambda_{2(1)}, \lambda_{3(2)}, \lambda_{3(1)})$ characterizes the relative storability of commodities perceived by all agents. *Define the parameter vector of the economy as* $(P_1, P_2, P_3; \lambda_{1(2)}, \lambda_{1(1)}, \lambda_{2(2)}, \lambda_{2(1)}, \lambda_{3(2)}, \lambda_{3(1)})$. *For a given parameter vector of the economy, the state of the economy at time t is defined by an ordered triple* $\left(P^t_{1(2)}, P^t_{2(2)}, P^t_{3(2)}\right)$, *where* $\left(P^t_{1(2)}, P^t_{2(2)}, P^t_{3(2)}\right) \in \{ (a,b,c) : a \in [0,1], b \in [0,1], c \in [0,1]\}$. *An equilibrium of the economy is defined to be a fixed point (or a steady state) under the dynamics F.*

As noted, in the dynamics F, all pure strategy vectors $(1,0,0)$, $(0,1,0)$, $(0,0,1)$, $(1,1,0)$, $(0,1,1)$, $(1,0,1)$, $(1,1,1)$, and $(0,0,0)$ constitute equilibria. These are the equilibria of concern in this chapter. For a fixed point (k_1, k_2, k_3), if $k_i = 1$ for some $i = 1,2,3$, then commodity $i-1$ is a medium of exchange. In other words agent i trades for any good in the morning and trades only for his or her own consumption good in the afternoon. If $k_i = 0$ for some $i = 1,2,3$, then agent i only trades for his or her consumption good in both trading sessions.

Among all these equilibria, which equilibrium can be selected under dynamics F in the long run needs to be addressed. This motivates the following definition.

For a given parameter vector of the economy, if there exists an open ball containing an equilibrium point such that, for any initial point ($P^0_{1(2)}, P^0_{2(2)}, P^0_{3(2)}$) in this open ball, the state of the economy converges to this equilibrium under the dynamics F, then this equilibrium is said to be supported by this open ball or the initial points in this ball. Such an equilibrium is asymptotically stable (see Luenberger (1979) for further discussion).

The initial trading strategies can be interpreted as the initial extrinsic beliefs. This initial extrinsic beliefs may have no rational basis and may only be due to some inherent social traditions. The perceived relative storability of commodities by different types of agents, as represented by $\lambda_{i(k)}$ need not reflect the actual relative storability of commodities. However, as long as all agents perceive the relative storability of commodities in the same way, there are three possible models which classify the relative storability of commodities relative to the agent types. Everything else is simply a relabeling. The first model coincides with all agents perceiving good 1 as the most storable good, good 3 as the least storable good, and good 2 as less storable than good 1, but more storable than good 3. This is represented by: $\lambda_{1(2)} > \lambda_{1(1)}$, $\lambda_{2(1)} > \lambda_{2(2)}$, $\lambda_{3(2)} > \lambda_{3(1)}$. The second model coincides with all goods perceived as being equally storable: $\lambda_{1(1)} = \lambda_{1(2)}$, $\lambda_{2(1)} = \lambda_{2(2)}$, $\lambda_{3(1)} = \lambda_{3(2)}$. The third model coincides with all agents perceiving good 1 as the most storable good, good 2 as the least storable good, and good 3 as less storable than good 1, but more storable than good 2. This is represented by $\lambda_{1(1)} > \lambda_{1(2)}$, $\lambda_{2(1)} > \lambda_{2(2)}$, $\lambda_{3(2)} > \lambda_{3(1)}$. The first and third model are analogous to Kiyotaki and Wright's (1989) Models A and B, respectively.

To facilitate comparisons with Kiyotaki and Wright (1989) and other similar papers, it is appropriate to distinguish between a fundamental and a speculative equilibrium. The storage cost is the intrinsic value of the commodity and it is "fundamental." If agents only look at the "fundamentals" – the storability; they will always trade in the morning for a more storable good relative to a less storable good, unless the latter good is his or her own consumption good. *If, in an equilibrium, everyone trades in the morning according to these fundamentals, the equilibrium is referred to as fundamental. If, in an equilibrium, some agents are trading a more storable good for a less storable good, not because they wish to consume it, but because they believe that they can use the less storable good to trade for their own consumption goods in the afternoon, the equilibrium is referred to as speculative.* In the first storability model, the fundamental equilibrium is the one where the most storable good 1 serves as a unique medium of exchange; and in the third storability model, the fundamental equilibrium is the one where the two most storable goods (3 and 1) serve as media of exchange. Except the equilibrium (0,0,0), where no medium of exchange is required, in each of the storability models, all the remaining equilibria are speculative.

7.3.3 Equilibria Selection

As just noted, for a given parameter vector of the economy, whether an equilibrium is asymptotically stable, depends on whether or not there exists an open ball containing this equilibrium such that for any distribution of initial trading strategies in the open ball, the state of economy converges to this equilibrium under dynamics F. There are many ways of illustrating this dependency. One way, which makes it easier for comparison with related literature, is to classify the economy on the basis of the three storability models and to make a further subclassification which distinguishes between economies with equal proportions of agent types (i.e., assumption of Kiyotaki and Wright's (1989) $P_1 = P_2 = P_3$) and economies with unequal proportions of agent types (i.e., not all P_1, P_2, and P_3 are equal). For the purpose of brevity, the third storability model where good 1 is the most storable good and good 2 is the least storable good will not be discussed in this chapter (see Luo (1995) for such discussion).

In the first subsection below, the discussion focuses on the first storability model where good 1 is the most storable good and good 3 is the least storable good. The second subsection below examines the second storability model where no differences in the storability of commodities are assumed. Each of two subsections focuses on two propositions, one corresponding to economies with equal proportions of agent types and the other to economies with unequal proportions of agent types. Each of the propositions identifies asymptotically stable equilibria and a corresponding set of possible starting points which leads the economy to converge to these respective equilibria under some parameter vectors of the economy. Where it is possible, equilibria which are not asymptotically stable are also identified.

7.3.3.1 Unequal Storability Among Commodities

In this section, it is assumed that good 1 costs least to store, and good 3 costs most to store, and the storage cost of good 2 is between those of goods 1 and 3. This is referred to as the first storability model, characterized by $\lambda_{1(2)} > \lambda_{1(1)}$, $\lambda_{2(1)} > \lambda_{2(2)}$, and $\lambda_{3(2)} > \lambda_{3(1)}$. This model is analogous to Model A in Kiyotaki and Wright (1989). Kiyotaki and Wright (1989) finds that both the fundamental equilibrium and the speculative equilibrium exist under different restrictions on the relative storage costs, the size of the discount factor and the size of the net utility from consumption and production. This is done within a stationary environment where representative and rational agents are assumed and the proportions of agent types are equal.

Within this section, the intention is to explore in the evolutionary model the implications of relaxing the assumption of equal proportions of agent types to include unequal proportions of agent types. This section begins by examining this model in the case of equal proportions of agent types. Proposition 7.1 shows that in this model, under equal proportions of agent types, the fundamental equilibrium $(0, 1, 0)$, where the most storable good is the unique medium of exchange, can be supported by a set of initial trading strategies for some parameter values of the economy; and also, the speculative equilibrium $(1, 1, 0)$, where the least storable and the most storable goods serve as media of exchange, can be supported by a set of initial trading strategies for some parameter values of the economy. Both of these are analogous to the results of Kiyotaki and Wright (1989). Furthermore, Proposition 7.1 shows that under equal proportions of agent types, another speculative equilibrium $(0, 1, 1)$, in which the two most storable goods are media of exchange, can also be supported by a set of initial trading strategies for some parameter values of the economy. This result is distinct from that of Kiyotaki and Wright (1989). Wright (1995), using the search theoretic framework of Kiyotaki and Wright (1989), but allowing for unequal proportions of agent types, finds the two equilibria of Kiyotaki and Wright (1989) and one other equilibrium, where the good which is the second least costly to store is the unique medium of exchange.

Within the current evolutionary framework, Proposition 7.2 illustrates that once the proportions of agent types are allowed to differ, all equilibria can be shown to be asymptotically stable, with the exception of two equilibria: one in which the least storable good serves as the only medium of exchange, and the other in which no medium of exchange is necessary. There is even an asymptotically stable equilibrium where the most storable good is not the medium of exchange, but the other two less storable commodities are the media of exchange (i.e., $(1, 0, 1)$).

The following begins by examining this model under equal proportions of agent types.

Equal Proportions of Agent Types: $P_1 = P_2 = P_3 = \frac{1}{3}$ Assuming equal proportions of agent types, Proposition 7.1 characterizes all the corner equilibrium points.

For the first storability model (where $\lambda_{1(2)} > \lambda_{1(1)}$, $\lambda_{2(1)} > \lambda_{2(2)}$, and $\lambda_{3(2)} > \lambda_{3(1)}$); and given $P_i = \frac{1}{3}$ for $i = 1, 2, 3$,

7.3 Evolution of Strategies

Proposition 7.1. *with condition (j) stated below, there exists an open ball B_j such that if the initial strategies lie in B_j then the state of the economy converges to equilibrium j, where for $j = 1, 2, 3$ the equilibria are $(0, 1, 0)$, $(1, 1, 0)$ and $(0, 1, 1)$, respectively;*

Condition (1): $\frac{4}{3} < \frac{\lambda_{1(2)}}{\lambda_{1(1)}}$, *and* $\frac{11}{9} < \frac{\lambda_{3(2)}}{\lambda_{3(1)}}$.

Condition (2): $\frac{3}{4} < \frac{\lambda_{1(1)}}{\lambda_{1(2)}}$.

Condition (3): $\frac{9}{11} < \frac{\lambda_{3(1)}}{\lambda_{3(2)}}$.

II. (1) there exists no initial point such that the economy converges to $(1, 0, 0)$, $(0, 0, 1)$, $(1, 0, 1)$ and $(0, 0, 0)$;

(2) the remaining equilibrium $(1, 1, 1)$ is not asymptotically stable under the specific dynamics in Example 1.

Proof. See Appendix B.

One interesting observation about Proposition 7.1 is that there exist some common parameter values of the economy under which different initial points support different equilibrium points. For example, consider the parameter vector of the economy $\Phi = (P_1, P_2, P_3; \lambda_{1(2)}, \lambda_{1(1)}, \lambda_{2(2)}, \lambda_{2(1)}, \lambda_{3(2)}, \lambda_{3(1)}) = (\frac{1}{3}, \frac{1}{3}, \frac{1}{3}, \lambda_{1(2)}, \lambda_{1(1)}, \lambda_{2(2)}, \lambda_{2(1)}, \lambda_{3(2)}, \lambda_{3(1)})$. Using the definition of the open balls B_1, B_2, and B_3 of Appendix B, it can be shown that with two different initial trading strategies, each sufficiently close to its respective equilibrium, $(1, 1, 0)$ or $(0, 1, 1)$, each equilibrium is asymptotically stable under particular common parameter vectors of the economy.

Notice that a methodology for computing the open balls (basins of attraction) for Proposition 7.1 and all of the following propositions is provided in Theorem 1 and Lemmas 1 and 2 of Appendix A.[12] These basins of attraction can be computed without detailed knowledge about the specific functional form of the dynamics.

Proposition 7.1 indicates that any equilibrium, where population 2 plays strategy 2(1), is not asymptotically stable under the equal proportions of agent types in this model. The reason is that any agent in population 2 has a higher probability (discounted by the storability parameter) of being successful in acquiring the consumption good by playing strategy 2(2) than by playing strategy 2(1), regardless of what populations 1 and 2 do. In other words, the evolutionary pressure in this economy pushes agents in population 2 away from playing strategy 2(1) and toward playing strategy 2(2). However, as will be seen below, if unequal proportions of agent types are allowed, some of those equilibria can be supported by some initial strategies.

---

[12] If the focus is not in finding basins of attraction (described by the open balls B_j) and the interest is only in determining the asymptotic stability of equilibria, for asymptotic stability, one only has to show that the equilibrium is a strict Nash equilibrium.

Unequal Proportions of Agent-Types: Not All P_1, P_2, and P_3 are Equal Under the assumption of unequal proportions of agent types, the following proposition finds more equilibria that are asymptotically stable.

For the first storability model (where $\lambda_{1(2)} > \lambda_{1(1)}$, $\lambda_{2(1)} > \lambda_{2(2)}$ and $\lambda_{3(2)} > \lambda_{3(1)}$); and given that not all P_1, P_2 and P_3 are equal,

Proposition 7.2. *With condition (j) stated below, there exists an open ball $\widetilde{B}_j$ such that if the initial strategies lie in $\widetilde{B}_j$, then the state of the economy converges to equilibrium j, where for $j = 1, 2, 3, 4, 5, 6$, the equilibria are $(0, 1, 0)$, $(1, 1, 0)$, $(0, 1, 1)$, $(0, 0, 1)$, $(1, 0, 1)$, and $(1, 1, 1)$, respectively;*

Condition (1): $P_1 + P_3 < \frac{\lambda_{1(2)}}{\lambda_{1(1)}}$ and $1 + P_1(P_1 + P_3) < \frac{\lambda_{3(2)}}{\lambda_{3(1)}}$.

Condition (2): $2(P_1 + P_3) > \frac{\lambda_{1(2)}}{\lambda_{1(1)}}$ and $\frac{1+P_1(P_2+P_3)}{1+P_1(P_1+P_3)} < \frac{\lambda_{3(2)}}{\lambda_{3(1)}}$.

Condition (3): $\frac{1+P_2(P_1+P_3)}{1+P_2(P_1+P_2)} < \frac{\lambda_{1(2)}}{\lambda_{1(1)}}$, $2(P_1+P_2) > \frac{\lambda_{2(2)}}{\lambda_{2(1)}}$ and $1+P_1(P_1+P_2) > \frac{\lambda_{3(2)}}{\lambda_{3(1)}}$.

Condition (4): $1 + P_3(P_2 + P_3) < \frac{\lambda_{1(2)}}{\lambda_{1(1)}}$ and $2(P_1 + P_2) < \frac{\lambda_{2(2)}}{\lambda_{2(1)}}$.

Condition (5): $1+P_2(P_2+P_3) > \frac{\lambda_{1(2)}}{\lambda_{1(1)}}$, $\frac{1+P_3(P_1+P_2)}{1+P_3(P_2+P_3)} < \frac{\lambda_{2(2)}}{\lambda_{2(1)}}$ and $2(P_2+P_3) > \frac{\lambda_{3(2)}}{\lambda_{3(1)}}$.

Condition (6): $\frac{1+P_2(P_1+P_2)}{1+P_2(P_1+P_3)} < \frac{\lambda_{1(1)}}{\lambda_{1(2)}}$, $\frac{1+P_3(P_2+P_3)}{1+P_3(P_1+P_2)} < \frac{\lambda_{2(1)}}{\lambda_{2(2)}}$ and $\frac{1+P_1(P_1+P_3)}{1+P_1(P_2+P_3)} < \frac{\lambda_{3(1)}}{\lambda_{3(2)}}$.

II. *if $P_1 \geq P_3$ then there exists no initial point such that the economy converges to the remaining equilibrium points $(1, 0, 0)$ and $(0, 0, 0)$; furthermore, the equilibria $(1, 0, 0)$ and $(0, 0, 0)$ are not asymptotically stable under the specific dynamics in Example 1.*

Proof. See Appendix B.

In comparison with the results in Proposition 7.1, some interesting observations about Proposition 7.2 are made:

1. The three asymptotically stable equilibria under equal proportions of agent types characterized in Proposition 7.1 are also asymptotically stable under unequal proportions of agent types. However, as Proposition 7.2 I(1), I(2) and I(3) in Appendix B show, the respective open ball which supports each equilibrium point is a function of the proportions of agent types.
2. The proportion of agent types is one of the important factors in determining which equilibrium evolves.

    (i) For example, under equal proportions of agent types, the fundamental equilibrium $(0, 1, 0)$ is supported by some initial trading strategies. However, under unequal proportions of agent types, from the same set of initial strategies, a speculative equilibrium can evolve. For example, consider these parameters: $\lambda_{1(1)} = 0.02$, $\lambda_{1(2)} = 0.70$, $\lambda_{2(1)} = 0.80$, $\lambda_{2(2)} = 0.20$, $\lambda_{3(1)} = 0.58$, $\lambda_{3(2)} = 0.80$, $P_{1(2)}^0 = 0.03$, $P_{2(2)}^0 = 0.95$, and $P_{3(2)}^0 = 0.09$. With an equal distribution of agent types, $P_1 = P_2 = P_3 = \frac{1}{3}$, and the initial point $\left(P_{1(2)}^0, P_{2(2)}^0, P_{3(2)}^0\right) = (0.03, 0.95, 0.09)$, under F, the economy converges to the fundamental equilibrium, $(0, 1, 0)$. However, for

7.3 Evolution of Strategies

the same set of parameters $\lambda_{i(k)}$ ($i = 1, 2, 3; k = 1, 2$) and the same initial values $(P^0_{1(2)}, P^0_{2(2)}, P^0_{3(2)}) = (0.03, 0.95, 0.09)$, the economy converges to the speculative equilibrium $(0, 1, 1)$ if $(P_1, P_2, P_3) = (0.475, 0.475, 0.05)$.

(ii) The importance of unequal proportions of agent types can also be seen from the fact that, in addition to the asymptotically stable equilibrium points under equal proportions of agent types characterized in Proposition 7.1, more equilibrium points (i.e., $(0, 0, 1)$, $(1, 0, 1)$, and $(1, 1, 1)$) are supported by some initial strategies under unequal proportions of agent types. The following provides some detailed characterizations of each of such equilibria.

(a) The equilibrium $(0, 0, 1)$, where good 2 is the medium of exchange, is not asymptotically stable under the assumption of equal proportions of agent types characterized in Proposition 7.1, but is asymptotically stable under the assumption of unequal proportions of agent types characterized in Proposition 7.2 (see Appendix B, Proposition 7.2 I(4)). Good 2 can be the medium of exchange if the economy $(P^0_{1(2)}, P^0_{2(2)}, P^0_{3(2)})$ is sufficiently close to $(0, 0, 1)$ and $1 + P_3(P_2 + P_3) < \frac{\lambda_{1(2)}}{\lambda_{1(1)}}$ and $2(P_1 + P_2) < \frac{\lambda_{2(2)}}{\lambda_{2(1)}}$.

(b) Where there are unequal proportions of agent types, it is possible that the most storable good does not serve as one of the media of exchange, and instead the two least storable goods serve as the media of exchange (see Appendix B, Proposition 7.2 I(5)). Good 1 not serving as the medium of exchange in equilibrium could be caused by the situation where $P^0_{1(2)}$ and $P^0_{3(2)}$ are both sufficiently close to 1 and $P_1 < P_3$. In this case (see $\widetilde{g}_2^{B_5}$ of Appendix B) the discounted probability (discounted by the storability parameter) of agent 2(1) being successful in acquiring his or her consumption good in the afternoon is higher than the discounted probability of agent 2(2) being successful in the afternoon. (Both agents 2(1) and 2(2) have the same discounted probability of being successful in the morning.) Furthermore, the less storable that good 2 is relative to good 1 $\left(\text{the bigger the ratio } \frac{\lambda_{3(2)}}{\lambda_{3(1)}}\right)$, the smaller P_1 must be for $(1, 0, 1)$ to be supported.

(c) All commodities can serve as the media of exchange under the following conditions. For a given $\frac{\lambda_{1(1)}}{\lambda_{1(2)}} < 1$, if P_2 is sufficiently smaller than P_3, the discounted probability of agent 1(2) being successful in acquiring his or her consumption good is higher than the discounted probability of agent 1(1) being successful (see $\widetilde{g}_1^{B_6}$ of Appendix B). Eventually, population 1 is dominated by 1(2) agents. Similarly, for a given $\frac{\lambda_{3(1)}}{\lambda_{3(2)}} < 1$, if P_1 is sufficiently smaller than P_2, eventually population 3 is dominated by 3(2) agents (see $\widetilde{g}_3^{B_6}$ of Appendix B). In population 2, for strategy 2(2) to become the unanimously played strategy, good 3 must be sufficiently costly to store relative to good 1 for a given initial proportion of 1(2) and 3(2) agents (see $\widetilde{g}_2^{B_6}$ of Appendix B).

(d) Given $\lambda_{2(1)} > \lambda_{2(2)}$ and $P_1 \geq P_3$ the discounted probability of agent 2(2) being successful in acquiring his or her own consumption good is always greater than that of agent 2(1) being successful in any time period. Therefore, subtype agent 2(2) will eventually take over population 2 and the economy cannot possibly converge to any one of the equilibria $(1,0,0)$ and $(0,0,0)$ (see Appendix B Proposition 7.2 II(i)).

3. Another important factor in determining which equilibrium evolves is the position of the initial trading strategies. Different initial strategies can lead the economy to different equilibria under the same parameter vectors of the economy. For example, consider a parameter vector $(P_1, P_2, P_3; \lambda_{1(2)}, \lambda_{1(1)}, \lambda_{2(2)}, \lambda_{2(1)}, \lambda_{3(2)}, \lambda_{3(1)})$, characterized by the following: $\frac{1}{2(P_3+P_1)} < \frac{\lambda_{1(1)}}{\lambda_{1(2)}} < \frac{1+(P_1+P_2)P_2}{1+(P_1+P_3)P_2}$, $\frac{1}{2(P_2+P_1)} < \frac{\lambda_{2(1)}}{\lambda_{2(2)}}$, and $\frac{1+P_1(P_3+P_2)}{1+P_1(P_3+P_1)} < \frac{\lambda_{3(2)}}{\lambda_{3(1)}} < 1+P_1(P_2+P_1)$. Given this parameter vector, Proposition 7.2 (see Appendix B Proposition 7.2 I(2) and I(3)) guarantees that a starting point $(P_{1(2)}^0, P_{2(2)}^0, P_{3(2)}^0)$ that is sufficiently close to one of the equilibrium points $(1,1,0)$ or $(0,1,1)$ can support either $(1,1,0)$ or $(0,1,1)$, respectively.

The intrinsic value of commodities is another important factor in determining which equilibrium point will evolve. This is best illustrated by comparing the above results with the results in the equal storability model in the following section.

7.3.3.2 Equal Storability Among Commodities

The purpose of this section is to stress the importance of varying intrinsic values. In contrast to the unequal storability assumed in Subsect. 7.3.3.1, in this subsection, no differences in storability perceived by agents are assumed. This is referred to as the second storability model, characterized by $\lambda_{1(1)} = \lambda_{1(2)}, \lambda_{2(1)} = \lambda_{2(2)}$, and $\lambda_{3(1)} = \lambda_{3(2)}$. Proposition 7.3 below shows that in this model the only asymptotically stable equilibrium under equal proportions of agent types is the one where all commodities are the media of exchange. However, Proposition 7.4 below shows that with unequal proportions of agent types, the equilibria where two goods serve as media of exchange are asymptotically stable. Both propositions illustrate that without having unequal intrinsic values (storability), a unique medium of exchange is not asymptotically stable under Example 1. The following subsection begins by examining this model under equal proportions of agent types.

Equal Proportions of Agent Types: $P_1 = P_2 = P_3 = \frac{1}{3}$ Assuming equal proportions of agent types the following proposition finds that only one equilibrium is asymptotically stable.

Proposition 7.3. *For the second storability model (where $\lambda_{i(2)} = \lambda_{i(1)}$ for $i = 1, 2, 3$) and given that $P_1 = P_2 = P_3 = \frac{1}{3}$, with any starting point other than any of the fixed points, the state of the economy converges to $(1,1,1)$.*

Proof. See Appendix B.

Since goods are equally storable and since each agent has an equal probability of meeting an agent from each population, agent $i(2)$ always has a higher probability of acquiring his or her consumption good than agent $i(1)$, for all i. As a result, $(1, 1, 1)$ evolves from any initial trading strategies other than any of the fixed points.

Unequal Proportions of Agent Types: Not All P_1, P_2 and P_3 are Equal

Proposition 7.4. *If not all P_1, P_2, and P_3 are equal, then the equilibria, where two goods serve as the media of exchange, are asymptotically stable.*

For the second storability model (where $\lambda_{i(1)} = \lambda_{i(2)}$ for $i = 1, 2, 3$),

I. *With $2(P_{j-1} + P_j) > 1$, $\frac{1+P_{j-1}(P_{j-1}+P_{j+1})}{1+P_{j-1}(P_j+P_{j+1})} < 1$ and $\frac{1+P_j(P_{j+1}+P_{j-1})}{1+P_j(P_j+P_{j-1})} < 1$, there exists an open ball $\widehat{B}_j$ such that if an initial strategies lie in $\widehat{B}_j$, then the state of the economy converges to equilibrium j, where for $j = 1, 2, 3$, the equilibria are $(1, 1, 0)$, $(0, 1, 1)$, and $(1, 0, 1)$, respectively;*

II. *the remaining equilibria, $(1,0,0)$, $(0,1,0)$, $(0,0,1)$, $(1,1,1)$, and $(0,0,0)$, are not asymptotically stable under the specific dynamics of Example 1.*

Proof. See Appendix B.

Using Appendix B, the open ball $\widehat{B}_j$ in Proposition 7.4 (I) is

$$\left\{ \left(P_{1(2)}^0, P_{2(2)}^0, P_{3(2)}^0 \right) \in [0, 1] \times [0, 1] \times [0, 1] : P_{j-1} + P_j P_{(j-1)(1)}^0 \right.$$
$$> P_{j+1}, P_j + P_{j-1} P_{(j-1)(1)}^0 > P_{j-1} P_{(j-1)(2)}^0, P_j P_{j(2)}^0 > P_{j+1}$$
$$\left. + P_{j-1} P_{(j+1)(1)}^0 + P_j P_{j(1)}^0 \right\}.$$

As noted above, for $j = 1, 2, 3$, if P_{j+1} is sufficiently small, the probability of agent $j(2)$ being successful in acquiring his or her consumption good is always greater than the probability of agent $j(1)$ being successful. With a sufficiently low initial $P_{(j-1)(2)}^0$, the probability of agent $(j+1)(2)$ being successful in acquiring his or her consumption good is always greater than the probability of agent $(j+1)(1)$ being successful. Furthermore, if, for a given initial point $\left(P_1^0, P_2^0, P_3^0\right)$, P_{j+1} is sufficiently low relative to P_j, and if the initial proportions $P_{j(2)}^0$ and $P_{(j+1)(2)}^0$ are sufficiently close to 1, then the probability of agent $(j-1)(1)$ being successful in acquiring his or her consumption good is greater than the probability of agent $(j-1)(2)$ being successful. All of the above contribute to the economy converging to the equilibrium where goods j and $j-1$ serve as the media of exchange.

7.4 Mutation

In this section, the concept of mutation is added to the above model. This is done for two reasons. The first is to capture a randomness in imitation. In addition to imitating other successful agents, agents may sometimes imitate unsuccessful agents. The second reason is that adding the element of mutation provides a method for selecting a smaller number of more plausible equilibria from several equilibria which may occur in an economy without mutation. This latter principle, illustrated in Kandori et al. (1993) and based on the earlier work of Foster and Young (1990), asserts that in the presence of multiple evolutionary stable strategies some equilibria are more likely to emerge than others when there are continual mutations. Specifically, the approach for selecting a unique equilibrium (see Kandori et al. 1993, pp. 53–54) is to select the equilibrium which requires the largest mutation rate for moving the dynamic system toward the basin of attraction containing this equilibrium. Below, Proposition 7.6 shows that with sufficiently large mutation rates, the number of asymptotically stable equilibria can be reduced to only one.

The following is an example which incorporates the idea of mutation.

Example 1a: Random Sampling Among The Same Population With Mutation
Example 1 captured the hypothesis that with some positive probability, agents imitate the successful strategies. This is now combined with the introduction of mutation rates to reflect the idea that agents imitate strategies regardless of the success of these strategies. Suppose at the end of day t, $t = 1, 2, \ldots$, agent $i(k)$ randomly meets another agent in the population i; if this agent is an agent of subtype $i(k')$, where $k' \neq k$, then agent $i(k)$ mimics and plays the strategy of agent $i(k')$ with probability $\mu_{i(k)}$ ($\mu_{i(k)} \in (0, 1)$) in day $t + 1$ if agent $i(k')$ is unsuccessful, and plays the strategy of agent $i(k')$ with probability $\mu_{i(k)} + \lambda_{i(k)}$ ($\mu_{i(k)} + \lambda_{i(k)} \in (0, 1)$) in day $t + 1$ if agent $i(k')$ is successful; otherwise, agent $i(k)$ will continue to play the same strategy in day $t+1$ as in day t. In other words, there is a base mutation rate $\mu_{i(k)}$ which plays a role regardless of the success of the encountered strategy, and an incremental imitation rate $\lambda_{i(k)}$ which plays a role only in the case of meeting a successful agent.[13] The sizes of $\mu_{i(k)}$ and $\lambda_{i(k)}$ can be related to the intrinsic characteristic of the commodities, here defined to be storability. If an i–type agent's production good $(i + 1)$ is more storable than the indirect traded good $(i - 1)$, $\mu_{i(2)} > \mu_{i(1)}$ and $\lambda_{i(2)} > \lambda_{i(1)}$; otherwise, $\mu_{i(1)} \geq \mu_{i(2)}$ and $\lambda_{i(1)} \geq \lambda_{i(2)}$.

The resulting dynamic equations of motion for Example 1a, are as follows: for $i = 1, 2, 3$,

---

[13]In the above, mutations produce mistakes in the sense that the imitation is irrational. An alternative interpretation of $\mu_{i(k)}$ is that it represents noise in imitation. The more extensive the noise in the information structure regarding the success of the mimiced agent, the higher would be $\mu_{i(k)}$ relative to $\lambda_{i(k)}$. Agents imitate others, regardless of the success of others. Another type of mistake would occur if agents arbitrarily moved away from steady states (i.e., arbitrary perturbations of the steady state). However, as noted by Weibull (1995), this type of mutation in the form of small perturbations is indirectly taken care of by the way of dynamic stability criteria. By the definition of asymptotic stability, such arbitrarily small movements imply that the economy returns to the steady state. However, with such perturbations away from an asymptotically unstable equilibrium or very large perturbations away from any equilibrium, the economy could evolve into another steady state.

$$P_{i(2)}^{t+1} = P_{i(2)}^t + P_{i(1)}^t \left(\mu_{i(1)} + \lambda_{i(1)}\right) \frac{P_{i(2)}^t(s)}{P_i} - P_{i(2)}^t \left(\mu_{i(2)} + \lambda_{i(2)}\right) \frac{P_{i(1)}^t(s)}{P_i}$$

$$+ P_{i(1)}^t \mu_{i(1)} \left(P_{i(2)}^t - \frac{P_{i(2)}^t(s)}{P_i} \right) - P_{i(2)}^t \mu_{i(2)} \left(P_{i(1)}^t - \frac{P_{i(1)}^t(s)}{P_i} \right),$$

i.e. $P_{i(2)}^{t+1} = P_{i(2)}^t + P_{i(1)}^t \lambda_{i(1)} \dfrac{P_{i(2)}^t(s)}{P_i} - P_{i(2)}^t \lambda_{i(2)} \dfrac{P_{i(1)}^t(s)}{P_i} + P_{i(1)}^t \mu_{i(1)} P_{i(2)}^t$

$$- P_{i(2)}^t \mu_{i(2)} P_{i(1)}^t.$$

7.4.1 The General Class of Dynamics

A more general class of dynamics encompassing mutation is defined as follows.

Definition 7.2. A class of dynamics F' for this economy is described by the system of equations of motion

$$P_{i(2)}^{t+1} - P_{i(2)}^t = f_i'(P_{1(2)}^t, P_{2(2)}^t, P_{3(2)}^t; \lambda, \mu), \quad \text{for } i = 1, 2, 3,$$

where, $\lambda = (\lambda_{1(2)}, \lambda_{1(1)}, \lambda_{2(2)}, \lambda_{2(1)}, \lambda_{3(2)}, \lambda_{3(1)})$, $\mu = (\mu_{1(2)}, \mu_{1(1)}, \mu_{2(2)}, \mu_{2(1)}, \mu_{3(2)}, \mu_{3(1)})$, and $f_i'(\cdot)$ has the following properties:[14]

1. $f_i'(P_{1(2)}^t, P_{2(2)}^t, P_{3(2)}^t; \lambda, \mu)$ is continuous in the first three arguments,
2. $f_i'(P_{1(2)}^t, P_{2(2)}^t, P_{3(2)}^t; \lambda, \mu) = 0$ for $P_{i(2)}^t \in \{0, 1\}$, $i = 1, 2, 3$, and
3. $f_i'(P_{1(2)}^t, P_{2(2)}^t, P_{3(2)}^t; \lambda, \mu) > 0$ if and only if

---

[14] In a model of N goods and N agents, where agent i consumes only good i and produces only good $i + 1$ (modulo N), one could specify s_i^j as the probability that agent i is willing to trade his or her production good for j where $j \neq i$ and $j \neq i + 1$, when agent i meets an agent holding good j.

Suppose traders only play pure strategies. That is, $s_i^j \in \{0, 1\}$. If $s_i^j = 0$ then agent i is not willing to trade for consumption good j. Agent i is willing to trade for commodity j when $s_i^j = 1$. The proportion of agent i choosing $s_i^j = 1$ at time t could be referred to as $P_{ij(2)}^t$ and the proportion of agent i choosing $s_i^j = 0$ could be referred to as $P_{ij(1)}^t$. One could further define μ_i^j as the probability of agent i imitating strategy s_i^j regardless of the success of s_i^j and λ_i^j as the incremental probability of agent i imitating a successful strategy s_i^j. Furthermore, the sizes of λ_i^j and μ_i^j could be modeled as a function of the degree of storability. That is $\lambda_i^j > \lambda_i^{j'}$ and $\mu_i^j > \mu_i^{j'}$ if commodity j is more storable than commodity j'. The number of dynamic equations of motion would then equal to $N \times (N - 2)$. Thus, the model becomes more intricate as N goes beyond 3. While the number of possible asymptotically stable equilbria undoubtedly grows, similar to the conclusions of this paper, increasing the size of the mutation rates further selects a reduced set of long run equilibria.

$$\frac{P^t_{i(2)}(s)}{\lambda_{i(2)}\overline{P}^t_{i(2)}} + \frac{\mu_{i(1)}}{\lambda_{i(1)}\lambda_{i(2)}} > \frac{P^t_{i(1)}(s)}{\lambda_{i(1)}\overline{P}^t_{i(1)}} + \frac{\mu_{i(2)}}{\lambda_{i(1)}\lambda_{i(2)}} \quad \text{for } P^t_{i(2)} \in (0,1).$$

Example 1a is a special case of F' where

$$f'_i\left(P^t_{1(2)}, P^t_{2(2)}, P^t_{3(2)}; \lambda, \mu\right)$$

$$= P^t_{i(1)}\lambda_{i(1)}\frac{P^t_{i(2)}(s)}{P_i} - P^t_{i(2)}\lambda_{i(2)}\frac{P^t_{i(1)}(s)}{P_i} + P^t_{i(1)}\mu_{i(1)}P^t_{i(2)} - P^t_{i(2)}\mu_{i(2)}P^t_{i(1)}.$$

If $\mu = 0$, the dynamics F' is the same as the dynamics F (described in the previous section). Under the dynamics F', properties (1) and (2) are the same as the corresponding properties under the dynamics F and property (3) is more general than property (3) under the dynamics F. Property (3) indicates that, subject to mutation flows across strategies, fitter strategies should increase relative to less fit strategies. Under the dynamics F', the parameter vector of this mutation economy becomes $(P_1, P_2, P_3; \lambda, \mu)$ and the equilibria of the economy are the fixed points under the dynamics F', which are the same as the ones under the dynamics F.

7.4.2 Equilibria Selection with Mutation

In this subsection, the implications of adding mutation rates into the model are explored under the dynamics F'. Proposition 7.5 below shows that for sufficiently small mutation rates, the results in Propositions 7.1, 7.2, 7.3, and 7.4 continue to hold. Thus, the previous results seem robust. However, suppose the mutation rates become sufficiently large that each agent, regardless of the success of agent subtypes in acquiring the desired consumption goods, has a higher probability of switching to a subtype who trades for a more storable good in the event of meeting another agent who does not have the desired consumption good. Then, with any initial strategy other than any of the fixed points, the economy will converge to a unique fundamental equilibrium $(0, 1, 0)$, where the most storable good (good 1) serves as a unique medium of exchange. This is seen in Proposition 7.6. The following begins with Proposition 7.5.

Proposition 7.5. *Under the dynamics F', there exists an $\epsilon > 0$ such that, if $\mu_{i(k)} < \epsilon$, for $i = 1, 2, 3$ and $k = 1, 2$, then the results in Propositions 7.1, 7.2, 7.3, and 7.4 still hold.*

Proof. See Appendix C.

The above proposition suggests that the introduction of small mutation rates into the dynamics F' changes the open ball by a very small amount, and it does not change the number of asymptotically stable equilibria in economies discussed in the previous section. The number of asymptotically stable equilibria remains the same. This is not surprising, given the existence of the previously defined basins of attraction which support asymptotically stable equilibria in previous propositions. By the definition of asymptotic stability, such small perturbations, however they are caused, do not upset the convergence of the economy to the steady state. However, if the mutation rates become so large that each agent, regardless of the success of agent subtypes in acquiring the desired consumption good, has a higher probability of switching to a subtype who trades for a more storable good, in the event of meeting another agent who does not have the desired consumption good, the number of asymptotically stable equilibria is reduced to one. That is, if $\mu_{i(2)} > \lambda_{i(1)} + \mu_{i(1)}$ for $i = 1, 3$ and $\mu_{2(1)} > \lambda_{2(2)} + \mu_{2(2)}$, then the economy converges to a unique fundamental equilibrium $(0, 1, 0)$ regardless of the initial strategies and regardless of the proportions of agent types.[15] This is formally stated as follows.

Proposition 7.6. *In the first storability model, where $\lambda_{1(2)} > \lambda_{1(1)}, \lambda_{2(1)} > \lambda_{2(2)}$ and $\lambda_{3(2)} > \lambda_{3(1)}$, if $\mu_{i(2)} > \lambda_{i(1)} + \mu_{i(1)}$, for $i = 1, 3$ and $\mu_{2(1)} > \lambda_{2(2)} + \mu_{2(2)}$, then with any starting point other than any of the fixed points, the state of the economy under the dynamics F' converges to a unique fundamental equilibrium $(0, 1, 0)$, where the most storable good (good 1) serves as a unique medium of exchange.*

Proof. See Appendix D.

The intuition for the convergence of the economy to the fundamental equilibrium $(0, 1, 0)$ is straightforward. It essentially says that if each agent, regardless of the success of agent subtypes in consumption, pays more attention to the fundamentals (the storability) in the sense that he or she is more likely to switch to trading for the more storable good if he or she meets an agent whose production good is not his or her consumption good, then only the fundamental equilibrium evolves from any initial strategies other than any of the fixed points.[16] Specifically, the condition says that in population i, where $i = 1, 3$, agents of subtype $i(2)$ have a sufficiently high probability of mutating into subtype $i(1)$ relative to the probability of agents of subtype $i(1)$ mutating into $i(2)$; and in population 2, agents of subtype $2(1)$ have a sufficiently high probability of mutating into subtype $2(2)$ relative to the probability of agents of subtype $2(2)$ mutating into subtype $2(1)$. This means that good 1 is perceived by all agents of all types as the most storable good, and furthermore, that each agent is more likely to switch to trading for a more storable good with an encountered agent whose production good is not his or her consumption good. As

---

[15] It should be noted that if agents make large enough mistakes, under different restrictions with respect to mutation and storability parameters, the system could move from one basin of attraction to another. Nevertheless, Proposition 7.6 focuses on the set of restrictions under which mutation rates become sufficiently large to produce a unique fundamental equilibrium.

[16] If we interpret the $\mu_{i(k)}$ as representing noise in imitation and since all agents perceive the relative storability of commodities in the same way, then Proposition 7.6 could be loosely interpreted as saying: "If agents know very little about what other agents are doing, then the fundamental equilibrium is the most likely to occur."

time goes by, under the dynamics F', the economy will eventually be populated with agents of subtype $i(1)$ in population i for $i = 1, 3$ and with agents of subtype $2(2)$ in population 2; and consequently, good 1 will emerge as a unique medium of exchange.

7.5 Conclusions

This evolutionary model illustrates how media of exchange evolve in a primitive economy. In this framework, agents specialize in production for the purpose of trading for their own consumption goods. They meet randomly in pairs and trade bilaterally. It is assumed that agents begin with given initial trading strategies. On a population basis, the evolution of agents' strategies is consistent with Darwinian dynamics. In turn, this is consistent with micro stories of individual agents following very simple rules of imitation. Strategies evolve gradually. As time goes by, agents myopically imitate the more successful strategies and eventually, in each population, one strategy may be observed. Even though the unconcerted efforts of individuals are directed toward the pursuit of very myopic strategies, an equilibrium evolves producing generally accepted media of exchange.

This evolutionary approach is distinct from recent literature. Agents are presumed to be unsophisticated and a general class of dynamics, which is compatible with Darwinian dynamics, is applied to the selection of strategies. Some may argue that the evolutionary approach is extreme in its adoption of the bounded rationality hypothesis. On the other hand, if some of the well-known results primarily supported under models of rationality are now generated by an evolutionary model, the robustness of those results is further enhanced. By using the evolutionary approach, this chapter is able to highlight some of the key factors which determine the media of exchange. Similar to Kiyotaki and Wright (1989), it is found that the relative intrinsic value (here storability) of commodities is a critical determinant. Similar to Wright (1995), this chapter also finds that the proportion of agents specializing in different production-consumption activities is an important determining factor. In addition, the agents' initial trading strategies also matter in the determination of the media of exchange. Nevertheless, the chapter shows that the importance of these initial strategies, in terms of determining which equilibrium will evolve, may be reduced by the introduction of mutation. If the extent of random play, expressed by mutation rates, is linked to the storability of commodities, then when these mutation rates get sufficiently large, starting with any initial strategy other than any of the fixed points, the economy converges to a unique equilibrium – the fundamental equilibrium.

An advantage of evolutionary analysis is that it allows the analysis of the model outside of the steady state equilibria; and furthermore, it allows a selection of equilibria based on stability. However, the selection of long run equilibria under the dynamics F' does depend on the size of storability parameters, the proportions of agent types, the initial strategies, and the mutation rates.

7.5 Conclusions

The importance of having different intrinsic values in commodities can be seen by comparing the results of Propositions 7.3 and 7.1 (where in both propositions the proportions of agent types are equal) and the results of Propositions 7.4 and 7.2 (where in both propositions not all of the proportions of agent types are equal). In Proposition 7.1, where differences in storability are assumed, the most storable good can serve as the unique medium of exchange. In contrast, in Proposition 7.3, where there are no differences in storability, a unique medium of exchange cannot occur. Proposition 7.2 shows that among the equilibria that are asymptotically stable, the most storable good can serve as a unique medium of exchange and the second most storable good can serve as a unique medium of exchange. However, in Proposition 7.4, where there are no differences in storability, an equilibrium with a unique medium of exchange is not asymptotically stable in Example 1.

Similar to Wright (1995), the relaxation of the assumption about equal distribution of agents who specialize in different consumption-production activities leads to other equilibria not found in Kiyotaki and Wright (1989). This evolutionary model further emphasizes this result. In comparing the results of Proposition 7.2 with Proposition 7.1 and Proposition 7.4 with Proposition 7.3, with the relaxation of equal proportions of agent types, the number of asymptotically stable equilibria is increased.

The importance of initial extrinsic beliefs, as reflected by agents' initial trading strategies, is clearly evident. Given the same parameter vector of the economy, different starting points may lead the economy to different equilibria.

The introduction of sufficiently small mutation rates changes the open balls by a very small amount in comparison to economies without mutation, and leaves the asymptotic nature of the equilibria virtually unchanged. Therefore, with sufficiently small mutation rates, the initial trading strategies still matter in the sense that an initial starting point can still put the dynamic system on an equilibrium path toward one of the many steady states. However, if the mutation rates become so large that each agent, regardless of the success of agent subtypes in acquiring the desired consumption good, has a higher probability of switching to a subtype who trades for a more storable good in the event of meeting another agent who does not have the desired consumption good, then the economy converges to a unique equilibrium – the fundamental equilibrium, where the most storable good serves as a unique medium of exchange.

In conclusion, this evolutionary approach has offered further insights on the evolution of money. Nevertheless, other illuminations from this approach may be possible. Although it is beyond the scope of this chapter, it is hoped that this evolutionary approach offers a framework for such future research topics as the inclusion of fiat money, varying the number of agents, allowing for some presence of double coincidence of wants, and the introduction of credit, stores or banks. Also, it would be interesting to explore whether or not any of the specific dynamic models encompassed within the general class of dynamics show any cyclical paths.

Appendix A

The following theorem is used in the proof of propositions in Appendix B.

Theorem 7.1. *Under the dynamics F', described by the system of equations of motion*

$$P_{i(2)}^{t+1} - P_{i(2)}^{t} = f_i'\left(P_{1(2)}^{t}, P_{2(2)}^{t}, P_{3(2)}^{t}; \lambda, \mu\right) \quad \text{for } i = 1, 2, 3 \quad (7.8)$$

($f_i'(\cdot)$ having the properties defined in Definition $1'$), if a fixed point $\left(P_{1(2)}^{*}, P_{2(2)}^{*}, P_{3(2)}^{*}\right) = (k_1, k_2, k_3)$ for $k_1, k_2, k_3 \in \{0, 1\}$ is contained in the ball B defined by

$$B = \left\{\left(P_{1(2)}^0, P_{2(2)}^0, P_{3(2)}^0\right) \in [0, 1] \times [0, 1] \times [0, 1] : g_i^B\left(P_{1(2)}^0, P_{2(2)}^0, P_{3(2)}^0\right) < 0, \ i = 1, 2, 3\right\},$$

where for $i=1,2,3$, $g_i^B(\cdot) : R_+^3 \to R$ is characterized by the following two properties:

(1) if for any $t = 1, 2, \ldots$, $g_i^B(P_{1(2)}^t, P_{2(2)}^t, P_{3(2)}^t) < 0$ for $P_{i(2)}^t \in (0, 1)$ implies that

$$\text{for } \delta_i = \begin{cases} -1 \text{ if } k_i = 0 \\ 1 \text{ if } k_i = 1 \end{cases}, \quad \delta_i \left[\frac{P_{i(2)}^t(s)}{\lambda_{i(2)} \overline{P}_{i(2)}^t} + \frac{\mu_{i(1)}}{\lambda_{i(1)} \lambda_{i(2)}}\right]$$

$$> \delta_i \left[\frac{P_{i(1)}^t(s)}{\lambda_{i(1)} \overline{P}_{i(1)}^t} + \frac{\mu_{i(2)}}{\lambda_{i(1)} \lambda_{i(2)}}\right]$$

and
(2) for $j = 1, 2, 3$,

$$\frac{\partial g_i^B(\cdot)}{\partial P_{j(2)}^t} \delta_j \leq 0,$$

then for every initial point $\left(P_{1(2)}^0, P_{2(2)}^0, P_{3(2)}^0\right)$ in the ball B, the state of the economy must converge to the fixed point $(P_{1(2)}^{*}, P_{2(2)}^{*}, P_{3(2)}^{*})$.

Proof. The proof consists of two steps.

Step I: Show that for any $\left(P_{1(2)}^0, P_{2(2)}^0, P_{3(2)}^0\right) \in B$, and for

$$\delta_i = \begin{cases} -1 \text{ if } k_i = 0 \\ 1 \text{ if } k_i = 1 \end{cases}, \text{ for any } t = 1, 2, \ldots,$$

Appendix A

(i) $\delta_i P_{i(2)}^{t+1} > \delta_i P_{i(2)}^t$ for $i = 1, 2, 3$; and
(ii) $g_i^B\left(P_{1(2)}^{t+1}, P_{2(2)}^{t+1}, P_{3(2)}^{t+1}\right) \leq g_i^B\left(P_{1(2)}^t, P_{2(2)}^t, P_{3(2)}^t\right) < 0$, for $i = 1, 2, 3$.

(Remark: Condition (ii) means that the path of the dynamic system described by equation (7.8) remains in B for $t \geq 0$.)

Proof of Step I: Since $\left(P_{1(2)}^0, P_{2(2)}^0, P_{3(2)}^0\right) \in B$, property (1) implies that under the dynamics F', for $t = 0$, $\delta_i P_{i(2)}^1 > \delta_i P_{i(2)}^0$ for $i = 1, 2, 3$. Since $P_{i(2)}^0$ increases to $P_{i(2)}^1$ if $\delta_i = 1$ and decreases if $\delta_i = -1$, and with property (2) this implies that for $t = 1$, $g_i^B\left(P_{1(2)}^1, P_{2(2)}^1, P_{3(2)}^1\right) \leq g_i^B\left(P_{1(2)}^0, P_{2(2)}^0, P_{3(2)}^0\right) < 0$, for $i = 1, 2, 3$. Using property (1) this in turn implies that

$$\delta_i \left[\frac{P_{i(2)}^1(s)}{\lambda_{i(2)} \overline{P}_{i(2)}^1} + \frac{\mu_{i(1)}}{\lambda_{i(1)} \lambda_{i(2)}} \right] > \delta_i \left[\frac{P_{i(1)}^1(s)}{\lambda_{i(1)} \overline{P}_{i(1)}^1} + \frac{\mu_{i(2)}}{\lambda_{i(1)} \lambda_{i(2)}} \right] \text{ for } i = 1, 2, 3,$$

which implies under F' that $\delta_i P_{i(2)}^2 > \delta_i P_{i(2)}^1$ for $i = 1, 2, 3$. In general, one can show inductively that for any $\left(P_{1(2)}^0, P_{2(2)}^0, P_{3(2)}^0\right) \in B$, and for

$$\delta_i = \begin{cases} -1 \text{ if } k_i = 0 \\ 1 \text{ if } k_i = 1 \end{cases}, \text{ for any } t = 0, 1, 2, \ldots,$$

(i) $\delta_i P_{i(2)}^{t+1} > \delta_i P_{i(2)}^t$ for $i = 1, 2, 3$; and
(ii) $g_i^B\left(P_{1(2)}^{t+1}, P_{2(2)}^{t+1}, P_{3(2)}^{t+1}\right) \leq g_i^B\left(P_{1(2)}^t, P_{2(2)}^t, P_{3(2)}^t\right) < 0$, for $i = 1, 2, 3$.

Step II: Under the dynamics F', for every initial point $\left(P_{1(2)}^0, P_{2(2)}^0, P_{3(2)}^0\right)$ in the ball B the state of the economy must converge to the fixed point $\left(P_{1(2)}^*, P_{2(2)}^*, P_{3(2)}^*\right)$.

Proof of Step II: Consider the function $V(\cdot) : [0, 1] \times [0, 1] \times [0, 1] \to R^+$

$$V\left(P_{1(2)}^t, P_{2(2)}^t, P_{3(2)}^t\right) = \left(P_{1(2)}^t - k_1\right)^2 + \left(P_{2(2)}^t - k_2\right)^2 + \left(P_{3(2)}^t - k_3\right)^2.$$

Since for any $t = 1, 2, \ldots$,

(i) $V(k_1, k_2, k_3) = 0$; and
(ii) $V\left(P_{1(2)}^t, P_{2(2)}^t, P_{3(2)}^t\right) > 0$ for all $\left(P_{1(2)}^t, P_{2(2)}^t, P_{3(2)}^t\right) \in B$ and $\left(P_{1(2)}^t, P_{2(2)}^t, P_{3(2)}^t\right) \neq (k_1, k_2, k_3)$; and
(iii) Step I has shown that for any $\left(P_{1(2)}^0, P_{2(2)}^0, P_{3(2)}^0\right) \in B$, for $\delta_i = \begin{cases} -1 \text{ if } k_i = 0 \\ 1 \text{ if } k_i = 1 \end{cases}$,

$\delta_i P_{i(2)}^{t+1} > \delta_i P_{i(2)}^t$ for all $i = 1, 2, 3$, then it follows that

$$V\left(P_{1(2)}^{t+1}, P_{2(2)}^{t+1}, P_{3(2)}^{t+1}\right) \leq V\left(P_{1(2)}^t, P_{2(2)}^t, P_{3(2)}^t\right), \tag{7.9}$$

where the inequality (7.9) is strict for $(P_{1(2)}^t, P_{2(2)}^t, P_{3(2)}^t) \neq (k_1, k_2, k_3)$. Therefore, $V(\cdot)$ is a strict Liapunov function for $f_i'(\cdot)$ (in Definition 1') at the fixed point $\left(P_{1(2)}^*, P_{2(2)}^*, P_{3(2)}^*\right)$ on the ball B.

Given the existence of the strict Liapunov function $V(\cdot)$, given that $f_i'(\cdot)$ is continuous, and given that every solution of equation (7.8) remains in B (by condition (ii) of Step I) then by Corollary 4.1 of Kelley and Peterson (1991), for any starting point in the ball B, the state of the economy $(P_{1(2)}^t, P_{2(2)}^t, P_{3(2)}^t)$ must converge to the fixed point $\left(P_{1(2)}^*, P_{2(2)}^*, P_{3(2)}^*\right)$.

The following two lemmas provide two methods for constructing the $g_i^B(\cdot)$ function which satisfies the two properties in Theorem 1.

Lemma 7.1. *Consider a fixed point* $v = (k_1, k_2, k_3)$ *for* $k_1, k_2, k_3 \in \{0, 1\}$, *and define* $\delta_j = \begin{cases} -1 \text{ if } k_j = 0 \\ 1 \text{ if } k_j = 1 \end{cases}$, *where* $j \in \{1, 2, 3\}$. *For* $i = 1, 2, 3$,

a) *if* $k_i = 1$ *and if there exists* $S_{i(1)}^t$ *and* $R_{i(2)}^t$ *such that*

$$S_{i(1)}^t\left(P_{1(2)}^t, P_{2(2)}^t, P_{3(2)}^t\right) \geq \frac{P_{i(1)}^t(s)}{\lambda_{i(1)} \overline{P}_{i(1)}^t} + \frac{\mu_{i(2)}}{\lambda_{i(1)} \lambda_{i(2)}}, \text{ where } \frac{\partial S_{i(1)}^t(\cdot)}{\partial P_{j(2)}^t} \delta_j \leq 0,$$

for $j = 1, 2, 3$,

and

$$R_{i(2)}^t\left(P_{1(2)}^t, P_{2(2)}^t, P_{3(2)}^t\right) \leq \frac{P_{i(2)}^t(s)}{\lambda_{i(2)} \overline{P}_{i(2)}^t} + \frac{\mu_{i(1)}}{\lambda_{i(1)} \lambda_{i(2)}}, \text{ where } \frac{\partial R_{i(2)}^t(\cdot)}{\partial P_{j(2)}^t} \delta_j \geq 0,$$

for $j = 1, 2, 3$,

then

$$g_i^B(\cdot) = \begin{cases} -1 & \text{if } R_{i(2)}^t(\cdot) > S_{i(1)}^t(\cdot) \text{ for all } \left(P_{1(2)}^t, P_{2(2)}^t, P_{3(2)}^t\right) \\ & \text{and all } t \\ S_{i(1)}^t(\cdot) - R_{i(2)}^t(\cdot) & \text{otherwise} \end{cases}$$

satisfies properties (1) and (2) of Theorem 1;
b) *if* $k_i = 0$ *and if there exists* $S_{i(2)}^t(\cdot)$ *and* $R_{i(1)}^t(\cdot)$ *such that*

$$S_{i(2)}^t(P_{1(2)}^t, P_{2(2)}^t, P_{3(2)}^t) \geq \frac{P_{i(2)}^t(s)}{\lambda_{i(2)} \overline{P}_{i(2)}^t} + \frac{\mu_{i(1)}}{\lambda_{i(1)} \lambda_{i(2)}}, \text{ where } \frac{\partial S_{i(2)}^t(\cdot)}{\partial P_{j(2)}^t} \delta_j \leq 0,$$

for $j = 1, 2, 3$,

Appendix A

and

$$R^t_{i(1)}(P^t_{1(2)}, P^t_{2(2)}, P^t_{3(2)}) \leq \frac{P^t_{i(1)}(s)}{\lambda_{i(1)}\overline{P}^t_{i(1)}} + \frac{\mu_{i(2)}}{\lambda_{i(1)}\lambda_{i(2)}}, \text{ where } \frac{\partial R^t_{i(1)}(\cdot)}{\partial P^t_{j(2)}}\delta_j \geq 0,$$

for $j = 1, 2, 3$,

then

$$g^B_i(\cdot) = \begin{cases} -1 & \text{if } R^t_{i(1)}(\cdot) > S^t_{i(2)}(\cdot) \text{ forall } \left(P^t_{1(2)}, P^t_{2(2)}, P^t_{3(2)}\right) \\ & \text{andall } t \\ S^t_{i(2)}(\cdot) - R^t_{i(1)}(\cdot) & \text{otherwise} \end{cases}$$

satisfies properties (1) and (2) of Theorem 1.

Proof of Part a): Since for $i \in \{1, 2, 3\}$, $g^B_i(\cdot) < 0$ implies that $S^t_{i(1)}(\cdot) < R^t_{i(2)}(\cdot)$ for any t, which further implies that

$$\left[\frac{P^t_{i(2)}(s)}{\lambda_{i(2)}\overline{P}^t_{i(2)}} + \frac{\mu_{i(1)}}{\lambda_{i(1)}\lambda_{i(2)}}\right] > \left[\frac{P^t_{i(1)}(s)}{\lambda_{i(1)}\overline{P}^t_{i(1)}} + \frac{\mu_{i(2)}}{\lambda_{i(1)}\lambda_{i(2)}}\right],$$

property (1) of Theorem 1 holds.

Since for $j = 1, 2, 3$,

$$\frac{\partial g^B_i(\cdot)}{\partial P^t_{j(2)}}\delta_j = \begin{cases} 0 \cdot \delta_j & \text{if } R^t_{i(2)}(\cdot) > S^t_{i(1)}(\cdot) \text{ for all } \left(P^t_{1(2)}, P^t_{2(2)}, P^t_{3(2)}\right) \\ & \text{and all } t \\ \frac{\partial S^t_{i(1)}(\cdot)}{\partial P^t_{j(2)}}\delta_j - \frac{\partial R^t_{i(2)}(\cdot)}{\partial P^t_{j(2)}}\delta_j & \text{otherwise} \end{cases}$$
$$\leq 0,$$

property (2) of Theorem 1 holds.

Proof of Part b) can be done similarly.

Lemma 7.2. *Consider a fixed point $v = (k_1, k_2, k_3)$ for $k_1, k_2, k_3 \in \{0, 1\}$, and define $\delta_j = \begin{cases} -1 \text{ if } k_j = 0 \\ 1 \text{ if } k_j = 1 \end{cases}$, where $j \in \{1, 2, 3\}$. For $i = 1, 2, 3$,*

a) *if $k_i = 1$ and $\frac{\lambda_{i(1)}}{\lambda_{i(2)}} \leq 1$ and $\mu_{i(2)} > \mu_{i(1)}$ and if there exists $K^t_i(\cdot)$, $M^t_{i(1)}(\cdot)$ and $N^t_{i(2)}(\cdot)$ such that $K^t_i(P^t_{1(2)}, P^t_{2(2)}, P^t_{3(2)}) \geq \overline{P}^t_{(i-1)(2)} + (P_i + \overline{P}^t_{(i-1)(1)})P_{i-1}\overline{P}^t_{(i+1)(2)}$, where $\frac{\partial K^t_i(\cdot)}{\partial P^t_{j(2)}}\delta_j \leq 0$, for $j = 1, 2, 3$; $M^t_{i(1)}(P^t_{1(2)}, P^t_{2(2)}, P^t_{3(2)}) \geq P_{i+1}P_{i-1}\overline{P}^t_{(i+1)(2)}$, where $\frac{\partial M^t_{i(1)}(\cdot)}{\partial P^t_{j(2)}(\cdot)}\delta_j \leq 0$, for $j = 1, 2, 3$;*

and $N^t_{i(2)}(P^t_{1(2)}, P^t_{2(2)}, P^t_{3(2)}) \leq P_{i+1}\left(P_i \overline{P}^t_{(i-1)(1)} + P_{i-1}\overline{P}^t_{(i+1)(1)} + (P_{i-1})^2\right)$,
where $\frac{\partial N^t_{i(1)}}{\partial P^t_{j(2)}}\delta_j \geq 0$, for $j = 1, 2, 3$,

then
$$g^B_i(\cdot) = \frac{M^t_{i(1)}(\cdot) + K^t_i(\cdot)}{N^t_{i(2)}(\cdot) + K^t_i(\cdot)} + \frac{[\mu_{i(2)} - \mu_{i(1)}]}{\lambda_{i(2)}N^t_{i(2)}(\cdot)} - \frac{\lambda_{i(1)}}{\lambda_{i(2)}}$$

satisfies properties (1) and (2) of Theorem 1;

b) if $k_i = 0$ and $\frac{\lambda_{i(2)}}{\lambda_{i(1)}} \leq 1$ and $\mu_{i(1)} > \mu_{i(2)}$ and if there exists $K^t_i(\cdot)$, $M^t_{i(2)}(\cdot)$ and $N^t_{i(1)}(\cdot)$ such that $K^t_i(P^t_{1(2)}, P^t_{2(2)}, P^t_{3(2)}) \geq \overline{P}^t_{(i-1)(2)} + \left(P_i + \overline{P}^t_{(i-1)(1)}\right)P_{i-1}\overline{P}^t_{(i+1)(2)}$, where $\frac{\partial K^t_i(\cdot)}{\partial P^t_{j(2)}}\delta_j \leq 0$, for $j = 1, 2, 3$;
$M^t_{i(2)}(P^t_{1(2)}, P^t_{2(2)}, P^t_{3(2)}) \geq P_{i+1}\left(P_i \overline{P}^t_{(i-1)(1)} + P_{i-1}\overline{P}^t_{(i+1)(1)} + (P_{i-1})^2\right)$,
where $\frac{\partial M^t_{i(2)}(\cdot)}{\partial P^t_{j(2)}}\delta_j \leq 0$, for $j = 1, 2, 3$; and $N^t_{i(1)}(P^t_{1(2)}, P^t_{2(2)}, P^t_{3(2)}) \leq P_{i+1}P_{i-1}\overline{P}^t_{(i+1)(2)}$, where $\frac{\partial N^t_{i(1)}(\cdot)}{\partial P^t_{j(2)}}\delta_j \geq 0$, for $j = 1, 2, 3$,

then
$$g^B_i(\cdot) = \frac{M^t_{i(2)}(\cdot) + K^t_i(\cdot)}{N^t_{i(1)}(\cdot) + K^t_i(\cdot)} + \frac{[\mu_{i(1)} - \mu_{i(2)}]}{\lambda_{i(1)}N^t_{i(1)}(\cdot)} - \frac{\lambda_{i(2)}}{\lambda_{i(1)}}$$

satisfies properties (1) and (2) of Theorem 1.

Proof of Part a): Since $\frac{P^t_{i(1)}(s)}{\overline{P}^t_{i(1)}} = \overline{P}^t_{(i-1)(2)} + \left(P_i + \overline{P}^t_{(i-1)(1)} + P_{i+1}\right)P_{i-1}\overline{P}^t_{(i+1)(2)}$
and $\frac{P^t_{i(2)}(s)}{\overline{P}^t_{i(2)}} = \overline{P}^t_{(i-1)(2)} + \left(P_i + \overline{P}^t_{(i-1)(1)}\right)P_{i-1}\overline{P}^t_{(i+1)(2)} + P_{i+1}\left(P_i \overline{P}^t_{(i-1)(1)} + P_{i-1}\overline{P}^t_{(i+1)(1)} + (P_{i-1})^2\right)$, it follows that,

$$\frac{\left[\frac{P^t_{i(1)}(s)}{P^t_{i(1)}P_i}\right]}{\left[\frac{P^t_{i(2)}(s)}{P^t_{i(2)}P_i}\right]} + \frac{[\mu_{i(2)} - \mu_{i(1)}]}{\lambda_{i(2)}\left[\frac{P^t_{i(2)}(s)}{P^t_{i(2)}P_i}\right]} \leq \frac{M^t_{i(1)} + \overline{P}^t_{(i-1)(2)} + \left(P_i + \overline{P}^t_{(i-1)(1)}\right)P_{i-1}\overline{P}^t_{(i+1)(2)}}{N^t_{i(2)} + \overline{P}^t_{(i-1)(2)} + \left(P_i + \overline{P}^t_{(i-1)(1)}\right)P_{i-1}\overline{P}^t_{(i+1)(2)}}$$

$$+ \frac{[\mu_{i(2)} - \mu_{i(1)}]}{\lambda_{i(2)}N^t_{i(2)}}$$

$$= \frac{M^t_{i(1)} + K^t_i}{N^t_{i(2)} + K^t_i} + \frac{[\mu_{i(2)} - \mu_{i(1)}]}{\lambda_{i(2)}N^t_{i(2)}}.$$

Since for $i \in \{1, 2, 3\}$, $g_i^B(\cdot) < 0$, the above equation further implies that

$$\frac{\left[\frac{P_{i(1)}^t(s)}{P_{i(1)}^t P_i}\right]}{\left[\frac{P_{i(2)}^t(s)}{P_{i(2)}^t P_i}\right]} + \frac{[\mu_{i(2)} - \mu_{i(1)}]}{\lambda_{i(2)} \left[\frac{P_{i(2)}^t(s)}{P_{i(2)}^t P_i}\right]} < \frac{\lambda_{i(1)}}{\lambda_{i(2)}} \leq 1,$$

it follows that Property (1) of Theorem 1 holds.

Property (2) of Theorem 1 follows since for $j = 1, 2, 3$,

$$\frac{\partial g_i^B(\cdot)}{\partial P_{j(2)}^t} \delta_j = \frac{\partial M_{i(1)}^t}{\partial P_{j(2)}^t} \delta_j \frac{1}{N_{i(2)}^t + K_i^t} - \frac{\partial N_{i(2)}^t}{\partial P_{j(2)}^t} \delta_j \left[\frac{M_{i(1)}^t + K_i^t}{\left(N_{i(2)}^t + K_i^t\right)^2} + \frac{[\mu_{i(2)} - \mu_{i(1)}]}{\lambda_{i(2)} \left(N_{i(2)}^t\right)^2} \right]$$

$$+ \frac{\partial K_i^t}{\partial P_{j(2)}^t} \delta_j \frac{N_{i(2)}^t - M_{i(1)}^t}{\left(N_{i(2)}^t + K_i^t\right)^2} \leq 0.$$

Proof of Part b) can be done similarly.

Appendix B

For all of this appendix, when Lemmas 1 and 2 are used, $\mu_{i(k)} = 0 \ \forall i, k$.

Proof of Proposition 7.1: I. For the first three equilibria, to derive the open balls of attraction, use Theorem 1 of Appendix A. The open ball B_i, for $i = 1, 2, 3$, is

$$\left\{ \left(P_{1(2)}^0, P_{2(2)}^0, P_{3(2)}^0\right) \in [0, 1] \times [0, 1] \times [0, 1] : g_j^{B_i}\left(P_{1(2)}^0, P_{2(2)}^0, P_{3(2)}^0\right) \right.$$
$$\left. < 0, j = 1, 2, 3 \right\}, \text{ where}$$

(1) with $\frac{4}{3} < \frac{\lambda_{1(2)}}{\lambda_{1(1)}}$, $g_1^{B_1} = S_{1(2)}^t(\cdot) - R_{1(1)}^t$, which is constructed using Lemma 1 where $S_{1(2)}^t(\cdot) = \frac{\frac{1}{3}P_{3(2)}^t + \frac{4}{27} + \frac{1}{27}P_{2(1)}^t}{\lambda_{1(2)}}$ and $R_{1(1)}^t = \frac{\frac{1}{27}\left(2+P_{3(1)}^t\right)P_{2(2)}^t}{\lambda_{1(1)}}$; $g_2^{B_1} = S_{2(1)}^t(\cdot) - R_{2(2)}^t(\cdot)$, which is constructed using Lemma 1 where $S_{2(1)}^t(\cdot) = \frac{\frac{1}{3}P_{1(2)}^t + \frac{3}{27}P_{3(2)}^t}{\lambda_{2(1)}}$ and $R_{2(2)}^t(\cdot) = \frac{\frac{1}{27}\left(1+P_{1(1)}^t+P_{3(1)}^t\right)}{\lambda_{2(2)}}$; and with $\frac{11}{9} < \frac{\lambda_{3(2)}}{\lambda_{3(1)}}$, $g_3^{B_1} = S_{3(2)}^t(\cdot) - R_{3(1)}^t$, which is constructed using Lemma 1 where $S_{3(2)}^t(\cdot) = \frac{\frac{1}{3} + \frac{1}{27}\left(1+P_{2(1)}^t\right)P_{1(2)}^t + \frac{1}{27}\left(2+P_{2(1)}^t\right)}{\lambda_{3(2)}}$ and $R_{3(1)}^t = \frac{\frac{1}{3}P_{2(2)}^t}{\lambda_{3(1)}}$;

(2) with $\frac{3}{4} < \frac{\lambda_{1(1)}}{\lambda_{1(2)}}$, $g_1^{B_2} = \frac{M_{1(1)}^t(\cdot) + K_1^t(\cdot)}{N_{1(2)}^t(\cdot) + K_1^t(\cdot)} - \frac{\lambda_{1(1)}}{\lambda_{1(2)}}$, which is constructed using Lemma 2 where $K_1^t(.) = \frac{1}{3} P_{3(2)}^t + \frac{2}{27}$, $M_{1(1)}^t(\cdot) = \frac{1}{27}$ and $N_{1(2)}^t(\cdot) = \frac{1}{27}(1 + P_{3(1)}^t)$; $g_2^{B_2} = S_{2(1)}^t(\cdot) - R_{2(2)}^t(\cdot)$, which is constructed using Lemma 1 where $S_{2(1)}^t(\cdot) = \frac{\frac{1}{3} + \frac{1}{27}(2 + P_{1(1)}^t) P_{3(2)}^t}{\lambda_{2(1)}}$ and $R_{2(2)}^t(\cdot) = \frac{\frac{1}{3} P_{1(2)}^t + \frac{1}{27}(1 + P_{3(1)}^t)}{\lambda_{2(2)}}$; and $g_3^{B_2} = S_{3(2)}^t(\cdot) - R_{3(1)}^t$, which is constructed using Lemma 1 where $S_{3(2)}^t(\cdot) = \frac{\frac{1}{3} + \frac{2}{27}(1 + P_{2(1)}^t) + \frac{1}{27} P_{1(1)}^t}{\lambda_{3(2)}}$ and $R_{3(1)}^t = \frac{\frac{1}{3} P_{2(2)}^t + \frac{2}{27} P_{1(2)}^t}{\lambda_{3(1)}}$;

(3) $g_1^{B_3} = S_{1(2)}^t(\cdot) - R_{1(1)}^t$, which is constructed using Lemma 1 where $S_{1(2)}^t(\cdot) = \frac{\frac{11}{27} + \frac{2}{27} P_{3(1)}^t + \frac{1}{27} P_{2(1)}^t}{\lambda_{1(2)}}$ and $R_{1(1)}^t = \frac{\frac{1}{3} P_{3(2)}^t + \frac{2}{27} P_{2(2)}^t}{\lambda_{1(1)}}$; $g_2^{B_3} = S_{2(1)}^t(\cdot) - R_{2(2)}^t(\cdot)$, which is constructed using Lemma 1 where $S_{2(1)}^t(\cdot) = \frac{\frac{1}{3} P_{1(2)}^t + \frac{1}{9}}{\lambda_{2(1)}}$ and $R_{2(2)}^t(\cdot) = \frac{(1 + P_{1(1)}^t) \frac{1}{27}(1 + P_{3(2)}^t)}{\lambda_{2(2)}}$; and with $\frac{9}{11} < \frac{\lambda_{3(1)}}{\lambda_{3(2)}}$, $g_3^{B_3} = \frac{M_{3(1)}^t(\cdot) + K_3^t(\cdot)}{N_{3(2)}^t(\cdot) + K_3^t(\cdot)} - \frac{\lambda_{3(1)}}{\lambda_{3(2)}}$, which is constructed using Lemma 2 where $K_3^t(.) = \frac{1}{3} + \frac{1}{27}(1 + P_{2(1)}^t) P_{1(2)}^t$, $M_{3(1)}^t(\cdot) = \frac{1}{27} P_{1(2)}^t$ and $N_{3(2)}^t(\cdot) = \frac{1}{27}(1 + P_{1(1)}^t)$.

II(1). This is shown by contradiction. Suppose that there exists an initial point, say $(\widetilde{P}_{1(2)}^0, \widetilde{P}_{2(2)}^0, \widetilde{P}_{3(2)}^0)$, that leads the economy through a path $(\widetilde{P}_{1(2)}^t, \widetilde{P}_{2(2)}^t, \widetilde{P}_{3(2)}^t)_{t \geq 1}$ to $(1, 0, 1)$ or $(1, 0, 0), (0, 0, 1)$ and $(0,0,0)$. Then $\widetilde{P}_{2(1)}^{t+1} > \widetilde{P}_{2(1)}^t$, for some t. It follows that under dynamics F,

$$\frac{\widetilde{P}_{2(1)}^t(s)}{\lambda_{2(1)} \widetilde{P}_{2(1)}^t} > \frac{\widetilde{P}_{2(2)}^t(s)}{\lambda_{2(2)} \widetilde{P}_{2(2)}^t}, \text{ for some } t.$$

That is,

$$\frac{1}{\lambda_{2(1)}} \left(\frac{1}{3} \widetilde{P}_{1(2)}^t + \frac{1}{27}(2 + \widetilde{P}_{1(1)}^t) \widetilde{P}_{3(2)}^t \right)$$
$$> \frac{1}{\lambda_{2(2)}} \left(\frac{1}{3} \widetilde{P}_{1(2)}^t + \frac{1}{27}(1 + \widetilde{P}_{1(1)}^t) \widetilde{P}_{3(2)}^t + \frac{1}{27}(1 + \widetilde{P}_{1(1)}^t + \widetilde{P}_{3(1)}^t) \right).$$

(7.10)

However, since $\lambda_{2(1)} > \lambda_{2(2)}$, $\frac{1}{\lambda_{2(1)}} < \frac{1}{\lambda_{2(2)}}$, and since $\frac{1}{3} \widetilde{P}_{1(2)}^t + \frac{1}{27}(1 + \widetilde{P}_{1(1)}^t) \widetilde{P}_{3(2)}^t + \frac{1}{27} \widetilde{P}_{3(2)}^t \leq \frac{1}{3} \widetilde{P}_{1(2)}^t + \frac{1}{27}(1 + \widetilde{P}_{1(1)}^t) \widetilde{P}_{3(2)}^t + \frac{1}{27} + \frac{1}{27} \widetilde{P}_{1(1)}^t + \frac{1}{27} \widetilde{P}_{3(1)}^t$, equation (7.10) cannot be possibly true.

II(2). Consider the fixed point $(1, 1, 1)$. One of the eigenvalues of the Jacobian evaluated at $(1,1,1)$ for the Example 1 is $1 + \frac{11}{27}(\lambda_{1(2)} - \lambda_{1(1)}) > 1$ (due to $\lambda_{1(2)} > \lambda_{1(1)}$). Therefore $(1,1,1)$ in Example 1 is not asymptotically stable.

Proof of Proposition 7.2: I. For the first six equilibria, to derive the open balls of attraction, use Theorem 1 of Appendix A. The open ball $\widetilde{B}_i$, for $i = 1, 2, 3$, is

$$\left\{ \left(P_{1(2)}^0, P_{2(2)}^0, P_{3(2)}^0 \right) \in [0,1] \times [0,1] \times [0,1] : g_j^{\widetilde{B}_i} \left(P_{1(2)}^0, P_{2(2)}^0, P_{3(2)}^0 \right) \right.$$
$$\left. < 0, j = 1, 2, 3 \right\}, \text{ where}$$

(1) with $P_1 + P_3 < \frac{\lambda_{1(2)}}{\lambda_{1(1)}}$, $g_1^{\widetilde{B}_1} = S_{1(2)}^t(\cdot) - R_{1(1)}^t$, which is constructed using Lemma 1 where $S_{1(2)}^t(\cdot) = \frac{P_3 P_{3(2)}^t + (P_1 + P_3)P_2 P_3 + P_3 P_2 \left(P_3 + P_1 + P_2 P_{2(1)}^t \right)}{\lambda_{1(2)}}$ and $R_{1(1)}^t = \frac{\left(P_1 + P_2 + P_3 P_{3(1)}^t \right) P_2 P_{2(2)}^t P_3}{\lambda_{1(1)}}$;

$g_2^{\widetilde{B}_1} = S_{2(1)}^t(\cdot) - R_{2(2)}^t(\cdot)$, which is constructed using Lemma 1 where $S_{2(1)}^t(\cdot) = \frac{P_1 \left(P_{1(2)}^t + P_3 P_{3(2)}^t \right)}{\lambda_{2(1)}}$ and $R_{2(2)}^t(\cdot) = \frac{P_1 P_3 \left(P_1 + P_2 P_{1(1)}^t + P_3 P_{3(1)}^t \right)}{\lambda_{2(2)}}$; and with $1 + P_1(P_1 + P_3) < \frac{\lambda_{3(2)}}{\lambda_{3(1)}}$, $g_3^{\widetilde{B}_1} = S_{3(2)}^t(\cdot) - R_{3(1)}^t$, which is constructed using Lemma 1 where $S_{3(2)}^t(\cdot) = \frac{P_2 + \left(P_3 + P_2 P_{2(1)}^t \right) P_1 P_{1(2)}^t P_2 + P_1 P_2 \left(P_2 + P_3 P_{2(1)}^t + P_1 \right)}{\lambda_{3(2)}}$ and $R_{3(1)}^t = \frac{P_2 P_{2(2)}^t}{\lambda_{3(1)}}$;

(2) with $2(P_1 + P_3) > \frac{\lambda_{1(2)}}{\lambda_{1(1)}}$, $g_1^{\widetilde{B}_2} = \frac{M_{1(1)}^t(\cdot) + K_1^t(\cdot)}{N_{1(2)}^t(\cdot) + K_1^t(\cdot)} - \frac{\lambda_{1(1)}}{\lambda_{1(2)}}$, which is constructed using Lemma 2 where $K_1^t(.) = P_3 P_{3(2)}^t + (P_1 + P_3) P_2 P_3$, $M_{1(1)}^t(\cdot) = (P_2)^2 P_3$ and $N_{1(2)}^t(\cdot) = P_2 P_3 (P_3 + P_1 P_{3(1)}^t)$; $g_2^{\widetilde{B}_2} = S_{2(1)}^t(\cdot) - R_{2(2)}^t(\cdot)$, which is constructed using Lemma 1 where $S_{2(1)}^t(\cdot) = \frac{P_1 + \left(P_2 + P_3 + P_1 P_{1(1)}^t \right) P_3 P_{3(2)}^t P_1}{\lambda_{2(1)}}$ and $R_{2(2)}^t(\cdot) = \frac{P_1 P_{1(2)}^t + P_3 P_1 \left(P_1 + P_3 P_{3(1)}^t \right)}{\lambda_{2(2)}}$; and with $\frac{1 + P_1(P_2 + P_3)}{1 + P_1(P_1 + P_3)} < \frac{\lambda_{3(2)}}{\lambda_{3(1)}}$, $g_3^{\widetilde{B}_2} = S_{3(2)}^t(\cdot) - R_{3(1)}^t$, which is constructed using Lemma 1 where $S_{3(2)}^t(\cdot) = \frac{P_2 + \left(P_3 + P_2 P_{2(1)}^t \right) P_1 P_2 + P_1 P_2 \left(P_2 + P_3 P_{2(1)}^t + P_1 P_{1(1)}^t \right)}{\lambda_{3(2)}}$ and $R_{3(1)}^t = \frac{P_2 P_{2(2)}^t + (P_3 + P_1) P_1 P_{1(2)}^t P_2}{\lambda_{3(1)}}$;

(3) with $\frac{1 + P_2(P_1 + P_3)}{1 + P_2(P_1 + P_2)} < \frac{\lambda_{1(2)}}{\lambda_{1(1)}}$, $g_1^{\widetilde{B}_3} = S_{1(2)}^t(\cdot) - R_{1(1)}^t$, which is constructed using Lemma 1 where $S_{1(2)}^t(\cdot) = \frac{P_3 + \left(P_1 + P_3 P_{3(1)}^t \right) P_2 P_3 + P_2 P_3 \left(P_3 + P_1 P_{3(1)}^t + P_2 P_{2(1)}^t \right)}{\lambda_{1(2)}}$ and $R_{1(1)}^t = \frac{P_3 P_{3(2)}^t + (P_1 + P_2) P_2 P_{2(2)}^t P_3}{\lambda_{1(1)}}$; with $2(P_1 + P_2) > \frac{\lambda_{2(2)}}{\lambda_{2(1)}}$, $g_2^{\widetilde{B}_3} = S_{2(1)}^t(\cdot) - R_{2(2)}^t(\cdot)$, which is constructed using Lemma 1 where $S_{2(1)}^t(\cdot) = \frac{P_1 \left(P_{1(2)}^t + P_3 \right)}{\lambda_{2(1)}}$ and $R_{2(2)}^t(\cdot) = \frac{\left(P_2 + P_1 P_{1(1)}^t \right) P_3 P_{3(2)}^t P_1 + P_3 P_1 \left(P_1 + P_2 P_{1(1)}^t \right)}{\lambda_{2(2)}}$; and with $1 + P_1(P_1 + P_2) > \frac{\lambda_{3(2)}}{\lambda_{3(1)}}$, $g_3^{\widetilde{B}_3} = \frac{M_{3(1)}^t(\cdot) + K_3^t(\cdot)}{N_{3(2)}^t(\cdot) + K_3^t(\cdot)} - \frac{\lambda_{3(1)}}{\lambda_{3(2)}}$, which is constructed using Lemma 2 where $K_3^t(.) = P_2 + \left(P_3 + P_2 P_{2(1)}^t \right) P_1 P_{1(2)}^t P_2$, $M_{3(1)}^t(\cdot) = (P_1)^2 P_2 P_{1(2)}^t$ and $N_{3(2)}^t(\cdot) = P_1 P_2 (P_2 + P_1 P_{1(1)}^t)$;

(4) with $1 + P_3(P_2 + P_3) < \frac{\lambda_{1(2)}}{\lambda_{1(1)}}$, $g_1^{\widetilde{B_4}} = S_{1(2)}^t(\cdot) - R_{1(1)}^t$, which is constructed using Lemma 1 where $S_{1(2)}^t(\cdot) = \frac{P_3 + (P_1 + P_3 P_{3(1)}^t) P_2 P_{2(2)}^t P_3 + P_2 P_3 (P_3 + P_1 P_{3(1)}^t + P_2)}{\lambda_{1(2)}}$ and $R_{1(1)}^t = \frac{P_3 P_{3(2)}^t}{\lambda_{1(1)}}$; with $2(P_1 + P_2) < \frac{\lambda_{2(2)}}{\lambda_{2(1)}}$, $g_2^{\widetilde{B_4}} = \frac{M_{2(2)}^t(\cdot) + K_2^t(\cdot)}{N_{2(1)}^t(\cdot) + K_2^t(\cdot)} - \frac{\lambda_{2(2)}}{\lambda_{2(1)}}$, which is constructed using Lemma 2 where $K_2^t(\cdot) = P_1 P_{1(2)}^t + (P_2 + P_1) P_3 P_1$, $M_{2(2)}^t(\cdot) = P_3 P_1 (P_1 + P_2 + P_3 P_{3(1)}^t)$ and $N_{2(1)}^t(\cdot) = (P_3)^2 P_{3(2)}^t P_1$; and $g_3^{\widetilde{B_4}} = \frac{M_{3(1)}^t(\cdot) + K_3^t(\cdot)}{N_{3(2)}^t(\cdot) + K_3^t(\cdot)} - \frac{\lambda_{3(1)}}{\lambda_{3(2)}}$, which is constructed using Lemma 2 where $K_3^t(\cdot) = P_2 P_{2(2)}^t + (P_3 + P_2) P_1 P_{1(2)}^t P_2$, $M_{3(1)}^t(\cdot) = (P_1)^2 P_2 P_{1(2)}^t$ and $N_{3(2)}^t(\cdot) = P_1 P_2(P_2 + P_3 P_{2(1)}^t + P_1 P_{1(1)}^t)$;

(5) with $1 + P_2(P_2 + P_3) > \frac{\lambda_{1(2)}}{\lambda_{1(1)}}$, $g_1^{\widetilde{B_5}} = \frac{M_{1(1)}^t + K_1^t(\cdot)}{N_{1(2)}^t + K_1^t(\cdot)} - \frac{\lambda_{1(1)}}{\lambda_{1(2)}}$, which is constructed using Lemma 2 where $K_1^t(\cdot) = P_3 + (P_1 + P_3 P_{3(1)}^t) P_2 P_{2(2)}^t P_3$, $M_{1(1)}^t = (P_2)^2 P_{2(2)}^t P_3$ and $N_{1(2)}^t = P_2 P_3 (P_3 + P_2 P_{2(1)}^t)$; with $\frac{1+P_3(P_1+P_2)}{1+P_3(P_2+P_3)} < \frac{\lambda_{2(2)}}{\lambda_{2(1)}}$, $g_2^{\widetilde{B_5}} = \frac{M_{2(2)}^t(\cdot) + K_2^t(\cdot)}{N_{2(1)}^t(\cdot) + K_2^t(\cdot)} - \frac{\lambda_{2(2)}}{\lambda_{2(1)}}$, which is constructed using Lemma 2 where $K_2^t(\cdot) = P_1 + (P_2 + P_1 P_{1(1)}^t) P_3 P_1$, $M_{2(2)}^t(\cdot) = P_3 P_1 (P_1 + P_2 P_{1(1)}^t + P_3 P_{3(1)}^t)$ and $N_{2(1)}^t(\cdot) = (P_3)^2 P_{3(2)}^t P_1$; and with $2(P_2 + P_3) > \frac{\lambda_{3(2)}}{\lambda_{3(1)}}$, $g_3^{\widetilde{B_5}} = \frac{M_{3(1)}^t(\cdot) + K_3^t(\cdot)}{N_{3(2)}^t(\cdot) + K_3^t(\cdot)} - \frac{\lambda_{3(1)}}{\lambda_{3(2)}}$, which is constructed using Lemma 2 where $K_3^t(\cdot) = P_2 P_{2(2)}^t + (P_3 + P_2) P_1 P_2$, $M_{3(1)}^t(\cdot) = (P_1)^2 P_2$ and $N_{3(2)}^t(\cdot) = P_1 P_2(P_2 + P_3 P_{2(1)}^t)$;

(6) with $\frac{1+P_2(P_1+P_2)}{1+P_2(P_1+P_3)} < \frac{\lambda_{1(1)}}{\lambda_{1(2)}}$, $g_1^{\widetilde{B_6}} = \frac{M_{1(1)}^t + K_1^t(\cdot)}{N_{1(2)}^t + K_1^t(\cdot)} - \frac{\lambda_{1(1)}}{\lambda_{1(2)}}$, which is constructed using Lemma 2 where $K_1^t(\cdot) = P_3 + (P_1 + P_3 P_{3(1)}^t) P_2 P_3$, $M_{1(1)}^t = (P_2)^2 P_3$ and $N_{1(2)}^t = P_2(P_3)^2$; with $\frac{1+P_3(P_2+P_3)}{1+P_3(P_1+P_2)} < \frac{\lambda_{2(1)}}{\lambda_{2(2)}}$, $g_2^{\widetilde{B_6}} = S_{2(1)}^t(\cdot) - R_{2(2)}^t(\cdot)$, which is constructed using Lemma 1 where $S_{2(1)}^t(\cdot) = \frac{P_1 + (P_2 + P_3 + P_1 P_{1(1)}^t) P_1 P_3}{\lambda_{2(1)}}$ and $R_{2(2)}^t(\cdot) = \frac{P_1 P_{1(2)}^t + P_2 P_3 P_{3(2)}^t P_1 + P_3 (P_1)^2}{\lambda_{2(2)}}$; and with $\frac{1+P_1(P_1+P_3)}{1+P_1(P_2+P_3)} < \frac{\lambda_{3(1)}}{\lambda_{3(2)}}$, $g_3^{\widetilde{B_6}} = \frac{M_{3(1)}^t(\cdot) + K_3^t(\cdot)}{N_{3(2)}^t(\cdot) + K_3^t(\cdot)} - \frac{\lambda_{3(1)}}{\lambda_{3(2)}}$, which is constructed using Lemma 2 where $K_3^t(\cdot) = P_2 + (P_3 + P_2 P_{2(1)}^t) P_1 P_2$, $M_{3(1)}^t(\cdot) = (P_1)^2 P_2$ and $N_{3(2)}^t(\cdot) = P_1 (P_2)^2$.

II (i). The first part is shown by contradiction. Suppose that there exists an initial point, say $(\widetilde{P}_{1(2)}^0, \widetilde{P}_{2(2)}^0, \widetilde{P}_{3(2)}^0)$, that leads the economy through a path $(\widetilde{P}_{1(2)}^t, \widetilde{P}_{2(2)}^t, \widetilde{P}_{3(2)}^t)_{t \geq 1}$ to $(1, 0, 0)$ and $(0, 0, 0)$. Then the following must be true:

$$\widetilde{P}_{2(1)}^{t+1} > \widetilde{P}_{2(1)}^t, \text{ for some } t.$$

Under dynamics F,

$$\frac{\widetilde{P}^t_{2(1)}(s)}{\lambda_{2(1)}\overline{\widetilde{P}}^t_{2(1)}} > \frac{\widetilde{P}^t_{2(2)}(s)}{\lambda_{2(2)}\overline{\widetilde{P}}^t_{2(2)}}, \text{ for some } t.$$

That is,

$$\frac{1}{\lambda_{2(1)}}\left[P_1\widetilde{P}^t_{1(2)} + (P_2 + P_1\widetilde{P}^t_{1(1)} + P_3)P_1P_3\widetilde{P}^t_{3(2)}\right]$$

$$> \frac{1}{\lambda_{2(2)}}\left[P_1\widetilde{P}^t_{1(2)} + (P_2 + P_1\widetilde{P}^t_{1(1)})P_1P_3\widetilde{P}^t_{3(2)}\right.$$

$$\left. + \left(P_2P_1\widetilde{P}^t_{1(1)} + P_1P_3\widetilde{P}^t_{3(1)} + (P_1)^2\right)P_3\right]. \quad (7.11)$$

However, since $\lambda_{2(1)} > \lambda_{2(2)}$, $\frac{1}{\lambda_{2(1)}} < \frac{1}{\lambda_{2(2)}}$, and since $P_1 \geq P_3$, Equation (7.11) cannot be possibly true.

(ii) In Example 1, one of the eigenvalues of the Jacobian evaluated at $(1,0,0)$ is $1 + (\lambda_{2(1)} - \lambda_{2(2)})P_1 + \lambda_{2(1)}P_1P_3(P_1 + P_3)$. Since $\lambda_{2(1)} > \lambda_{2(2)}$, at least one of the eigenvalues in Example 1 is greater than one. Therefore, $(1,0,0)$ is not asymptotically stable.

In Example 1, one of the eigenvalues of the Jacobian evaluated at $(0,0,0)$ is $1 + \lambda_{1(1)}P_2P_3$. Therefore, in Example 1, $(0,0,0)$ is not asymptotically stable.

Proof of Proposition 7.3: Since $\lambda_{i(1)} = \lambda_{i(2)}$ and since for $t = 1, 2, 3, ...$, for $P^t_{i(2)} \in (0, 1)$, $\frac{P^t_{i(1)}(s)}{\lambda_{i(1)}\overline{P}^t_{i(1)}} - \frac{P^t_{i(2)}(s)}{\lambda_{i(2)}\overline{P}^t_{i(2)}} = \frac{\frac{1}{27}P^t_{(i+1)(2)} - \frac{1}{27}\left(1 + P^t_{(i+1)(1)} + P^t_{(i-1)(1)}\right)}{\lambda_{i(1)}} < 0$, it follows that $P^{t+1}_{i(2)} > P^t_{i(2)} \, \forall \, t$. With $k_1 = k_2 = k_3 = 1$ and $B = [0, 1] \times [0, 1] \times [0, 1]$, the proof in Step II of Theorem 1 in Appendix A applies here.

Proof of Proposition 7.4:

I. The open balls $\widehat{B}_j$ ($j = 1, 2, 3$ (modulo 3)) are constructed using Lemma 2 and Theorem 1 of Appendix A where with $2(P_{j-1} + P_j) > 1$, $g_j^{\widehat{B}_j}$ is constructed using $M^t_{j(1)} = (P_{j+1})^2 P_{j-1}$, $N^t_{j(2)} = (P_{j-1} + P_j P^t_{(j-1)(1)})P_{j+1}P_{j-1}$ and $K^t_j = \overline{P}^t_{(j-1)(2)} + (P_j + P_{j-1})P_{j-1}P_{j+1}$; with $\frac{1+P_{j-1}(P_{j-1}+P_{j+1})}{1+P_{j-1}(P_j+P_{j+1})} < 1$, $g_{j+1}^{\widehat{B}_j}$ is constructed using $M^t_{(j+1)(1)} = (P_{j-1})^2 P^t_{(j-1)(2)}P_j$, $N^t_{(j+1)(2)} = (P_j + P_{j-1}P^t_{(j-1)(1)})P_jP_{j-1}$ and $K^t_{j+1} = P_j + (P_{j+1} + \overline{P}^t_{j(1)})P_j\overline{P}^t_{(j-1)(2)}$; and with $\frac{1+P_j(P_{j+1}+P_{j-1})}{1+P_j(P_j+P_{j-1})} < 1$, $g_{j-1}^{\widehat{B}_j}$ is constructed using $M^t_{(j-1)(2)} = (P_{j+1} + P_{j-1}P^t_{(j+1)(1)} + P_jP^t_{j(1)})P_jP_{j+1}$, $N^t_{(j-1)(1)} = (P_j)^2 P^t_{j(2)}P_{j+1}$ and $K^t_{j-1} = P_{j+1} + (P_{j-1} + \overline{P}^t_{(j+1)(1)})P_{j+1}P_j$.

II. In all examples, without loss of generality, set $\lambda_{i(k)} = \lambda_{i'(k')} = 1$ for all i, i', k, k'.

Consider the dynamics under Example 1. (1,0,0) is not asymptotically stable since one of eigenvalue of the Jacobian is $1 + P_1 P_3(P_1 + P_3) > 1$. (0,1,0) is not asymptotically stable since one of eigenvalue of the Jacobian is $1 + P_1 P_2(P_1 + P_2) > 1$. (0,0,1) is not asymptotically stable since one of eigenvalues of the Jacobian is $1 + P_2 P_3(P_2 + P_3) > 1$. (0,0,0) is not asymptotically stable since one of eigenvalue of the Jacobian is $1 + P_1 P_3 > 1$. (1,1,1) is not asymptotically stable since the eigenvalues of the Jacobian are $1 + P_1 P_3(P_3 - P_1)$, $1 + P_1 P_2(P_1 - P_2)$, and $1 + P_2 P_3(P_2 - P_3)$ and for any given set of values of P_1, P_2, and P_3, at least one of the eigenvalues is greater than 1.

Appendix C

Proof of Proposition 7.5: Consider the $g_i^{X_j}$ for which $g_i^{X_j} < 0$ for $X_j = B_j, \widetilde{B}_j$ and $\widehat{B}_j$, and $i = 1, 2, 3$, found in the proof of Proposition 7.1, 7.2, and 7.4 in Appendix B. It follows that there exits an $\epsilon > 0$, such that if $\mu_{i(k)} < \epsilon$, for all $i = 1, 2, 3$ and $k = 1, 2$, then $g_i^{X_j} + \frac{|\mu_{i(k)} - \mu_{i(k')}|}{\lambda_{i(k)}\lambda_{i(k')}} < 0$ and $g_i^{X_j} + \frac{|\mu_{i(k)} - \mu_{i(k')}|}{\lambda_{i(k)} N_{i(k)}^t(\cdot)} < 0$. Hence, the same principles described in the proofs of Proposition 7.1, 7.2, and 7.4 can be used to construct the open balls. Specifically, the open ball $\overline{X}_j$, where

$$\overline{X}_j = \left\{ (P_{1(2)}^0, P_{2(2)}^0, P_{3(2)}^0) \in [0,1]^3 : g_i^{\overline{X}_j}(P_{1(2)}^0, P_{2(2)}^0, P_{3(2)}^0) < 0, i = 1, 2, 3 \right\},$$

is constructed as follows.

I(i). For the results in Part I of Proposition 7.1 to hold under dynamics F', $X_j = B_j$ for $j = 1, 2, 3$; (1) $g_1^{\overline{B}_1} = g_1^{B_1} + \frac{\mu_{1(1)} - \mu_{1(2)}}{\lambda_{1(1)}\lambda_{1(2)}}$, $g_2^{\overline{B}_1} = g_2^{B_1} + \frac{\mu_{2(2)} - \mu_{2(1)}}{\lambda_{2(1)}\lambda_{2(2)}}$ and $g_3^{\overline{B}_1} = g_3^{B_1} + \frac{\mu_{3(1)} - \mu_{3(2)}}{\lambda_{3(1)}\lambda_{3(2)}}$; (2) $g_1^{\overline{B}_2} = g_1^{B_2} + \frac{\mu_{1(2)} - \mu_{1(1)}}{\lambda_{1(2)} N_{1(2)}^t(\cdot)}$, $g_2^{\overline{B}_2} = g_2^{B_2} + \frac{\mu_{2(2)} - \mu_{2(1)}}{\lambda_{2(1)}\lambda_{2(2)}}$ and $g_3^{\overline{B}_2} = g_3^{B_2} + \frac{\mu_{3(1)} - \mu_{3(2)}}{\lambda_{3(1)}\lambda_{3(2)}}$; (3) $g_1^{\overline{B}_3} = g_1^{B_3} + \frac{\mu_{1(1)} - \mu_{1(2)}}{\lambda_{1(1)}\lambda_{1(2)}}$, $g_2^{\overline{B}_3} = g_2^{B_3} + \frac{\mu_{2(2)} - \mu_{2(1)}}{\lambda_{1(1)}\lambda_{1(2)}}$ and $g_3^{\overline{B}_3} = g_3^{B_3} + \frac{\mu_{3(2)} - \mu_{3(1)}}{\lambda_{3(2)} N_{3(2)}^t(\cdot)}$; (ii) The proofs for the remaining results in Proposition 7.1 under dynamics F' can be done similarly to that of Proposition 7.1;

II(i). For the results in Part I of Proposition 7.2 to hold under dynamics F', $X_j = \widetilde{B}_j$ for $j = 1, 2, 3, 4, 5, 6$; (1) $g_1^{\widetilde{B}_1} = g_1^{\widetilde{B}_1} + \frac{\mu_{1(1)} - \mu_{1(2)}}{\lambda_{1(1)}\lambda_{1(2)}}$, $g_2^{\widetilde{B}_1} = g_2^{\widetilde{B}_1} + \frac{\mu_{2(2)} - \mu_{2(1)}}{\lambda_{2(1)}\lambda_{2(2)}}$ and $g_3^{\widetilde{B}_1} = g_3^{\widetilde{B}_1} + \frac{\mu_{3(1)} - \mu_{3(2)}}{\lambda_{3(1)}\lambda_{3(2)}}$; (2) $g_1^{\widetilde{B}_2} = g_1^{\widetilde{B}_2} + \frac{\mu_{1(2)} - \mu_{1(1)}}{\lambda_{1(2)} N_{1(2)}^t(\cdot)}$, $g_2^{\widetilde{B}_2} = g_2^{\widetilde{B}_2} + \frac{\mu_{2(2)} - \mu_{2(1)}}{\lambda_{2(1)}\lambda_{2(2)}}$ and $g_3^{\widetilde{B}_2} = g_3^{\widetilde{B}_2} + \frac{\mu_{3(1)} - \mu_{3(2)}}{\lambda_{3(1)}\lambda_{3(2)}}$; (3) $g_1^{\widetilde{B}_3} = g_1^{\widetilde{B}_3} + \frac{\mu_{1(1)} - \mu_{1(2)}}{\lambda_{1(1)}\lambda_{1(2)}}$, $g_2^{\widetilde{B}_3} =$

Appendix D

$g_2^{\overline{B}_3} + \frac{\mu_{2(2)}-\mu_{2(1)}}{\lambda_{2(1)}\lambda_{2(2)}}$ and $g_3^{\overline{B}_3} = g_3^{\widetilde{B}_3} + \frac{\mu_{3(2)}-\mu_{3(1)}}{\lambda_{3(2)}N_{3(2)}^t(\cdot)}$; (4) $g_1^{\overline{B}_4} = g_1^{\widetilde{B}_4} + \frac{\mu_{1(1)}-\mu_{1(2)}}{\lambda_{1(1)}\lambda_{1(2)}}$, $g_2^{\overline{B}_4} = g_2^{\widetilde{B}_4} + \frac{\mu_{2(1)}-\mu_{2(2)}}{\lambda_{2(1)}N_{2(1)}^t(\cdot)}$ and $g_3^{\overline{B}_4} = g_3^{\widetilde{B}_4} + \frac{\mu_{3(2)}-\mu_{3(1)}}{\lambda_{3(2)}N_{3(2)}^t(\cdot)}$; (5) $g_1^{\overline{B}_5} = g_1^{\widetilde{B}_5} + \frac{\mu_{1(2)}-\mu_{1(1)}}{\lambda_{1(2)}N_{1(2)}^t(\cdot)}$, $g_2^{\overline{B}_5} = g_2^{\widetilde{B}_5} + \frac{\mu_{2(1)}-\mu_{2(2)}}{\lambda_{2(1)}N_{2(1)}^t(\cdot)}$ and $g_3^{\overline{B}_5} = g_3^{\widetilde{B}_5} + \frac{\mu_{3(2)}-\mu_{3(1)}}{\lambda_{3(2)}N_{3(2)}^t(\cdot)}$; and (6) $g_1^{\overline{B}_6} = g_1^{\widetilde{B}_6} + \frac{\mu_{1(2)}-\mu_{1(1)}}{\lambda_{1(2)}N_{1(2)}^t(\cdot)}$, $g_2^{\overline{B}_6} = g_2^{\widetilde{B}_6} + \frac{\mu_{2(2)}-\mu_{2(1)}}{\lambda_{2(1)}\lambda_{2(2)}}$ and $g_3^{\overline{B}_6} = g_3^{\widetilde{B}_6} + \frac{\mu_{3(2)}-\mu_{3(1)}}{\lambda_{3(2)}N_{3(2)}^t(\cdot)}$.

(ii) The proofs for the remaining results in Proposition 7.2 under dynamics F' can be done similarly to that of Proposition 7.2;

III(i). For the results in Part I of Proposition 7.4 to hold under dynamics F', $X_j = \widehat{B}_j$ for $j = 1, 2, 3$; (1) $g_1^{\overline{B}_1} = g_1^{\widehat{B}_1} + \frac{\mu_{1(2)}-\mu_{1(1)}}{\lambda_{1(2)}N_{1(2)}^t(\cdot)}$, $g_2^{\overline{B}_1} = g_2^{\widehat{B}_1} + \frac{\mu_{2(2)}-\mu_{2(1)}}{\lambda_{2(2)}N_{2(2)}^t(\cdot)}$ and $g_3^{\overline{B}_1} = g_3^{\widehat{B}_1} + \frac{\mu_{3(1)}-\mu_{3(2)}}{\lambda_{3(1)}N_{3(1)}^t(\cdot)}$; (2) $g_1^{\overline{B}_2} = g_1^{\widehat{B}_2} + \frac{\mu_{1(1)}-\mu_{1(2)}}{\lambda_{1(1)}N_{1(1)}^t(\cdot)}$, $g_2^{\overline{B}_2} = g_2^{\widehat{B}_2} + \frac{\mu_{2(2)}-\mu_{2(1)}}{\lambda_{2(2)}N_{2(2)}^t(\cdot)}$ and $g_3^{\overline{B}_2} = g_3^{\widehat{B}_2} + \frac{\mu_{3(2)}-\mu_{3(1)}}{\lambda_{3(2)}N_{3(2)}^t(\cdot)}$;(3) $g_1^{\overline{B}_3} = g_1^{\widehat{B}_3} + \frac{\mu_{1(2)}-\mu_{1(1)}}{\lambda_{1(2)}N_{1(2)}^t(\cdot)}$, $g_2^{\overline{B}_3} = g_2^{\widehat{B}_3} + \frac{\mu_{2(1)}-\mu_{2(2)}}{\lambda_{2(1)}N_{2(1)}^t(\cdot)}$ and $g_3^{\overline{B}_3} = g_3^{\widehat{B}_3} + \frac{\mu_{3(2)}-\mu_{3(1)}}{\lambda_{3(2)}N_{3(2)}^t(\cdot)}$. The proofs for the remaining results in Proposition 7.4 under dynamics F' can be done similarly to that of Proposition 7.4.

IV. Proving the result in Proposition 7.3 under dynamics F' : since $\lambda_{i(1)} = \lambda_{i(2)}$ and since for $t = 1, 2, 3, ...$, $P_{i(2)}^t \in (0, 1)$, there exists an $\epsilon > 0$, such that if $\mu_{i(k)} < \epsilon$, then $\frac{P_{i(1)}^t(s)}{\lambda_{i(1)}\overline{P}_{i(1)}^t} - \frac{P_{i(2)}^t(s)}{\lambda_{i(2)}\overline{P}_{i(2)}^t} + \frac{\mu_{i(2)}-\mu_{i(1)}}{\lambda_{i(1)}\lambda_{i(2)}} = \frac{\frac{1}{27}P_{(i+1)(2)}^t - \frac{1}{27}\left(1+P_{(i+1)(1)}^t+P_{(i-1)(1)}^t\right)}{\lambda_{i(1)}} + \frac{\mu_{i(2)}-\mu_{i(1)}}{\lambda_{i(1)}\lambda_{i(2)}} < 0$. This further implies that $P_{i(2)}^{t+1} > P_{i(2)}^t \; \forall \; t$. With $k_1 = k_2 = k_3 = 1$ and $B = [0, 1] \times [0, 1] \times [0, 1]$, the proof in Step II of Theorem 1 in Appendix A applies here.

Appendix D

Proof of Proposition 7.6: Consider the equilibrium $(0, 1, 0)$ Since,

$$\frac{P_{i(1)}^t(s)}{\lambda_{i(1)}\overline{P}_{i(1)}^t} + \frac{\mu_{i(2)}}{\lambda_{i(1)}\lambda_{i(2)}} \geq \frac{\mu_{i(2)}}{\lambda_{i(1)}\lambda_{i(2)}} \text{ and } \frac{P_{i(2)}^t(s)}{\lambda_{i(2)}\overline{P}_{i(2)}^t} + \frac{\mu_{i(1)}}{\lambda_{i(1)}\lambda_{i(2)}} \leq \frac{1}{\lambda_{i(2)}}$$

$$+ \frac{\mu_{i(1)}}{\lambda_{i(1)}\lambda_{i(2)}} \text{ for } i = 1, 3$$

and if $\mu_{i(2)} > \lambda_{i(1)} + \mu_{i(1)}$, then it follows that for $i = 1, 3$, $\frac{P_{i(1)}^t(s)}{\lambda_{i(1)}\overline{P}_{i(1)}^t} + \frac{\mu_{i(2)}}{\lambda_{i(1)}\lambda_{i(2)}} > \frac{P_{i(2)}^t(s)}{\lambda_{i(2)}\overline{P}_{i(2)}^t} + \frac{\mu_{i(1)}}{\lambda_{i(1)}\lambda_{i(2)}}$ for all $\left(P_{1(2)}^t, P_{2(2)}^t, P_{3(2)}^t\right)$. Also, since

$$\frac{P_{2(2)}^t(s)}{\lambda_{2(2)}\overline{P}_{2(2)}^t} + \frac{\mu_{2(1)}}{\lambda_{2(1)}\lambda_{2(2)}} \geq \frac{\mu_{2(1)}}{\lambda_{2(1)}\lambda_{2(2)}} \text{ and } \frac{P_{2(1)}^t(s)}{\lambda_{2(1)}\overline{P}_{2(1)}^t} + \frac{\mu_{2(2)}}{\lambda_{2(1)}\lambda_{2(2)}}$$

$$\leq \frac{1}{\lambda_{2(1)}} + \frac{\mu_{2(2)}}{\lambda_{2(1)}\lambda_{2(2)}}$$

and if $\mu_{2(1)} > \lambda_{2(2)} + \mu_{2(2)}$, then it follows that $\frac{P_{2(2)}^t(s)}{\lambda_{2(2)}\overline{P}_{2(2)}^t} + \frac{\mu_{2(1)}}{\lambda_{2(1)}\lambda_{2(2)}} > \frac{P_{2(1)}^t(s)}{\lambda_{2(1)}\overline{P}_{2(1)}^t} + \frac{\mu_{2(2)}}{\lambda_{2(1)}\lambda_{2(2)}}$ for all $(P_{1(2)}^t, P_{2(2)}^t, P_{3(2)}^t)$. Therefore, there exists a unique open ball $\overline{B}'$ with $g_i^{\overline{B}'} = \lambda_{i(1)} + \mu_{i(1)} - \mu_{i(2)} < 0$ for $i = 1, 3$ and $g_2^{\overline{B}'} = \lambda_{2(2)} + \mu_{2(2)} - \mu_{2(1)} < 0$, and, with Theorem 1, the equilibrium $(0, 1, 0)$ is the only stable equilibrium.

References

Aiyagari, S.R., and N. Wallace. 1991. Existence of steady states with positive consumption in the Kiyotaki–Wright model. *Review of Economic Studies* 58: 901–916.

Bjornerstedt, J., and J. Weibull. 1996. Nash equilibrium and evolution by imitation. In *The rational foundations of economic behavior* eds. K. Arrow and E. Colombatto. New York: Saint Martin's Press.

Einzig, P. 1966. *Primitive money in its ethnological, historical and economic aspects* (Oxford: Pergamon Press).

Foster, D., and P. Young. 1990. Stochastic evolutionary game dynamics. *Theoretical Population Biology* 38: 219–232.

Jones, R. 1976. The origin and development of media of exchange. *The Journal of Political Economy* 84: 757–775.

Kandori, M., G.J. Mailath and R. Rob. 1993. Learning, mutation, and long run equilibria in games. *Econometrica* 61: 29–56.

Kehoe, T.J., N. Kiyotaki and R. Wright. 1993. More on money as a medium of exchange. *Economic Theory* 3: 297–314.

Kelley, W.G. and A.C. Peterson. 1991. *Difference Equations*. London: Academic Press, Inc.

Kiyotaki, N. and R. Wright. 1989. On money as a medium of exchange. *The Journal of Political Economy* 97: 927–954.

Luenberger, D.G. 1979. *Introduction to Dynamic Systems*. (New York: Wiley).

Luo, G. 1995. Evolutionary models of market behavior. Ph.D. dissertation (Faculty of Graduate Studies, University of Western Ontario, London, Canada).

Mailath, G.J. 1992. Introduction: symposium on evolutionary game theory. *Journal of Economic Theory* 57: 259–277.

Marimon, R., E. McGrattan, and T.J. Sargent. 1990. Money as a medium of exchange in an economy with artificially intelligent agents. *Journal of Economic Dynamics and Control* 14: 329–373.

Menger, K. 1892. On the origin of money. *Economic Journal* 2: 239–255.

Oh, S. 1989. A theory of generally acceptable medium of exchange and barter. *Journal of Monetary Economics* 23: 101–119.

Quiggin, A.H. 1949. *A Survey of Primitive Money: The Beginning of Currency* (New York: Barnes and Noble, Inc.).

Renero, J.M. 1998. Unstable and stable steady states in the Kiyotaki–Wright model. *Economic Theory* 11: 275–294.

Sethi, R. 1999. Evolutionary stability and media of exchange, *Journal of Economic Behavior and Organization* 40(3): 233–254.
Smith, A. 1776. *The Wealth of Nations,* Books I–III (Harmondsworth, England: Penguin Books).
Taylor, P. and L. Jonker. 1978. Evolutionarily stable strategies and game dynamics. *Mathematical Biosciences* 40: 145–156.
Weibull, J.W. 1995. *Evolutionary Game Theory*. (Cambridge: MIT Press).
Wright, R. 1995. Search, evolution and money. *Journal of Economic Dynamics and Control* 19: 181–206.

Chapter 8
Conclusions

In responding to the challenge of justifying the existence of equilibria after abandoning individual market participants' rationality, this book has presented a series of analytical models applying the Darwinian evolutionary idea of natural selection to the markets to examine the occurrence of the perfectly competitive equilibrium, monopolistically competitive equilibrium, and informationally efficient equilibrium in various contexts. The model in Chap. 2 concludes that the perfectly competitive equilibrium can be achieved without assuming that firms are purposively maximizing their profits. The model in Chap. 3 proves that the monopolistically competitive equilibrium can emerge as a long run aggregate market outcome even if firms are totally irrational. Both models in Chaps. 2 and 3 assume that firms are totally irrational in the sense that firms enter the industry regardless of the existence of profits; firms' outputs are randomly determined rather than generated from profit maximization problems; and firms exit the industry if their wealth is negative.

The models in Chaps. 4, 5, and 6 shows that an informationally efficient equilibrium can also be achieved in the futures market or one-sided buyer auction market after removing the individual market participants' rationality. In these models, the market force serves as a natural selection process, that constantly shifts the wealth over times from traders with less accurate information to traders with more accurate information. In other words, the market selects against noise and selects for more accurate information.

One extension would be to examine the impact on market efficiency of conservative traders who are behaving conservatively in their trading activities to avoid potential losses. Till date, the consensus in the literature has been that the presence of informed traders is necessary for achieving informationally efficient equilibrium. However, Luo (2011) proves that without such informed traders, the presence of conservative traders is sufficient for market efficiency to occur. Specifically the model uses an evolutionary idea of natural selection in the context of a futures market. Traders act on their own predetermined trading characteristics in their trading activities. This includes a wide spectrum of trading behavior ranging from very aggressive behavior to very conservative behavior. This model shows theoretically, that even without informed traders, as long as there is the presence of a sufficient number of conservative traders, with probability one, the proportion of time, that the futures price is arbitrarily close to the spot price, converges to one. The presence of conservative traders plays a critical role in driving the futures price to the spot price.

Chapter 7 uses an evolutionary approach to explain the origin of money as media of exchange in a primitive economy, where agents specialize in production for the purpose of trading for their own consumption of goods.

In all evolutionary models in this book, the market aggregate rationality is established in the long run even though the individual market participants are irrational. The natural selection in the markets works to promote efficient outcomes.

The models presented here shed some lights on the validation of the concepts of the perfectly competitive equilibrium, monopolistically competitive equilibrium, and informationally efficient equilibrium. Undoubtedly, there are still a lot of other equilibria that need to be examined after abandoning the rationality of individual market participants.

Reference

Luo, G. 2011. Conservative Traders, Natural Selection and Market Efficiency, *Journal of Economic Theory*, doi: 10.1016/j.jet.2011.10.016.